PELICAN BOOKS

Penguin Library of Business and Management
Editor: T. Kempner

THE MANAGEMENT OF
INDUSTRIAL RELATIONS

Kevin Hawkins was educated at Keighley Grammar School and Gonville and Caius College, Cambridge, where he obtained a double first-class honours degree. He spent a year doing research at Nuffield College, Oxford, and then joined the research staff of the University of Bradford Management Centre and was appointed Lecturer in Industrial Relations in 1970. He is an associate member of the British Institute of Management, has acted as consultant to several organizations and worked extensively in the field of management training and development. Kevin Hawkins's previous publications include *Conflict and Change* (1972), *Business and Society* (1974, Pelican), *British Industrial Relations 1945-75* and numerous articles and contributions to other books.

THE MANAGEMENT OF
INDUSTRIAL RELATIONS

KEVIN HAWKINS

PENGUIN BOOKS

Penguin Books Ltd, Harmondsworth, Middlesex, England
Penguin Books, 625 Madison Avenue, New York, New York 10022, U.S.A.
Penguin Books Australia Ltd, Ringwood, Victoria, Australia
Penguin Books Canada Ltd, 2801 John Street, Markham, Ontario, Canada L3R 1B4
Penguin Books (N.Z.) Ltd, 182–190 Wairau Road, Auckland 10, New Zealand

—

First published 1978

—

—

Made and printed in Great Britain by
Hazell Watson & Viney Ltd,
Aylesbury, Bucks
Set in Monotype Times Roman

Contents

Preface 7

1. The New Militancy 11

2. New Pressures and Priorities 45

3. The Role of Incomes Policy 81

4. The New Legitimacy 117

5. The Role of Law 154

6. Policy and Practice 185

Postscript 229

Notes 231

Index 257

Preface

MANY people seem to believe that bad industrial relations have made a major contribution to the crises and problems which have beset the British economy over the past thirty years. They will say that British industry has too many strikes, that the British worker does not work hard enough and that British trade unions are greedy, irresponsible and over-mighty. The implication is, presumably, that if only the unions could somehow be 'put in their place', or at least compelled to behave in a much more reasonable manner (like the German unions), everyone would work harder and strike less, and Britain would be a lot better off. The most interesting thing about this popular line of argument, however, is its remarkable tenacity in the face of evidence to the contrary. It has often been pointed out, for example, that Britain is not exceptionally strike-prone by international standards and that the vast majority of British companies have never experienced a stoppage. It has further been argued that if productivity in British industry is low by international standards (which it is), the fault lies not so much with idle workers as with decades of inadequate investment in capital equipment and labour-saving technology. Again, the allegation that British trade unions are too powerful can hardly be sustained if one looks at their track record. Not only are British workers now among the lowest-paid in Western Europe, but the whole quality of their working lives seems greatly inferior in many respects to that of their continental brothers. Indeed, since 1974 the TUC has thrown its political weight behind a government whose policies have reduced living standards and raised unemployment to a postwar record. In these circumstances it would be difficult to argue that the unions are 'running the country'.

Nevertheless, the myth that they have acquired too much power and are using it irresponsibly persists. It is frequently forgotten that in practice trade union representatives do not and cannot determine the experience, attitudes and perceptions of

7

their members in the work situation. In the eyes of many employees, the union is something they can appeal to for protection if they should ever need it. Apart from its basic bargaining functions, a trade union does not generally play a salient role in the day-to-day working lives of its members. The role of management, by contrast, is of immense significance. Management determines the structure and organization of the enterprise, the technology and production arrangements, the physical conditions of the workplace and (in many cases) the nature of the payment system and the level of manning. It should be remembered that just over 50 per cent of the labour force actually belongs to a trade union and it must be assumed that in workplaces where collective organization is absent, management has considerable freedom to determine matters of substance unilaterally. Where there *is* a trade union presence, the scope of collective bargaining is often limited to basic bread-and-butter issues, beyond which management still retains considerable authority. Even in organizations where most issues of substance are subject to consultation and/or negotiation with trade union officials and shop stewards, management still has a vital role to play in establishing a framework of policies and procedures within which collective bargaining can take place.

Most experienced practitioners would probably agree that shop stewards tend to react both to initiatives from management and to the demands and aspirations of their constituents on the shop floor. In general, therefore, it would be misleading to see them as active trouble-makers, eccentrics or subversives, hell-bent on destroying the authority of management and wrecking the enterprise in which they are employed. On the contrary, it would seem that the role of the steward has in many ways become an integral part of the system of authority within the organization – a system which is, of course, ultimately determined by management, not the trade unions.

Any serious analyst of Britain's economic problems cannot, therefore, make the trade unions a scapegoat for the failures and shortcomings of management. Several criticisms can be levelled at the unions, but it is at least arguable that their shortcomings would not have assumed so much importance if the quality of management had been significantly better than it has been. However, it must now be apparent to most observers that if Britain's rate of economic growth is to be raised to a level comparable with that of our major competitors, measures will have to be taken at plant and company level which will have far-reaching implications for the management of industrial relations. Most organizations, whether in the private or the public sector, will find themselves under growing pressure over the next few years to increase productivity and use all their resources, including manpower, more efficiently. To some extent these pressures have been gradually making themselves felt since the 1960s, and the approach of many managements to collective bargaining has changed accordingly. But there is still a great deal of ground to cover and the pressures on management to initiate changes in the traditional relationship between motivation, effort and reward will undoubtedly grow. This will in turn pose a challenge for those managers and trade unionists who are wedded to a traditional conception of their respective roles. It will become increasingly difficult for managers to impose change on their employees, without consultation or negotiation, and equally difficult for trade union representatives to refuse to accept a degree of responsibility for those decisions which they take with management on a joint basis.

The purpose of this book is to analyse some of the factors which have influenced the development of British (and to some extent European) industrial relations in recent years and which may be expected to continue to play an important role in the future. This is *not* a 'how to do it' book; the writer would not presume to tell seasoned practitioners how they should manage their industrial relations. The object is to examine a number of general themes which are of some importance to those managers in all business enterprises and public organizations, including central and local government, who have the responsibility of formulating policies and strategies in industrial relations. One problem facing many practitioners is that they usually lack the time, or sometimes the inclination, to consider the wider implications of what they are doing. Consequently they frequently underestimate the complexity of the problems which confront them. If this book makes some contribution, however modest, to the task of broadening their understanding – as well as that of the student and general reader – then the writer will be more than satisfied.

Kevin Hawkins

University of Bradford Management Centre
September 1977

CHAPTER ONE

The New Militancy

> The very discovery of improved industrial methods, by
> leading to specialization, makes manual labourer and
> brain worker alike dependent on the rest of the commun-
> ity for the means of subsistence and subordinates them,
> even in their own crafts, to the action of others. In the
> world of civilization and progress, no man can be his own
> master. But the very fact that, in modern society, the in-
> dividual thus necessarily loses control over his own life,
> makes him desire to regain collectively what has become
> individually impossible.
>
> Sidney and Beatrice Webb

IT is widely believed that the economic strength of the Western
world and the unprecedentedly high standard of living which it
supports, ultimately depends on the continued dynamism of free
enterprise. The doctrines of classical liberalism may have been
modified during the present century – most notably by the
recognition that the state has an important regulatory role in the
economy and by the growing belief that businessmen should
behave in a 'socially responsible' manner – but their normative
influence is still pervasive. A recent survey of managerial attitudes
by Nicholls, for example, suggests that in Britain at least the
businessman believes

that economic prosperity, the furtherance of which is a common en-
deavour, is a good in itself; that the businessman's role is to pursue it;
and given the assumption that the company is essentially a cooperative
organization, that by facilitating the achievement of organizational
goals the businessman himself is furthering the interests of all partners
who give the company its existence.[1]

In other words the adoption of certain *substantive* norms, namely
the creation of wealth (including more goods, services and

11

employment) has had certain *procedural* implications, most notably that entrepreneurs and industrialists – the wealth creators – should not have to contend with unreasonable constraints in the performance of their role. In recent years, however, it has been argued that the growth of trade union power constitutes an increasingly unreasonable restriction on the freedom and dynamism of private – and indeed publicly owned – industry. It has also been alleged that the unions impose equally unreasonable constraints on the freedom of their members. In Paul Johnson's words:

In Britain today, a man can no longer freely sell his labour since the union stands between him and his potential employer. An employer cannot make a contract either, since the union tells him which categories of men are employable and which are not . . . The most important fact in an economic sense about a worker in Britain today is not his skill or his training or his character but his union membership – in short, his status.[2]

There is, of course, nothing new about these attacks on trade unionism. Complaints about the 'excessive' power of the unions can be traced back at least a hundred years. Yet despite numerous reverses, whether induced by economic downswings or by judicial and legislative hostility, trade unionism has steadily extended and strengthened its roots in British society. This development is in itself something of a paradox. Numerous public opinion polls have long indicated that the majority of people in Britain (including trade unionists themselves) think that the unions have too much power.[3] Yet, just as public hostility to the unions seems to have grown in recent years, so too has trade union membership. Indeed the unions have been particularly successful in recruiting new members among supposedly 'moderate' and 'responsible' groups of white collar employees. The renewed growth of collective organization, not just in Britain but in Western Europe as a whole, over the past ten years or so has of course been accompanied by significant increases in both the rate of inflation and the level of industrial conflict. Indeed some observers have concluded that there is a new (and largely unwelcome) spirit of militancy abroad which is symptomatic of a cumulative breakdown in the traditional framework of order and restraint.

This 'new militancy' must be analysed in its historical context. Traditionally in Britain collective bargaining has been regarded as the cornerstone of industrial peace. From the 1890s to the mid-1960s the popular assumption was that the most effective way of achieving orderly industrial relations lay in the industry-wide collective agreement, negotiated and maintained by trade unions and employers' federations. Thus in the early 1950s Zweig could reasonably claim that the unions

are at present the bulwark of industrial peace and lawfulness. With the employers' federations and associations, often within the framework of a joint industrial council, they have developed a whole code of industrial behaviour in hundreds of rules, regulations and standards which are kept by both sides. In fact the unions and employers' associations support one another in keeping up these rules.[4]

Twenty years later, however, few observers were prepared to take such an optimistic view. The framework of industry-wide regulation has been shaken by the growth of 'largely informal, largely autonomous and largely fragmented' bargaining at workplace level.[5] Workgroups are either ignoring or directly challenging the rules and restraints imposed on them from above. This new pattern of behaviour has revealed itself not merely in a higher rate of wage inflation but also in a growing dissatisfaction with traditional methods of making decisions. Many employers have found that their ability to control various aspects of the work situation has been eroded by shop stewards and workgroups. The willingness of these workgroups to accept the authority of their *own* organizations without question also appears to be declining. Indeed, since the mid-1960s a search has been going on for new methods of controlling workplace behaviour and thereby restoring 'order' to industrial relations. The rationale behind this search, however, is thoroughly traditional. The new militancy is generally viewed as a serious obstacle to the achievement of faster economic growth, which, since the mid-1960s, has been a national priority. Government ministers have exhorted managements to hold down their wage costs and increase the productivity of their labour force. A battery of new policies has been devised to assist managements in their task. Yet the new militancy continues to grow, and both governments and managements have now begun to realize that there is no quick and painless solution to the problem.

It must be recognized at the outset, of course, that the use of the word militancy in itself implies a value judgement. At its simplest it infers that employees and their representatives are behaving in a manner which in some way deviates from the norms laid down by managements and the state. In a complex and interdependent industrial society, deviant behaviour frequently entails an economic cost and is therefore regarded as a problem – particularly by those whose role is to create more wealth. Although in practice managements may devote a great deal of time and energy to the propagation of behavioural norms which emphasize industrial harmony and cooperation, many of them now recognize that a degree of conflict is more or less inevitable. The acid test of good management, therefore, is now regarded as the extent to which conflict can be predicted and controlled. As Fox has pointed out, 'The essence of organization is regular, standardized and recurrent behaviour. The social organization (of the business enterprise) therefore consists of patterned uniformities of behaviour which persist for varying lengths of time.'[6] Conflict is not incompatible with this perspective provided it can be anticipated and kept within certain bounds. In other words conflict is 'legitimate' as long as it does not challenge the structure of power in industry and thereby disrupt the central wealth-generating mechanisms of Western societies. Does the 'new militancy' pose such a challenge? Has the traditional framework of order broken down so completely that piecemeal reforms are unlikely to succeed? In order to answer these questions we must begin by analysing those factors which have in the past helped to produce the 'patterned uniformities of behaviour' which are commonly regarded as essential to the continued success of the business enterprise. Prominent among these factors are firstly the *expectations* of the parties themselves (i.e. employees, managements and governments) and secondly the framework of *institutions* through which these expectations have been traditionally expressed. This chapter will be concerned with the changing character of employee expectations and its implications for management.

The role of expectations (1)

Eighty years ago Sidney and Beatrice Webb observed that the thought and behaviour of many trade unionists was strongly influenced by social and economic conservatism; they noted, for example,

the abiding faith in the sanctity of vested interests; the strong presumption in favour of the *status quo*; the distrust of innovation, the liking for distinct social classes, marked off from each other by corporate privileges and peculiar traditions; the disgust at the modern spirit of self-seeking assertiveness; and the deep-rooted conviction that the only stable organization of society is that based on each man being secured and contented in his inherited station in life.[7]

These norms of behaviour obviously posed no threat to the established structure of power in industry, particularly since those groups for whom they had most appeal – the status-conscious craftsmen – effectively dominated the trade union movement during the late Victorian era. Indeed they were usually synonymous with a highly cooperative approach to the resolution of any disputes which arose between 'masters' and 'men'.[8] When major conflicts arose – as they did during the 1890s – the main cause was not so much a change in the expectations of the craftsmen themselves as in the economic environment in which they worked. As the Webbs pointed out, it was an integral part of the craft tradition that 'the wages and other conditions of employment hitherto enjoyed by any section of workmen ought under no circumstances to be interfered with for the worse'.[9] Indeed the success of Victorian craft unionism depended on the *unilateral* determination of wage rates and working practices by well-organized workgroups. In the closing years of the nineteenth century, however, the pace of technical change in manufacturing industry accelerated and many employers, now facing tough competition from abroad, were compelled to adopt measures which threatened the status and bargaining power of craftsmen. As Clegg *et al.* have argued: 'Craft controls were peculiarly exasperating obstacles. The craftsmen were apt to regard them as principles which they must never willingly submit to negotiated compromise, and where their societies were strong there was no way round. Consequently, the employers banded themselves together in order to break through.'[10] The late 1890s witnessed national disputes in several craft-dominated trades, the best-known of which was the lock-out by the engineering employers.[11] The main substantive implication of these disputes was that neither the working practices nor the wages of craftsmen could be insulated from the economic environment.

Yet even in the competitive environment of the early 1900s, when most trade unions found themselves under attack, there was strong resistance to reductions in wages, particularly from the rank-and-file membership. The idea that every working man was entitled to a 'living wage', regardless of fluctuations in prices and profits, was beginning to exert a powerful normative influence among trade unionists. The Webbs noted that this idea would, if widely adopted, reinforce the 'established expectations' of a fair and reasonable standing of living.[12] There was as yet no expectation that real wages would or should rise rapidly – the demand was merely that wages should be 'steady'. When established bargaining machinery proved incapable of ensuring that wages kept pace with the cost of living – as it did during the inflationary conditions of the First World War – workgroups took matters into their own hands and negotiated their own increases with individual employers. By 1920 it was generally accepted that 'a wage sufficient to afford a man an adequate and decent livelihood must be regarded as a first charge on industry' and, equally significant, 'that pay for public employees should be guided by the level of wages paid to men of similar qualifications in industry generally'.[13] But some strategic industries, notably coal, cotton and engineering, were still vulnerable to international competition and when these economic pressures became severe (as they did in the coal industry after 1925), there was prolonged conflict between employers and unions which invariably resulted in wage reductions. The reality of high and sustained unemployment prevented most unions and work-groups from pressing their claims for a 'living wage' too far, although it did nothing to weaken their attachment to the idea. In fact those who worked in the more sheltered industries found that, taking the inter-war period as a whole, their wages fell more slowly than the cost of living.

From 1940 onwards, however, the economic climate became much more secure and optimistic. Governments committed themselves to the maintenance of full employment and made the achievement of higher standards of living a major plank in their political platforms. Given conditions of high and rising demand and a structure of industry-wide wage agreements, the resistance of employers to inflationary pay claims weakened. Increases in unit labour costs could now be passed on to the consumer without fear of losing business; the last vestiges of the discipline long imposed by a hard market environment disappeared. Phelps Brown has summarized the consequences for employee expectations:

> When rises in pay were no longer constrained by the market, what rise was it reasonable to expect? A first answer was, at least as much as the others are getting. A certain level of settlements came to be regarded as predominant in the annual round. The parties to negotiations, on both sides of the table, came to be concerned to conform with it, so that the employees concerned should not slip in the 'league table' ... there grew up an expectation of annual betterment – an expectation that is taken for granted today, but is a recent innovation that stands in striking contrast with 'the traditional fatalism of the working class'.[14]

Increases in the cost of living – which became a permanent feature of practically all Western societies after 1945 – were regarded as a *prima facie* justification for higher pay. The principle of 'fair comparison' was also widely recognized as central to the process of wage bargaining, regardless of its inflationary implications. Under conditions of full employment and high demand, collective bargaining – originally a market transaction – became more and more remote from market forces. As Barbara Wootton observed in the early 1950s:

In general, the shift of emphasis away from economic and towards social and ethical considerations cannot fail to strike anyone who has followed the trend of wage discussions over the past thirty or forty years. The contrasts are striking. Once a battleground in which rivals fought each other over the division of the proceeds of their joint plundering activities, today wage negotiations have developed into a conference of industrial statesmen debating questions of justice, precedent and public interest.[15]

Since the words quoted above were written, however, wage bargaining has become more contentious in character. Between 1951 and 1966, strikes caused by disputes over pay generally constituted less than half the total number of stoppages in any given year. Since 1966 the relative importance of pay has increased.

Table 1

Causes of stoppages, 1966–77

Causes of stoppages	*Number of stoppages (percentage of total in brackets)*				
	1966–74 (average)	*1974*	*1975*	*1976*	*1977 (first half)**
Pay disputes	1,509 (57)	1,922 (66)	1,318 (58)	875 (44)	671 (52)
Hours of work	56 (2)	53 (2)	26 (1)	66 (3)	22 (2)
Redundancy questions	99 (4)	85 (3)	116 (5)	86 (4)	50 (4)
Trade union matters	211 (8)	184 (6)	142 (6)	166 (8)	119 (9)
Working conditions	166 (6)	156 (5)	156 (7)	215 (11)	123 (10)
Manning and work allocation	204 (11)	263 (9)	276 (12)	398 (20)	180 (14)
Dismissal/ disciplinary measures	308 (12)	259 (9)	248 (11)	210 (10)	121 (9)
Miscellaneous	12 (–)	– (–)	– (–)	– (–)	– (–)
TOTAL	2,565	2,922	2,282	2,016	1,286

*Provisional.
Source: *Department of Employment Gazette*, various issues.

Clearly the overall level of strike activity and the pattern of causation can both be affected by incomes policy. A policy which commands the support, or at least the grudging acquiescence, of trade union representatives and their members naturally tends to reduce the number of pay disputes – hence the relatively low levels of strike activity recorded in years such as 1973 and 1976. When, however, a policy has either been widely challenged or largely ignored, as in 1970 and 1974, stoppages over pay have rapidly increased. Overall, therefore, the tendency has been for strikes over pay to become more important within the total pattern of strike activity in Britain. The prominence of pay disputes is even greater when the number of working days lost is taken as an index. Over the four-year period 1966–70, stoppages over pay accounted on average for 66·1 per cent of all working days lost. In the succeeding five-year period, 1970–75, this proportion rose to 85·2 per cent, largely because the incidence of big, industry-wide stoppages increased significantly – particularly in the public sector – and almost all these strikes occurred in pursuit of pay claims. In the years 1969–70 the rate of wage inflation nearly doubled, despite a relatively high *and rising* level of unemployment, and since then average earnings have increased by not less than 10 per cent every year. As a result, successive governments have placed an extremely high priority on strategies designed to restrain the growth of wages and salaries. Indeed, one government even felt obliged to fight a general election in order to preserve the credibility of its incomes policy.

Does the pattern of events since 1969 suggest, therefore, that employee expectations are becoming even more ambitious? If expectations were indeed set on an ever-rising trend, one would expect to see a breakdown in the traditional structure of wage and salary relativities. Groups who, because of their position in the economy, command considerable bargaining power would be breaking through the barriers of custom and practice which have long determined their place in the hierarchy of incomes. Long-established relativities and differentials would be dissolving in inflationary chaos. In fact, however, this does not appear to be happening. Indeed one can only agree with Daniel that 'what is remarkable about our present society is that people are so content with their situation and that their demands are so limited rather than that there is so much pressure on pay'.[16] The general

19

acceptance of the *status quo* is particularly significant in view of the fact that the structure of wages and salaries in Britain is little more than 'the accumulated deposit laid down by a rich mixture of economic and social forces, operating through considerable periods of history'.[17] Many differentials and relativities cannot be justified on either economic or ethical grounds, yet they continue to be regarded as firm, fixed and irremoveable. How can this overwhelming conservatism be explained? According to Daniel, the reason lies in the fact that people have

very narrow social horizons for evaluating their own position. They compare their own situation with those who are socially and geographically close to them, those whom they define as being of their own kind, and if they feel that they are doing all right and are justly treated in relation to such people they are generally content. In terms of pay, semi-skilled or unskilled manual workers are more aggrieved by other semi-skilled or unskilled manual workers, who they feel are doing much the same kind of work, doing marginally better than them, than they are by professional and managerial workers earning five times as much as them or top executives with gross earnings ten or twenty times as much.[18]

Daniel's research suggests that, despite an increasingly popular argument to the contrary, feelings of injustice about the distribution of income and dissatisfaction with the existing structure of differentials and relativities have *not* in general become widespread in recent years.

How, then, can we account for the recent growth of militancy associated with pay claims? Expectations undoubtedly have played a significant role. Over the postwar period as a whole the vast majority of employees (including middle and senior managers) have become accustomed to expect a steady increase in their real incomes. The average rate of growth has not been as high in Britain as in most other Western countries but it has nevertheless been historically very significant. Most groups experienced moderate but generally continuous increases in their living standards until the late 1960s, when the situation began to change. Firstly, for reasons that need not concern us here, there was a sharp and sustained acceleration in the cost of living which, despite all the efforts of successive governments, has not been reversed. The decline in the value of the pound, the dramatic increase in world energy prices and the excessive growth of the domestic money supply have at various times since 1969 contributed to the explosive rise in the cost of living, and the effect on wage bargaining has been far-reaching. An individual's view of whether his wage or salary is 'fair' depends not only on what is happening to the income of those groups with whom he customarily compares himself but also on the extent to which it keeps rising ahead of the cost of living. The more rapidly the cost of living is rising at a given point in time, the more demanding employees are likely to be in their approach to wage and salary bargaining, particularly if their last increase has been overtaken by inflation.[19]

Secondly, during the 1960s more and more manual workers entered the net of direct taxation for the first time and saw a rising proportion of their money wages 'lost' at source. Turner, Jackson and Wilkinson have shown that whereas the typical manual worker was hardly liable for tax until the late 1950s, by 1970/71 his tax and social security contributions took nearly 20 per cent of his earnings and by 1975 this proportion had risen to over 25 per cent.[20] This development has not, of course, been peculiar to Britain. Throughout the Western world the growing burden of government expenditure has found its way through to the employee's pay packet in the form of higher taxation. Resentment against these impositions has been reported from several European countries in recent years, notably Sweden and West Germany, where it has shown up in the form of increasingly militant attitudes to pay claims.[21] It can, of course, be argued that higher direct taxation has been accompanied by, and indeed has helped to finance, a much-improved 'social wage' and that the pressure for higher money wages can to a great extent be neutralized by increases in social benefits of various kinds. This comfortable theory has, however, been shattered by the British experience in 1974/5, when incomes policy was based on the assumption that in a period of rapid inflation workers would be prepared to forego higher real wages in return for increases in the 'social wage'. The assumption soon proved to be erroneous. In Britain (and probably to a greater extent here than elsewhere) the trade unions are overwhelmingly interested in money wages.

It is on the size of their pay packets that most rank-and-file union members assess the performance and credibility of their organizations.

The new militancy which appeared throughout Western Europe during the late 1960s should therefore be seen, at least in part, as a protest by workers against the slower rate of growth in their real incomes which set in about that time and has continued in most years ever since. In order to make this protest effective, many employees joined a trade union. In Britain the unions gained nearly one million new members between 1968 and 1971 – a rate of growth which was far in excess of anything seen since the explosion in union membership which accompanied the extraordinarily rapid inflation of 1919 and 1920. Equally significant was the fact that most of the growth occurred in white-collar occupations. In 1964 the total membership of white-collar unions in Britain stood at 2·6 million; by 1970 this figure had risen to 3·6 million and four years later reached 4·2 million. This growth of white-collar unionism must, of course, be related to the rapid increase in the white-collar labour force which has been a marked feature of the postwar period. But whereas initially white-collar union *membership* merely kept abreast of the growth of white-collar *employment*, from the mid-1960s onwards the unions greatly increased their penetration of these occupational groups.[22] It is probably safe to assume that the vast majority of white-collar workers (including middle managers) who joined a union did so for instrumental rather than ideological reasons. One study of technicians, for example, has emphasized that those who had joined a union

were concerned with using bargaining strength to improve or restore their absolute and relative levels of earnings. In particular they wanted to see their own perceptions of their status compared with that of shop floor workers rewarded equitably . . . Unionization was seen as a means by which technical staff could emulate the successes of the manual workers and achieve the restoration of the traditional salary differentials. This view of the possible achievement of technicians' unions was assiduously fostered by the unions seeking to organize technicians.[23]

Consequently those union leaders who promised the most in terms of tangible rewards did best in the race to recruit new members. The leadership of ASTMS, for example, adopted a particularly aggressive recruitment campaign in which they stressed the white-collar worker's eroded differentials, his relative lack of employment security and his generally weak bargaining position *vis-à-vis* top management. Thus in only three years (1968–71) ASTMS nearly trebled its membership.

Much of the 'deviant' behaviour associated with the new militancy can therefore be attributed to the increasing frustration of many workgroups, manual and white-collar alike, in the face of a rapidly rising cost of living and higher taxation. As a result some workgroups and unions traditionally noted for their quiescence and moderation have become considerably more aggressive in recent years – hence the rise in both union membership and in the incidence of strikes from 1968 onwards. In the words of Bacon and Eltis

... all too often those who sought higher living standards, or the mere continuation of car and home ownership (which have risen in cost far more than prices in general) found that they could only obtain these by making full use of their trade union power, with the result that ordinary workers turned to aggressive union leaders to produce results. That a politically moderate population has chosen to be represented by immoderate trade unions is plausibly explained once it is appreciated that this was in many cases a response to a situation where a rising cost of living and rising taxation made the preservation of living standards increasingly difficult.[24]

It should not be assumed, however, that a resumption in the growth of real incomes will in itself remove *all* manifestations of the new militancy, firstly because faster growth raises the possibility that some groups will move ahead more quickly than others, and secondly because certain non-monetary factors are involved. It is to these non-monetary causes of the new militancy to which we must now turn.

The role of expectations (2)

Any contract of employment is a 'wage–work' bargain – in other words a defined amount of money is offered in return for the performance of specified work tasks. But the 'work' side of the bargain is necessarily imprecise compared with the 'wage' side. Wage norms are based, as was argued above, on the principle of fair comparison and on the sanctity of customary standards of living, and these norms have long been embodied in collective agreements. Work norms, however, are much more difficult to quantify and in any case have been generally regarded as falling within the ambit of managerial prerogative. The situation described by the Webbs probably remained typical of many workplaces until the postwar period:

The hiring of a workman, unlike a contract for the purchase of a commodity, necessarily leaves many conditions not precisely determined, still less expressed in any definite form. This indeterminateness of the labour contract is in some respects a drawback to the employer. In return for the specified wage, the workman has impliedly agreed to give work of the currently accepted standard of quantity and quality. The lack of definiteness in this respect leaves him free to skulk or to scamp. But against this the employer protects himself by providing supervision and by requiring obedience to his foreman, if not also by elaborate systems of fines and deductions ... When an additional 'hand' is taken on in a manufacturing establishment, practically the only point explicitly agreed upon between him and the foreman is the amount of the weekly wage, or possibly the scale of piece-work rates. How many hours he shall work, how quickly or how intensely he is to exert himself, what intervals will be allowed for meals, what fines and deductions he will be subject to, what provision is made for warmth and shelter, the arrangements for ventilation and the prevention of accidents, the sanitary accommodation, the noise, the smell and the dirt, the foreman's temper and the comrades' manners – all this has to be taken for granted, it being always implied in the engagement that the workman accepts the conditions existing in the employer's establishment, and obeys all his lawful commands.[25]

It should, of course, be remembered that the imprecision of work obligations was not always as overwhelmingly in favour of the employer as the passage quoted above might imply. In workplaces where well-organized groups of craftsmen were present, the employer's control over the effort bargain might well be limited by traditional craft norms. Moreover, as the Webbs themselves pointed out, the effort bargain for all employees was strongly influenced by custom and practice which, in effect, meant a level of effort generally thought to be consistent with 'a fair day's work'. Standards of fairness naturally varied from one industry to another and depended to a great extent firstly on the kind of technology employed, secondly on the character of the labour force and thirdly on the market situation in which the industry concerned operated. But these customary standards, whatever they were, proved remarkably resistant to change. Even in an industry like the docks, where employment practices were condemned by successive investigators as grossly unfair and inhuman, both employers and workers preferred to go on living with the structure of work norms to which they had become accustomed over many years.[26] The right of management to determine work norms unilaterally was therefore widely accepted, the only proviso being that managerial decisions should respect the established framework of custom and practice. Only when managers sought to overturn customary norms, as in the engineering industry during the 1890s, did workgroups and their organizations openly challenge managerial authority.[27]

The dominant position of the employer rested not only on a widespread acceptance of his 'right to manage' but also on the relative lack of countervailing power in the labour market. In the economic conditions which prevailed up to 1914 and again from 1921 to 1940, many manual workgroups found themselves at a continuing disadvantage in the labour market. The external reality of too many men chasing too few jobs buttressed the internal authority of the employer.[28] The dissatisfied worker could of course resort to the strike weapon, but in a climate of low demand and excess labour supply this was unlikely to be effective. In addition, workers contemplating a withdrawal of labour had to face the prospect of a sharp cut in their standard of living for the duration of the dispute, with no certainty of ultimate victory, and the likelihood of victimization or unemployment after the strike was over. However, when the market environment changed, as it did temporarily in the period from 1914 to 1920 and then permanently after 1940, there was much more scope for collective action designed to redress the inequality of the traditional 'wage–work' bargain. During the First World War the overriding priority of most managements in manufacturing industry was higher output. Traditional working practices, however, stood in the way of this objective. In the pre-war environment the problem would have been resolved by unilateral action on the part of the employers, backed by a lock-out. In a climate of full employment and high demand, however, employers found themselves obliged to negotiate on working practices (i.e. the effort bargain) at plant level with representatives of the workforce. The same conditions reappeared from 1940 onwards and this time the effect on workers' expectations was more permanent and far-reaching. In Phelps Browns' words:

Lengthening experience of high levels of employment has given the employee a heightened appreciation of the demand for his services, and a greater independence and self-reliance, or reliance on the power of his working group. That experience has also removed the fear that if he walks out of his job he may not get it back. In several ways the resources available for the maintenance of the striker have been increased. Meanwhile the leverage of the strike has been raised by changes in the organization of industry. Increased complexity and integration of processes has given some quite small groups the power to halt wide sectors of production. Increased capital per employee has raised the cost of a stoppage relatively to the cost of the settlement that will avoid it.[29]

The type of collective action described above began to emerge in the motor-car industry during the 1950s, and by the mid-1960s, when the Donovan Commission began its investigations, had become almost synonymous with the popular image of Britain's strike problem. Turner, Clack and Roberts examined the nature of strikes in the car industry at this time and concluded that there had been a rise in the 'horizon of labour expectations' which manifested themselves in the form of two normative standards – that wages should be 'fair' in comparative terms and that the performance of a job established 'property rights' in it for the employee.[30] The importance of fair comparison in wage bargaining was touched upon earlier in this chapter and all we need to add here is that in the motor-car industry it was reinforced by a growing concern with the *instability* of earnings levels in a sector unusually prone to sharp fluctuations in demand and also with the inequities and anomalies thrown up by the incentive schemes commonly used in the industry. The 'deep popular sentiment' in favour of the achievement of fair wages and stable earnings through negotiation led naturally to the demand for *work-loads* which were fair in comparative terms. The idea that work-loads should be 'regulated by agreeably comparative standards' was a potent source of conflict in a mass-production industry in which management had hitherto insisted on the right to speed up the assembly line when production requirements demanded a higher level of activity. In Beynon's words: 'The history of the assembly line is a history of conflict over speed-up, the process whereby the pace of work demanded of the operator is systematically increased.'[31]

The growing normative influence of 'job property rights', however, posed a more radical challenge to the traditional managerial concept of the effort bargain. As Turner *et al.* pointed out:

In manual workers' terms it extends not merely to the sense that operatives should not be turned off *en masse* when it is no longer profitable to employ them, or that the individual worker should not be deprived of his property rights established by service without appeal from the decision of a management which now finds his presence undesirable: it also includes the idea of rights to a particular job at a particular place, and may extend to the right to consultation in anything which may affect the future value of his 'property' . . . In a large sense the idea of 'property in the job' is the employee's compensation for his relative lack of property in the capital that employs him.[32]

The same authors also observed that stoppages in protest against the dismissal or suspension of individual workers had not only doubled over the postwar period but had also become 'considerably more obdurate'. At first glance it may seem paradoxical that workers' resistance to individual and collective dismissals should have stiffened at a time when employment was at a historically high level and the main complaint from employers was of labour shortages. The paradox can only be explained if one starts from the proposition that full employment not only strengthened the worker's market position as a seller of labour (which is self-evident), but that it also enabled him to question and if necessary challenge the rules imposed on him by management in respect of the 'work' side of the employment relationship. The notion of 'job property rights' challenged the traditional prerogatives of management not only to hire and fire labour as necessary, but also to determine unilaterally the nature of the effort bargain. Thus the Donovan Commission concluded that the frequency of unofficial strikes in the motor industry arising over substantive issues such as working arrangements, rules and discipline, redundancy, dismissal and suspension 'indicates that there is considerable confusion as to what management does and does not have the right to do; or, where it is conceded to have the right, whether it is or is not making reasonable use of it'.[33]

The normative disorder to which Donovan referred, and which Allan Flanders labelled the 'challenge from below', was by no means common to all workplaces. It was conspicuous only in industries where technological and organizational change was beginning to challenge the relevance of procedural and substantive rules laid down at national level. In other words the source and focus of action lay not with the trade unions as formal organizations but with groups of union members whose bargaining power had been greatly increased during the postwar period. As Flanders pointed out at the time:

This power is strategically greatest in industries with the most advanced technologies where a single, small group of workers can disrupt production at considerable cost to the employer. It has been used by craft union groups – though not by them alone – to enhance their job security by erecting stronger defences around their job territory and, where possible, by gaining more ground.[34]

These 'defences' included many working practices which managements and outside observers condemned as inefficient, outdated and conducive to low productivity. As governments became increasingly concerned with Britain's low rate of economic growth, so the whole issue of 'job property rights' and managerial control over the effort bargain became central to public policy. The overriding need was to achieve radical changes in working practices and simultaneously preserve or even improve the job security of those affected by the changes.

Some managements successfully reconciled these two needs. At Esso's Fawley refinery, for example, two comprehensive productivity agreements were negotiated in the early 1960s which abolished unnecessary overtime, reduced the average working week, raised output and increased average earnings by 35 per cent. Subsequent agreements at the refinery sought to tackle the related problems of overmanning and rigid demarcation lines between craftsmen. The success of these agreements proved conclusively that long-established job defences could be overcome through collective bargaining at workplace level to the benefit of both management and workers. In Brown's words: 'The central lesson of Fawley was that a powerful workforce can only be persuaded to give up its protective practices and adapt to new technologies if it is given alternative guarantees of security: and that can only be done through formal negotiations with representatives at the workplace.'[35] Several other companies in advanced technology industries such as oil refining, chemicals and steel followed Esso's example and negotiated similar agreements. Indeed for a while the comprehensive productivity agreement was generally regarded as easily the most promising method yet devised of constructing a new framework of normative order at the workplace.[36] This surge of optimism was by no means as misplaced as it seems in retrospect to have been. The traditional situation on the shop floor 'was one of management in principle refusing to recognize the legitimacy of workers' rights to have an effective say over work organization while in practice yielding all the time to the exercise of their informal power'.[37] But, as the Donovan Commission observed, both sides appeared quite satisfied with this situation. Unofficial strikes were still confined to a relatively small number of industries and workplaces, thus belying the popular impression that managements and shop stewards throughout British industry were continually at one another's throats. Yet the incidence of direct conflict was a deceptive criterion with which to measure the effectiveness of the industrial relations system. As Flanders pointed out at the time '... peace may be preserved by constant capitulation of one side to the other's demands, or by joint acquiescence in stagnation and the avoidance of any change that would stir up resistance'.[38] Comprehensive productivity bargaining explicitly recognized that the introduction of much-needed improvements in efficiency was likely to *provoke* direct conflict, and that the best way to deal with this problem was to recognize openly the need for extended joint regulation of the effort bargain at work-place level.

The primary focus of the classic productivity deals of the early 1960s was the effort bargain; improvements on the 'wage' side of the employment relationship were regarded as *consequent* upon the achievement of radical changes in working methods. From 1967 onwards, however, productivity bargaining was formally incorporated into the Labour government's incomes policy and the emphasis of the classic agreements was reversed. The policy established a flat norm of $3\frac{1}{2}$ per cent for pay increases but permitted above-the-norm settlements where improvements in productivity were negotiated. In other words the policy held out the prospect of higher earnings provided that managements and union representatives could do something, or pretend they were doing something, to justify them. Not surprisingly productivity bargaining spread rapidly from 1967 onwards and by the end of 1969 some 4,000 agreements covering about seven million employees had been negotiated. But by comparison with the earlier comprehensive agreements, those negotiated under the quasi-compulsion of incomes policy were small-scale, sectional bargains whose contribution either to higher productivity or to the reform of workplace bargaining was marginal. In Flanders' words, 'usually they were just another way, the latest fashionable way, of permitting management to do what it had done before, namely yield to group pressures when they became too threatening with no overall policy in mind'.[39] By 1970, therefore, the climate of opinion had swung decisively against productivity bargaining. It was believed, firstly, that by raising the level of pay expectations they were an important cause of the 'wage explosion' which began towards the end of the 1960s. Secondly, because productivity bargaining was most appropriate to, and most widely practised in, private manufacturing industry, many groups in other sectors of employment saw their relative pay fall further behind. Thirdly, the rising level of unemployment associated with the severe economic recession of 1970 to 1972 made many workers even more security-conscious than before. In this kind of environment it seemed extremely unwise for workers to concede changes in working practices which *might* ultimately lead to redundancy and fewer employment opportunities.

Since the collapse of productivity bargaining, workers' expectations with regard to their 'job property rights' have, if anything increased, largely in reaction to the dramatic and sustained increase in the customary level of unemployment. When unemployment began to climb steeply in 1971 from an already high plateau, some relatively well-organized workgroups who were threatened with redundancy resorted to direct action (usually in the form of a 'work-in' or a 'sit-in' on their factory premises) in order to preserve their jobs. The appearance of a more militant attitude towards loss of employment underlined the inadequacy of public policy as it then stood. The Redundancy Payments Act of 1965 introduced a limited recognition of 'job property rights' by establishing an entitlement to monetary compensation for loss of employment, geared to length of service. The objective of the Act was to lessen workers' resistance to redundancy and thereby achieve greater mobility of labour in the interests of technological innovation and faster economic growth.[40] Several studies of the impact of redundancy on workgroups, however, have cast doubt on the extent to which the mere availability of compensatory payments does in fact remove the deep-seated psychological barriers involved.[41] In Clegg's words:

> In so far as they reduce the hardship of dismissal they may also be expected to diminish hostility to redundancy, but that is not to say they constitute an adequate solution, for workers want security, and these palliatives do no more than begin to diminish insecurity . . . But even handsome payments do not put an end to objections to redundancy, for the best form of security is the knowledge that the worker's present employment will continue as long as he wants it.[42]

By 1974 the limitations of the approach to redundancy embodied in the 1965 Act were self-evident. Above all, the theory that cash compensation could reconcile most workers to the idea of redundancy seemed less and less realistic as a basis for public policy. If the number of strikes arising over redundancy issues is any guide, then resistance to redundancy appears to have *increased*. Between 1966 and 1969 an annual average of seventy-seven strikes over redundancy was recorded; between 1970 and 1973 the corresponding figure was 124. Consequently the emphasis of public policy began to move towards greater protection for the employee and away from the essentially managerial priorities embodied in the 1965 Act. The first clear indication of a change in official thinking was given in the Code of Practice which accompanied the Industrial Relations Act of 1971. This emphasized the need for prior warning and consultation with employees and trade unions before management made decisions involving redundancy. As the economic climate deteriorated once again in 1974, industrial tribunals began to insist that in redundancy situations managements should use selection criteria which recognized the importance of long service. One tribunal, for example, declared that 'Regardless of the nature of the employment, the principle must apply that the longer an employee goes on working for the same employer, the more dependent he becomes on him and the employer owes a corresponding moral duty to avoid dismissing that employee if reasonably possible.'[43] Tribunals also advised management firstly to consult their employees about forthcoming redundancies wherever and whenever possible, secondly to find ways of avoiding dismissals if the contraction of business was expected to be only temporary, and thirdly to try and find alternative work within the organization for employees who would otherwise be made redundant. The Employment Protection Act of 1975 continues this trend in favour of an explicit recognition of 'job property rights' by laying down minimum time periods for consultation and negotiation with trade union representatives where redundancy is envisaged. It also compels managements to disclose comprehensive information about proposed redundancies to union representatives and be prepared to negotiate on alternatives to redundancy. Finally, the Act also instructs tribunals to consider *reinstatement* as the first remedy for unfair dismissal, as distinct from compensation.

It could of course be argued that the growing concern of both employees and governments with the defence of 'job property rights' may well inhibit the ability of managements to respond to the pressures of structural and technological change. It is now generally realized (even within the TUC) that over the last fifteen years too many jobs have been created in the non-market sector of the economy and that there must be a shift of manpower back into manufacturing industry. It is also accepted that the *under-*employment of manpower is still a major problem in many industries and services and that some jobs have survived only because investment in new and more capital-intensive methods of production have been inadequate. In these circumstances it would obviously be dangerous to assume that any employee can be given a cast-iron guarantee that his job will be preserved indefinitely and somehow insulated from the changing economic environment. What *should* be guaranteed is the right of all employees to receive adequate retraining so that they may be in a position to move to expanding areas of employment. In Britain, however, governments have been comparatively reluctant to invest resources in retraining and job-creation programmes. It may well be, therefore, that the growing resistance to redundancy has been fuelled by the knowledge that in Britain this usually means a period of enforced idleness, loss of social status and a feeling of being thrown 'on the scrap heap'.[44] As the *Economist* has recently observed, with only a little exaggeration:

Fear of the dole is the biggest obstacle to industrial change in Britain. It forces governments to bale out lame ducks when they should be slaughtered. It conditions workers to spin out the available work, to surround their jobs with mysterious restrictive practices and to resist productivity improvements lest they produce themselves out of a job. It encourages unions to fight to preserve work in unpleasant, badly paid industries. It reduces managers to weary cynicism in which innovation is replaced by careful calculation of the least that must be done. It gives militants a following: they can always count on plenty of moderates to line up behind them when the 'right to work' is at stake. In short, the spectre of redundancy has helped to make stagnation a way of life in British industry.[45]

In summarizing this section of the argument, therefore, we must note that the traditional imprecision of the 'work' side of the employment contract which long buttressed the authority of the employer has in recent years been challenged and modified by the new normative aspirations of workgroups. Traditional norms emphasized the right of managements to 'manage', including the right to hire and fire, change work-loads, and remove inefficient working practices, without let or hindrance by employees and their organizations. These norms fitted in easily with a system of collective bargaining which merely established a narrow framework of basic terms and conditions of employment at industry level and reflected a labour market situation which favoured buyers rather than sellers. When labour market conditions changed, however, as they did during the First World War, the traditional framework of managerial norms came under attack from the shop floor. As the first Whitley Report (1917) observed: 'A permanent improvement in the relations between employers and employed must be founded upon something other than a cash basis. What is wanted is that workpeople should have a greater opportunity of participating in the discussion about and adjustment of those parts of industry by which they are most affected.' The Report advocated the establishment of a structure of joint councils at industry, local and workplace level in order to secure to workers 'a greater share in and responsibility for the determination and observance of the conditions under which their work is carried on' and 'the greatest possible security of earnings and employment' in the interests of industrial peace and efficiency.

Forty years later the problems which confronted the Whitley Commission had become even more acute. Full employment was a reality, the disruptive power of the strike had increased and the level of expectations on the shop floor had risen. In these circumstances many employers found themselves unable to prevent the 'frontier of control' moving against them. Workgroups were in a position to insist that inefficient practices of all kinds must be preserved in the interests of job security. A few managements attempted to meet this challenge by openly recognizing the need for extended *joint* regulation of the effort bargain in place of unilateral regulation by either side. For a time it seemed that in comprehensive productivity bargaining management had found a rational and effective solution to the problem of reconciling the need for greater efficiency (i.e. changes in the effort bargain) with employees' expectations of greater job security, higher earnings and a greater say in the making of decisions affecting their interests. But productivity bargaining withered away in face of the rapid increase in both inflation *and* unemployment from 1970 onwards. In Britain, as in most other Western countries, the 1970s have witnessed relatively high levels of unemployment, inflation and industrial conflict. Workers are becoming increasingly militant in defence of their 'right to work' and this has clear implications for the regulation of the effort bargain. The notion of 'job property rights' embraces not merely the preservation of the job itself but the way in which it is done, the work-load it involves and many other related matters of substance. Many managements have resisted formal recognition of the legitimacy of joint regulation of the effort bargain while making informal concessions when pressure has been applied from the shop floor. Public policy has not, at least until recent years, helped either side to face the realities of promoting industrial change by negotiation and agreement. As a result, the feeling has undoubtedly grown that direct action is the only way of asserting or defending established and, at least in the eyes of most employees, wholly fair and reasonable expectations.

A crisis of authority?

It is of course possible to see the new militancy as a manifestation of a deep-seated change in popular attitudes towards the established structure of power in Western industrial society. Revans, for example, has argued that

A fundamentally cultural change, irreversible and historically determined, is taking place throughout Western society; it is manifest as a crisis in authority and calls into question traditional assumptions about the nature of command and obedience . . . All organizations that are to survive – and transformation may be a form of survival – must examine the assumptions upon which their contracts of command and obedience are based, with a view to legitimizing these contracts in the light of changing assumptions.[46]

Some of these changes have already been touched upon – in particular the marked decline in the 'fatalism' of working people. The expectation of higher standards of living, the insistence that the possession of a job carries certain 'property rights' and the desire for a greater say in managerial decision-making on matters closely related to the work situation may all be regarded as part and parcel of the 'crisis of authority'. The use of such phrases, however, though widespread, begs a number of questions. Any structure of authority rests on a set of social values which supports and legitimizes the role of those who exercise this authority. Although, as Fox has pointed out, authority relations are compatible with the use of sanctions by those in the upper reaches of the organization for the purpose of securing the necessary 'patterned uniformities of behaviour' from those beneath them, they also imply that such sanctions will be used in support of norms of behaviour which the subordinates themselves ultimately support.[47] If, therefore, there is indeed a real crisis of authority in modern industry, it follows that the social values on which Western capitalism has long been based must be losing their normative influence over a large and growing section of the employed population.

These values have been briefly discussed earlier in this chapter. First and foremost is the belief that the continued prosperity of Western society – and thus the quality of life itself – depends on the vitality and dynamism of private enterprise. This belief legitimizes not only the 'profit motive' but, more especially, the right of management to organize and direct the human, technological and financial resources of the business enterprise. Indeed, it could be argued that the legitimacy of management's role has if anything been strengthened over the past few decades by the growing emphasis on merit and professional expertise rather than on the simple fact of property ownership. The case for the professional manager now rests on the belief that, because of his expertise, he can achieve the traditional objectives of the enterprise – survival, profit and growth – and thereby enrich society as a whole more effectively and efficiently than anyone else.[48] Despite all that has been written in recent years about the 'costs' of economic growth, there is little evidence of any widespread rejection of the social and economic benefits of material prosperity. Indeed, the current debate on worker participation is couched in overwhelmingly utilitarian terms – will extended participation by employees in managerial decision-making, particularly at board level, improve or inhibit the efficiency and success of the enterprise? In short, worker participation will be judged by politicians, managers and employees alike on its relevance to the rate of economic growth, the level of industrial efficiency and the improvement of living standards. As far as employees and trade unions are concerned, there is, to be sure, some evidence that they are becoming more critical of what they see as managerial inefficiency. But this concern should not necessarily be interpreted as a *rejection* of the social values which have long justified managerial control over the organization. On the contrary, it may well be that some employees and their organizations have over the past few years been made more aware than ever before that they have a direct and material interest in the efficiency and competitiveness of the enterprise.[49] Without this awareness it is doubtful that the demand for extended participation in managerial decision-making would be strong enough to warrant the attention of managers and politicians alike.

Social values which legitimize the role of management obviously have a generally conservative and stabilizing influence on the aspirations and behaviour of employees. In Hyman's words: 'Because massive inequalities in the rewards and deprivations associated with work are conventionally regarded as natural and inevitable, major disparities between and within classes are not a serious and persistent source of discontent.'[50] Indeed these disparities have to a great extent become institutionalized through the spread of collective bargaining. They are also cocooned in the language of 'fairness'. The notion of 'a fair day's pay for a fair day's work' formed an important strand in the ideology of late Victorian trade unionism and its normative influence in industrial relations has greatly increased over the last few decades. As Zweig has pointed out:

'Fair' and 'unfair' are words which are always on the lips of the worker. He asks for a fair day's wage and offers a fair day's work, he asks for a fair chance in his work and play and for fair treatment . . . The idea of fairness is linked strongly with the best customs and traditions and the best social rules. It is a social measure which is accepted by most men as binding. The strange thing about 'fairness' is that it is never defined, but all the same its application in practice provides no difficulties. Out of a hundred men asked whether a particular thing is fair or not a big majority will agree on what should be done.[51]

Standards of fairness are embodied in the customary expectations of workgroups and naturally reveal considerable variations from group to group. The process of comparison enables groups to decide whether or not their own pay and general conditions are as fair as they ought to be, or have been in the past. But, as we noted earlier, this process has also become institutionalized through collective bargaining and the formation of *new* comparative reference groups is in practice greatly discouraged by the force of tradition. Consequently, provided that 'proper' relationships are maintained, there is little disposition among the great mass of employees and their representatives to challenge the established hierarchy of incomes.

It must also be recognized, however, that the framework of custom and practice cannot be insulated from the changing economic and social environment. Established relations and expectations have frequently been challenged by technical change, and industrial relations have consequently become markedly more unstable and disputatious. The effects of the engineering employers' attack on the established framework of craft rules in the late 1890s have been noted above. Many other examples, however, can be quoted. In the early 1920s the British coal industry became uncompetitive in international markets, leaving the owners with the choice of rationalizing output or cutting wage costs. They chose the latter option and took on the miners, with immense repercussions on labour relations both inside and outside the mining industry. Fifty years later, with the mines in public ownership, a dramatic increase in world energy prices enhanced the importance of coal and gave the miners a powerful case for a major improvement in their relative pay. Once again the wider ramifications of the miners' claim (and the action they took in pursuit of it) exerted a powerful, destabilizing effect on industrial relations as a whole, particularly as the government of the day was attempting to restrain inflation by means of a statutory incomes policy. Initially, however, the miners themselves were merely reacting to adverse movements in their own pay relative to the pay of certain other manual workgroups. It was noted above that over the postwar period as a whole, a combination of full employment and growing technological interdependence enabled some workgroups (e.g. those employed in the motor-car industry) to raise their earnings through the determined use of bargaining power. As well-organized groups of manual workers have improved their relative position, so a number of traditionally unorganized white-collar groups have sought to re-establish what they consider to be 'proper' relationships – hence, in part, the growth of white-collar unionism. Moreover, the rapid expansion of the white-collar labour force as a whole over the past few decades has brought with it several new occupational groups 'whose proper place within the established pay hierarchy constitutes a source of controversy and conflict'.[52]

The pressures of technical and economic change have introduced other sources of conflict and instability. Mergers, closures and the general drive towards rationalizing production and distribution systems have undoubtedly created a sense of insecurity among manual and white-collar groups alike, thereby stimulating a new awareness of the importance of job property rights and the relevance of collective action. This point is best illustrated by the experience of Electrolux Ltd in the late 1960s. A series of redundancies at the company's Luton plant caused by fluctuations in demand led to 'a breakdown of trust between management and employees', the situation being aggravated by a unilateral tightening up of discipline by management in order to secure higher productivity. When the Commission on Industrial Relations (CIR) investigated industrial relations problems at the plant in 1971 they found that the gap between management and workers was wide and growing:

Workpeople feel that management has become remote and no longer takes an interest in employees. The feeling increased during 1970 because of the company's refusal, as the employees saw it, to give any information about the possibility of (further) redundancies. The fact that in the autumn the company declared thirty employees redundant with little prior warning and no consultation with the unions (as apparently also happened in 1966) tended to confirm their feelings.[53]

The main symptom of this fundamental lack of trust was a growth in short sharp unofficial stoppages, go-slows, etc. throughout the factory, ostensibly in pursuit of sectional pay claims. A similar situation was diagnosed by the CIR at the East Kilbride plant of Standard Telephones and Cables Ltd. Here, a major product change in 1966 resulted in several departmental closures and redundancies, imposed by management without adequate consultation. The climate of labour relations at the plant steadily deteriorated, despite (or perhaps partly because of) repeated threats by management to close down the whole operation, and matters came to a head in the form of a nine-week official stoppage in the spring of 1970. The CIR criticized both management's insensitivity to the needs and problems of its (largely female) workforce and its consequent tendency to impose changes without consultation: 'It appeared to the workforce that a management who had rendered the consultative process useless, and drawn up rules and regulations affecting employees and their representatives unilaterally, lacked any commitment to the making and operation of joint agreements.'[54]

These examples illustrate how the problems of trying to remain competitive in a changing market environment have forced some managements not only to reduce their manpower requirements but also to change the traditional balance in their plants between wages and work standards. In the late 1960s these changes in the effort bargain were frequently embodied in productivity agreements and/or in the development of more formal disciplinary and negotiating procedures. While generally in line with the Donovan Commission's recommendations on the need for more effective control over workplace relations by management, these initiatives for change inevitably increased the interest of many workgroups in the extension of *joint* regulation. Consequently, when changes were introduced without sufficient consultation, workgroups reacted by challenging not only specific managerial decisions but also, implicitly, procedural norms which denied them the right to influence the making of those decisions. Yet the emergence of more formal and comprehensive bargaining structures at workplace level did not in itself guarantee that changes in the effort bargain would always be acceptable to those affected. Occasionally these changes, even where they were fully negotiated, resulted in strikes which typically were longer and involved more employees than the short, localized unofficial stoppage with which the Donovan Commission was so concerned.[55] British Leyland experienced a considerable number of these 'post-Donovan' strikes between 1971 and 1974 as the company slowly replaced its chaotic piecework system by a job-evaluated wages structure. In doing so management also recognized that the workforce, acting through its trade union officials, had a formal role to play in determining both rates of pay and levels of output. One of the major problems which management encountered after the implementation of the new wage structure, however, was that the attitudes fostered by piecework did not disappear with the system itself. Three years after the introduction of measured daywork at the Cowley plant, for example, the old habits were still very much in evidence:

The old system prevented any growth of collective solidarity among the workers. It stressed the individual over the group and injected an abrasive climate into the workplace. That fragmentation is still visible in the readiness that so many groups still have to take industrial action with little thought for its impact on other workers in the plant ...[56]

It may be said, therefore, that over the past few years the 'patterned uniformities of behaviour' regarded as essential to the efficiency of the business organization have been challenged and modified by the changing aspirations of both workgroups and managements. The former have become increasingly preoccupied with higher standards of living, greater security of employment and the extension of joint decision-making machinery through which these substantive gains can be achieved and preserved. Some writers have argued that this preoccupation with pay and security is in turn only symptomatic of a growing *alienation* from work. One well-established school of thought believes, in general terms, that the spread of modern technology has so increased the division of labour and fragmented so many work tasks that many jobs are now incapable of providing the job-holders with any real satisfaction or self-realization. Consequently, it is said, more and more employees are coming to regard work only as a means to an end – namely the achievement of a reasonable and secure standard of living. As long as work continues to fulfil these instrumental goals then most workers may well appear to be quite satisfied with their lot. When, however, these goals are jeopardized – say by the onset of a tougher economic climate which restrains the growth of incomes and creates greater insecurity of employment – then the workgroups will become more 'militant' and direct conflict will increase. Other writers, following Marx, assert that the roots of alienation lie not so much in the 'de-humanizing' effects of modern technology as in the very nature of the wage–work contract: 'It is because man is forced to work for money, and thus places himself under the direction of "an alien will" that he is unable to realize himself in work through the exercise of physical and mental energies.'[57] It follows, therefore, that the wage–work relationship *by its very nature* contains 'a constant potential for disorder'.[58] Seen in these terms, industrial relations are in reality a constant struggle for power between managements and workgroups – a struggle which is expressed primarily in cash terms (i.e. demands for higher pay) because these are the only terms on offer in a capitalist society. Consequently the 'crisis of authority' is and always has been an integral part of employer–employee relations:

Management commands, employees are expected to obey; but the *limits* of management authority and worker obedience are imprecise and shifting. The frontier of control over work relations is in principle too fluid and dynamic to achieve stable definition through formally agreed rules: it must be constantly negotiated and renegotiated through a permanent process of pressure and counter-pressure, the mobilization by both sides of sanctions and resources, at the point of production.[59]

If, however, the Marxist analysis is valid, why is there *so little* direct conflict in industry? Surveys of attitudes and behaviour in the workplace in recent years suggest that the vast majority of managements and workers, far from being locked in continual guerrilla warfare, seem to get along quite reasonably with very little trouble at all. Marxists occasionally pose the same question and answer it largely in terms of the stabilizing force of trade unionism and collective bargaining and the unwillingness of either side to engage in prolonged and costly confrontations. This of course underlines the importance of collective bargaining as a force for order and restraint in industrial relations. But the relative infrequency of direct conflict and the prevalence of cooperative attitudes on the shop floor may also challenge one of the assumptions which many 'alienation' theorists – Marxists and non-Marxists alike – invariably make, namely that work is, at least for most people, *the* most important avenue for self-realization. It is at least possible to argue that, on the one hand, *some* employees and workgroups may find pay and security a positive source of satisfaction whatever the nature of their jobs and, on the other hand, that others may regard their lives *outside* work to be a more satisfying source of personal fulfilment even though their job may not be 'alienating' in any sense.[60] In short, we still have much to learn about employee motivation, orientations to work and priorities in work and the present state of our empirical knowledge does not really lend itself to sweeping generalizations. Consequently the contention that management is currently facing a 'crisis of authority' which may well result in the destruction of the established structure of power in industry must be treated with considerable reserve.

In summary, it has been argued that the new militancy can only be understood in historical perspective. Changes in employee expectations, of which the new militancy is symptomatic, have not appeared unannounced; they did not suddenly burst forth in the late 1960s – although a combination of economic and political factors gave them a peculiar emphasis at that time. On the contrary, the roots of these changes can be traced back several decades. Industrial societies are never entirely static and indeed at most times *change* is the norm. The norms and institutions of industrial relations cannot, therefore, be frozen at any given point in time. Yet, paradoxically, managements and trade union leaders alike have long placed a high priority on preserving tradition, order and stability in workplace relations. In Britain, as in other Western countries, these values have been realized increasingly through a framework of institutional controls, principally collective bargaining. The problem is, of course, that institutions are by their very nature resistant to *rapid* change and may, in periods of economic instability, lose at least some of their regulatory force. In any case it must be remembered that, ultimately, institutions only represent collective arrangements made by people – and human attitudes, customs and practices seldom change at the speed required by economic growth and technological innovation. It follows that the new militancy can only be understood in terms of the underlying conflict in industrial relations between pressures for order and stability and contrary pressures for disorder and change. In Britain this conflict has in many ways intensified over the past ten years as governments have become increasingly concerned with the overall performance of the economy. The pressures for change have increased and, as a result, the relevance of traditional institutional arrangements has been questioned. New priorities have been emerging and these in turn have major implications for all those involved in the management of industrial relations.

CHAPTER TWO

New Pressures and Priorities

> It is important to realize that it is only the fear of the large-
> scale strike which renders governments impotent to stop
> inflation. If it were not for the strike threat, a pay and
> prices freeze could be imposed, followed by a régime of
> strict monetary policy which, in a free competitive market,
> could be expected to produce price stability without ex-
> cessive unemployment.
>
> Brendon Sewill, Special Assistant to
> the Chancellor of the Exchequer, 1970–74

IT is almost a truism that the institutional framework of British
industrial relations is in many respects an historical monument.
The principles and values on which this framework is based are
essentially Victorian in origin. Yet it is only in the past fifteen
years or so that the relevance of these principles has been
seriously questioned. Until the early 1960s the level of confidence
in the system remained high, primarily because there was relatively little disquiet about the performance of the British economy.
However, with the commencement of the great debate about the
failure of the economy to grow at the rate of our major trading
rivals the effectiveness of the industrial relations system was
called into question. Initially its weaknesses were analysed largely
in *moral* terms. The 'irresponsibility' of shop stewards, the
frequency of unofficial strikes, the 'selfishness' of the unions in
pursuing inflationary wage claims and the 'bloody-mindedness'
of workgroups in hanging on to outdated restrictive practices
were all condemned. Gradually, however, the scope of the debate
was widened and a more comprehensive analysis of Britain's
industrial relations problems emerged, in which the effectiveness
of our institutional arrangements occupied a prominent position.
As Allan Flanders observed in 1965:

Whether trade union structure is under debate, or the organization
of employers' associations, or the prospect of an incomes policy, or the

frequency of unofficial strikes, or the relaxing of restrictive practices, or the failure of joint consultation to realize the earlier hopes that were placed in it, no one is any longer disputing that pressing and largely unresolved problems abound. More than that, there is a widespread uneasiness that they are not being resolved because our system of industrial relations, praised in the past for its adaptability, is suffering from an excessive institutional rigidity. The actual texture of relations in industry is being continually transformed along with their technological and economic background, yet they remain pressed uncomfortably into the mould of institutions which though outmoded are strongly resistant to reform.[1]

The institutional framework of any system of industrial relations is important for several reasons. First and foremost, it expresses the values and priorities which the parties themselves (including the state) commonly observe when conducting their business on a day-to-day basis. Second, it controls the level and character of industrial conflict by setting limits to what can be achieved by either side and by laying down a body of 'Queensberry rules' in order to prevent even the most overt clashes of interest from becoming too disruptive. In Hyman's words:

The *aims* of strikers are normally such as to permit scope for compromise; trade unions do not seek to expropriate the employers, or employers to smash the unions. The remarkable fact about most industrial disputes is that, given the wide range of demands which *could* reasonably be raised by workers, union aspirations in bargaining are unambitious and the gap between the disputing parties is thus relatively narrow.[2]

In this sense a strong institutional framework can be a powerful force for order and restraint. Finally, it is ultimately through the collective organizations on both sides of industry that the state seeks to regulate pay, prices, employment and productivity. The success with which any government can pursue its economic policy objectives therefore depends to a large degree on how far the institutional framework of industrial relations and – no less important – the attitudes of those who work within it, are in sympathy with those objectives. Many of Britain's problems in this field stem from the fact that the institutional framework which emerged in the late Victorian period, and has survived largely intact up to the present day, assumed that the role of the state in economic and industrial affairs would be minimal. The most that employers and trade union officials were required to do was to show that they could preserve industrial peace through their own efforts and institutional arrangements. In recent years, however, governments have demanded far more from both sides and some major conflicts have arisen when the parties themselves have attempted to meet these demands.

The institutional legacy

The official attitude towards the conduct of industrial relations in the late Victorian era – an attitude which was to be maintained, at least in peacetime, for another fifty years – was succinctly expressed by the Royal Commission on Labour in 1896:

> ... in some of the principal industries a steady extension has for many years past taken place in the scale and importance of trade unions and employers' associations ... When organizations on either side are so strong as fairly to balance each other, the result is a disposition, already realized in certain cases, to form a mixed board, meeting regularly to discuss and settle questions affecting their relations ... The most successful of these institutions are those which have been formed in the trades where organizations on either side are strongest and most complete ... We hope and believe that the present rapid extension of voluntary boards will continue.

In other words, collective organization was regarded as the prerequisite of order and stability in industrial relations. But it was also widely believed that since the organizations of employers and unions were essentially voluntary and unregulated by statute law, the procedural and substantive rules which they made through collective bargaining must also be voluntary in character. As the Council on Industrial Agreements observed in 1913:

> The whole organization of collective bargaining is based on the principle of consent. We have found that such collective agreements have as a rule been kept and we are loath to interfere with the internal organization of the associations on both sides by putting upon them the legal necessity of exercising compulsion on their members.[3]

In other words the state would put no pressure on employers to recognize trade unions for bargaining purposes, nor would it attempt to influence the substantive content of collective agreements. Nor would it even seek to regulate the use by either side of the ultimate bargaining weapons, the strike and the lock-out, except in so far as its services would be available to help resolve disputes which the parties themselves could not settle.[4]

The refusal of the state to assume a more active role in industrial relations – a refusal which was strongly endorsed by the vast majority of employers and trade union officials – had important consequences. Firstly, it gave neither side any incentive to develop strong centralized institutional controls over the conduct of labour relations at workplace level. Many employers' associations emerged in the 1880s and 1890s primarily in response to changing economic circumstances, the net effect of which was to underline the need to push back the frontier of trade union control over working practices. The success of the employers' counter-attack gave them no further incentive to coordinate their policies on a national rather than an industry-wide basis. During the First World War the rapid growth of state intervention in the economy as a whole prompted some employers to think more in terms of nationwide organization, but interest declined when the government reverted to its traditional role after 1919.[5] If the General Strike of 1926 had succeeded there might easily have been a radical change in the attitude of both employers and politicians to voluntarism, and this might in turn have led to a more centralized system. But the strike failed and an opportunity to break with the past was lost.[6] Indeed, even by 1926 employers' associations had in general become a force for conservatism in industrial relations. Each association was anxious to preserve its autonomy and even when the Confederation of British Industry was formed in 1965 many employers' organizations did not join it. As the Donovan Commission observed, from 1914 onwards 'every important innovation in industrial relations which was not the work of the unions came from the government or from individual companies'.[7] By the 1960s many large firms were leaving their federations, believing that they could make better procedural and substantive agreements with the unions on their own.

The absence of a centralized, authoritative negotiating body on the employers' side gave the unions no incentive to strengthen their own national organization, the TUC. When the TUC was established in 1868 it represented 'an annual demonstration of trade union strength, an expression of solidarity and an opportunity for leaders of the movement to discuss their problems'.[8] In other words it was more of a symbolic gesture than a high command. Over the next few decades little progress was made towards turning the TUC into a genuine policy-making institution. Not until 1921 did the affiliated unions consent to the establishment of a thirty-two-member General Council and a full-time secretariat. The reason was, quite simply, that most union leaders, and particularly those representing the older craft organizations, were determined not to lose any of their traditional autonomy. By contrast with their counterparts in Sweden, British trade unions revealed little sense of solidarity.[9] Parochial loyalties, occupational consciousness and a strong attachment to customary differentials together constituted a formidable barrier against any centralizing tendencies. They also prevented any rationalization of trade union structures, despite the growing conviction of some trade unionists that the overlapping and illogical distribution of membership was a source of weakness. The TUC never had more than a general moral authority over the policies and actions of its affiliated members. During the Second World War this authority was enhanced by the close involvement of the TUC in decision-making at government level. Indeed until the end of the 1940s it was strong enough to bear the weight of the policy of wage restraint which the postwar Labour government requested. The eventual repudiation of wage restraint by rank-and-file members on the shop floor, however, exposed the fundamental weakness of the TUC – a weakness which became even more evident over the next two decades with the growth of workplace bargaining and the corresponding decline in the authority of trade union officials. Difficulties arose when successive governments from 1961 onwards solicited the cooperation of the TUC in restraining wage inflation, in return for which the latter wanted more influence over an ever-widening range of economic and social policies. The result was a gradual institutionalization of the process of central bargaining between governments and the TUC with the CBI trying, never very successfully, to participate on equal terms. But the TUC could rarely offer a convincing guarantee that whatever agreement it made with the government would be observed by all its affiliated unions and, more especially, their members on the shop floor. This was not so much due to any bad faith or cynicism on the part of the General Council members as an inevitable consequence of the inherent constitutional weakness of the TUC.

Another result of the state's reluctance to regulate the conduct of industrial relations on a systematic basis was that the structure and coverage of collective bargaining remained haphazard and illogical. What Marsh has described as the 'cults of privacy, unstructure and negotiation' flourished in the absence of any reforming pressure from outside.[10] Employers and trade union officials, or at any rate those outside the public sector, were led to believe that the agreements they made were of no concern to anyone but themselves – hence the 'cult of privacy'. By the same token it was also generally believed that bargaining rights could and should be agreed only after a trial of strength. Although the government in its role as a major employer accepted that collective bargaining was appropriate for its own employees, it exerted little or no pressure (except in wartime) on employers in the private sector. The absence of any legal right to join a trade union meant that where an employer enjoyed a strong bargaining position in the local labour market, trade union members and activists could be dismissed or otherwise discriminated against with impunity. Even when, in the 1950s, full employment blunted this weapon in respect of many manual workers, it was still frequently applied in order to discourage white-collar employees from joining a union. Yet there was no pressure from the TUC in favour of legal support for trade union recognition and the extension of collective bargaining. The leaders of most manual unions prided themselves on the achievements of 'voluntarism' and feared that legal support would inevitably bring some form of government supervision in its train. Finally, where bargaining arrangements were already well established (as they were in all the major industries by 1945, at least for manual workers), both sides strongly believed that all disputes should be settled by negotiation, without recourse to any assistance from 'outsiders'. The government provided a conciliation service for those who wanted it and could in extreme cases appoint a court of inquiry, but the parties themselves much preferred to settle their own problems by means of their own machinery and behind closed doors.

This strong attachment to the voluntary principle would perhaps have received a more favourable press if it had in fact achieved the objectives which enthusiasts claimed for it. In reality, however, it was ironical that while British trade union leaders repeatedly claimed that free collective bargaining was superior to the methods of conducting industrial relations in the USA and continental Europe, which relied on a varying mixture of collective bargaining and legal regulation, the substantive achievements of the British system were generally more modest.[11] Almost every British industry had its own national procedure agreement which in turn permitted the regular negotiation of substantive terms and conditions, including wage rates, hours of work, overtime payments and other basic items, covering manual workers in the industry. But very few national agreements, at least in the private sector, even attempted to regulate matters of substance at *workplace* level. This did not matter greatly while labour market conditions favoured unilateral decision-making by management. The onset of full employment, however, gradually eroded the traditional shop-floor acquiescence in unilateral managerial rule. In the motor-car industry, for example, the growing insistence by workgroups that their wages should be fair in comparative terms and that the possession of a job gave the worker certain 'property rights' was reflected in the pattern of strike action. In most other industries, however, the traditional absence of comprehensive joint regulation in the workplace did not lead to such overt and direct conflict. In engineering, for example, the volume of *ad hoc* bargaining at plant and company level gradually increased during the 1960s and the frequency of unofficial stoppages also increased, but the vast majority of establishments still remained almost entirely strike-free.[12] In other words the spread of workshop bargaining was typically slow and uneven and consequently did not result in a *general* upsurge in the level of direct conflict.

Successive investigations since the mid-1960s have in fact made the following salient points about the institutional characteristics of workplace relations in British industry. Firstly, *formal machinery* for bargaining purposes is much more likely to be found in large companies than in small ones, and is generally more common in the public sector than in private industry.[13] Secondly, *unilateral decision-making* by management, even on matters of substance regarded as important by the workforce, is more widespread than is commonly supposed, particularly where the level of union membership is low.[14] Thirdly, both the degree of mutual *satisfaction* with existing arrangements and the level of *cooperation* on the shop floor seem to be considerably greater than the popular image of British industrial relations would suggest.[15] Fourthly, the importance of *workplace bargaining* in general and of *shop stewards* in particular is growing and the influence of both employers' associations and trade union officials is correspondingly on the wane.[16] Finally the significance of *informal practices*, even in workplaces where there is a relatively high level of formality, remains strong. The following observation by one researcher is particularly relevant:

The pattern of industrial relations at plant level would appear to be one of continuous adjustment to change, which is carried on without recourse to formal procedures. This does not mean that there is no dialogue between management and workers, but that it does not always take place within an easily definable system. The process of participation is part of a complex web of arrangements that have been built up over time and are particular to a company or a department and to specific managers, foremen and shop stewards. This kind of continuous participation is highly dependent upon personal understandings and perceptions. Where these fail to satisfy needs they may result in conflict and open dispute, with a stoppage of work as the ultimate consequence.[17]

Strikes, however, are still largely confined to a minority of plants and companies, which presumably means that traditional methods of adapting to a continuously changing environment still seem to be generally effective. Recent statistics issued by the Department of Employment suggest that even in the relatively strike-prone manufacturing sector, stoppages are peculiar to a small number of establishments. The size of the employment unit appears to have some influence on strike-proneness.

The figures given in Table 2 lend some support to the view that there are certain features of life in small plants which are conducive to cooperative employee relations, notably the emphasis on informality, flexibility and one-to-one communications. Yet even among the firms with over a thousand employees

Table 2

Strikes in British manufacturing industries, 1971–3

	1971	1972	1973	Average
Percentage of firms with *no* strikes	98·1	97·5	97·7	97·8
Percentage of strike-free firms with:				
11–24 employees	99·9	99·8	99·9	99·8
25–99 employees	99·0	98·9	98·9	98·9
100–199 employees	97·3	96·3	96·7	96·7
200–499 employees	94·8	92·0	92·5	93·1
500–999 employees	86·5	82·1	82.4	83·7
1,000 or more employees	59·7	54·1	54·4	56·1
Average of all firms	83·1	80·0	80·3	81·1

Source: *Department of Employment Gazette*, December 1976.

nearly 44 per cent did not experience a single stoppage during the three-year period, so that direct conflict is not an inevitable consequence of large-scale organization. The plain fact is that even in manufacturing, strikes are exceptional. More than three quarters of all industries in this sector, accounting for almost 70 per cent of manufacturing employment, had at least nine out of ten establishments which were *totally* free of stoppages during the period.

If, then, the established framework of institutional arrangements at plant level is effective and commands the support of both managements and shop stewards, why has it attracted so much criticism in recent years? The Donovan Commission, in discussing this paradox, pointed out that the present system had much to commend it. Firstly, the tradition of workplace autonomy and the weakness of the central organizations on both sides (trade unions and employers' associations) seemed to suit the preferences of everyone concerned: 'Managers have considerable freedom to run their own industrial relations affairs without interference from outside. This also means that shop stewards enjoy considerable authority; but, since stewards are for the most part reasonable people, managers can normally come to an arrangement with them.' Secondly, said the Commission, the system was extremely flexible; the absence of rigid and detailed rules enabled the parties to settle their disputes on an *ad hoc* basis 'without having to worry too much about the consequences elsewhere'. Thirdly, the system had conferred 'a very high degree of self-government' on the parties concerned: 'Not only do managers and shop stewards have a considerable freedom from outside interference, but above all workgroups are given scope to follow their own customs and take their own decisions.'

The Commission felt, however, that these benefits were outweighed by the following costs: 'the tendency of extreme decentralization and self-government to degenerate into indecision and anarchy; the propensity to breed inefficiency; and the reluctance to change – all of them characteristics which become more damaging as they develop, as the rate of technical progress increases, and as the need for economic growth becomes more urgent'.[18] In other words, Donovan was saying that the traditional justification for the voluntary principle – the preservation of industrial peace through self-regulation – was no longer adequate in the economic environment of the 1960s. Instead, the conduct of industrial relations and the framework of institutional arrangements on which this was based would henceforward be evaluated according to their contribution to technological change and economic growth. The implication was that if voluntarism inhibited the introduction and implementation of necessary change then, even though it preserved 'flexibility' and avoided stoppages, the cost to the community was unacceptably high.

Donovan was particularly concerned with the relationship between the shortcomings of the formal system of industry-wide procedures and the tendency for unofficial and unconstitutional stoppages to increase. Indeed, the Commission's emphasis on unofficial strikes was partly rooted in the growing national preoccupation with economic growth, industrial efficiency and international competitiveness. Thus the Commission was concerned not merely with the effect on the economy of those strikes which *did* take place but also with the wider implications of the threat that strikes *might* occur:

If an employer forestalls a strike by making concessions in the face of threats which it might have been better to resist, or by refraining from introducing changes which he believes to be necessary in the interests of efficiency, then the economic consequences of his doing so may be more serious than those to which a strike would have given rise.[19]

The implication of this argument was that a *higher* level of direct conflict in industry would not necessarily be a bad thing if it was the result of faster technological innovation and organizational change. If, therefore, the members of the Commission had not been as preoccupied as politicians and the media were with the supposedly damaging effect of strikes, they might have reflected on the point that far from having too many stoppages, British industry did not in fact have enough. The real problem was not that managements as a whole were being deterred from taking much-needed initiatives for change by a militant and 'bloody-minded' workforce but that, on the contrary, there was too *little* pressure on managements from the shop floor.

It is now frequently argued that one reason for the declining competitiveness of British industry over the past decade is a growing relative deficiency in the amount of capital investment which the British worker has at his elbow. This deficiency has in turn been caused, at least in part, by the relative cheapness of British labour (see Table 3).

In some foreign countries, notably the USA and Sweden, the trade unions have long accepted that it is very much in the interests of their members that companies should invest as much

Table 3

Labour costs in manufacturing, 1964–75
*Total hourly labour costs, including
social charges (UK = 100)*

	1964	1970	1975
Belgium	105	124	184
Denmark	119	141	195
France	103	103	128
UK	100	100	100
Italy	93	111	127
Japan	42	66	99
Netherlands	95	126	188
Sweden	153	179	219
USA	268	253	185
West Germany	119	145	176

Source: NIESR, *Economic Review*, November 1976; all
costs expressed in Swedish Kroner.

as possible in labour-saving machinery. The best way of encouraging managements to improve the efficiency (and thus the competitiveness) of the organization is, of course, to press for the highest possible wages and fringe benefits, and this is precisely what American and Swedish unions have done. By comparison, most trade union officials and shop stewards in Britain, despite popular impressions to the contrary, have been far less demanding. It was noted in the previous chapter that the general expectation of a rising standard of living, while significant in historical terms, has not assumed as radical a form as it might have done. The economic consequences of this relative moderation have not, therefore, been as beneficial as one might have supposed. In Tessler's words:

> More successful bargaining (by trade unions) might have sent management hurrying round the corner, into the City, to raise funds for modernization and cost-saving equipment . . . As it was – with wages rising relatively slowly – management could indulge in a hoarding of labour which in some plants assumed proportions that frequently astonished observers from similar industries abroad.[20]

The institutional framework of British industrial relations has undoubtedly helped to keep the level of aspirations relatively low on both sides of the bargaining table. The Donovan Commission argued that the 'formal' system of industry-wide agreements was becoming less and less relevant to the real issues of substance in the workplace and yet at the same time was inhibiting many managements from seeking to develop a more formal and comprehensive framework of joint regulation at plant and company level:

What is required is effective and orderly collective bargaining over such issues as the control of incentive schemes, the regulation of hours actually worked, the use of job evaluation, work practices and the linking of changes in pay to changes in performance, facilities for shop stewards and disciplinary rules and appeals. In most industries industry-wide collective agreements cannot deal effectively with these issues because individual companies have not delegated authority to settle them to their associations, and they have no intention of doing so now.[21]

Donovan regarded the formal, written company-wide agreement, backed by a comprehensive industrial relations policy decided at board level, as a much more appropriate framework within which *change* could be introduced. The Donovan model, which was itself based on the standard North American collective agreement, presupposed that the scope of collective bargaining in the workplace would have to be greatly increased and that procedures would have to be formalized. Yet the Commission also pointed out that 'fragmented bargaining and informal workshop understandings' could not be abolished simply by introducing formal plant agreements – everything depended on the willingness of managements to take initiatives and the readiness of trade union representatives to 'respond positively' to such initiatives. In retrospect, however, it is evident that the 'formal' system has not declined to anything like the extent predicted by Donovan. On the contrary, in recent years the regulative importance of industry-wide agreements, at least in respect of earnings, has increased.[22] By the same token Donovan's enthusiasm for the formalization of plant and company agreements does not seem to have been shared by either managements or shop stewards. Thus while the substantive scope of workplace bargaining has generally increased since the late 1960s, and the status of the shop steward has correspondingly continued to grow, the preference of both sides for informality and privacy has in no way diminished.[23] This continuing attachment to traditional habits and institutional arrangements suggests that aspirations on both sides are still relatively modest and that internally generated pressure for change is therefore weak.

The growth of state regulation (I)

If the pressure for change from within industry is weak, can central government provide the missing impetus? In the 1960s the conventional wisdom was that it could. A major cause of low productivity in British industry was held to be the failure of managers to use their manpower resources efficiently, a failure which was frequently compounded by the refusal of workgroups to 'give up' their restrictive practices. Low productivity was in turn responsible for the apparent tendency of British industry's unit costs to rise faster than those of our major competitors, spilling over into a balance of payments deficit and a rising rate of domestic inflation. Thus the efficient use of manpower quickly became a matter of priority for the government of the day and in 1965 a new agency, the National Board for Prices and Incomes, was set up in order to further this objective. As the Board's *First General Report* pointed out:

There are two possible causes lying behind the phenomenon of rising prices. First, demand may be too high ... Second ... old habits, inherited attitudes and institutional arrangements may all combine to exert an upward pressure on prices ... Experience has shown that attitudes are not changed by a use of the fiscal and monetary weapons at the disposal of the government. Nor are they susceptible to legislation – habits are not changed by law. We see ourselves as promoting change by conducting a continuing dialogue with managements, unions and indeed government.

In short the traditional freedom of managements and unions to conduct their business in their own way, regardless of the wider implications of their decisions, was being questioned.

The government and the Board took the view that the only practicable way of inducing managements and unions to negotiate and agree upon more efficient working practices was to make pay increases above the prevailing norm of $3\frac{1}{2}$ per cent conditional on the achievement of measurable improvements in productivity. It was also anticipated, largely on the basis of the experience which companies such as Esso had had with productivity bargaining, that managerial initiatives to increase efficiency would also involve the reform of bargaining habits and institutions at plant and company level. Thus the Board (and subsequently the Donovan Commission) regarded the comprehensive productivity agreement as the model for the reform of workplace relations. The problem was that in practice relatively few managements were capable of initiating changes which involved such a radical break with tradition. Many of the productivity deals agreed under the auspices of incomes policy between 1967 and 1969 were small-scale affairs whose contribution to either higher productivity or institutional reform was to say the least marginal. Research has in fact shown that those managements who approached productivity bargaining seriously were *already* thinking of taking an initiative of some kind in order to improve their labour relations. In the words of Daniel and McIntosh, 'the effect of the productivity criterion, where it was effective, was to give events a very firm push in the direction in which they were already going'.[24]

In short it was the most enlightened and progressive section of British management which responded to the challenge of productivity bargaining. The Board was never able to solve the problem of how to induce the mass of employers who did not fall into this category to do likewise. The Donovan Commission faced the same problem in relation to the implementation of its general ideas for the reform of workplace bargaining. How could managements and trade unionists who saw no need for change and were quite satisfied with existing arrangements be persuaded that the Commission's recommendations were relevant to *them*? Since Donovan's objective was to strengthen the voluntary principle, the emphasis had to be on voluntary action. However, a new institution – the Commission on Industrial Relations – was established in order to promote and publicize the need for fundamental (and necessarily long-term) changes in institutions and attitudes at plant and company level. Because such changes could only be achieved with the active co-operation of the parties concerned, the CIR was given no power to enforce its recommendations. Some observers, including one or two members of the Donovan Commission itself, doubted whether a CIR without legal powers would have much credibility in cases where the parties themselves were not convinced of the need for change. In practice, however, the CIR sought to win the confidence of both sides by producing detailed, practical suggestions for improving particular situations which it had investigated in depth. While its early reports were usually based on the Donovan themes of formalizing workplace relations and extending collective bargaining, they nevertheless spoke directly to the managements concerned. The Commission sensibly took the view that its analyses of specific problems and the solutions proposed should stand or fall on their own merits, without recourse to legal penalties. The difficulty was that the adherents of this strategy could not, and never claimed to be able to, transform British industrial relations overnight. Unfortunately by the late 1960s a large and increasingly influential school of thought had become impatient with 'voluntary' reforms and clamoured for the imposition of a more restrictive legal framework on British industrial relations, in the hope that this would bring about a radical change in behaviour on the shop floor.

From 1969 until 1974 public policy towards industrial relations was strongly influenced by the belief that British industry as a whole was inordinately prone to strikes and that the 'irresponsibility' of trade unions and workgroups was the root of the problem. In his 'Note of Reservation' to the Donovan Report, Andrew Shonfield advanced the proposition that 'the deliberate abstention of the law from the activities of mighty subjects tends to diminish the liberty of the ordinary citizen and place his welfare at risk'.[25] Implicit in this proposition was the 'David and Goliath' view of trade unionism. It was frequently asserted that trade unions had become 'mighty subjects' *because* the state had stood apart from the conduct of industrial relations for so long. It followed therefore that the alleged imbalance of power in the workplace could only be redressed by the introduction of a new, interventionist framework of law. However the basic assumption that a permissive framework of law had encouraged the abuse of collective power was totally at variance with reality. If certain sections of British industry were becoming more strike-prone during the 1960s the main reason lay in the changing nature of employee expectations. Nevertheless, this basic misconception about the normative role of the law led the authors of the Conservative government's Industrial Relations Act (1971) into making several erroneous assumptions about the nature of industrial conflict. These assumptions were (1) that many unofficial strikes occurred because of a failure by trade union leaders to control their rank-and-file members, especially their shop stewards; (2) that disruptive behaviour on the shop floor could be discouraged by the threat of legal penalties; (3) that trade unions habitually imposed unreasonable limitations on the freedom of their members; (4) that many large-scale official stoppages took place in defiance of the wishes of the 'silent majority' of trade unionists and (5) that most managers were eager to reassert their control over workplace relations and would therefore exploit whatever legal avenues were opened to them. As soon as the Act was put to the test, however, it quickly emerged that the new legal framework would be of little practical use. Unfortunately a high price was paid in terms of working days lost before the politicians' faith in the law as a remedy for industrial conflict was broken.

It would of course be very misleading to regard the Industrial Relations Act as little more than a partisan attack on the trade unions. In the post-Donovan era only the most blinkered critic of the unions could ignore the role of bad management and inappropriate bargaining structures in generating industrial conflict. Various sections of the Act were therefore predominantly reformist in intention. Following Donovan the authors of the Act wanted to bring more formality into workplace bargaining and to encourage managements to develop a stronger procedural framework at company and plant level.[26] The Act also attempted to resolve the problems posed both by multi-union bargaining structures and by the unreasonable opposition of some employers to trade union recognition.[27] Finally the Act broadly followed

Donovan in introducing new, if limited, safeguards for the employee against unfair dismissal.[28] In practice, however, the reformist objectives of the Act were largely frustrated by the authors' obsession with trade union power. Trade unionists regarded the Act as an attack on their traditional freedom. Consequently, with the exception of the new safeguards against unfair dismissal, which met a real need, the reformist provisions of the Act were either ignored or tarred with the same brush as the restrictive sections. Even before the Act had reached the statute book the TUC decided to adopt a policy of 'non-co-operation' and most affiliated unions stuck doggedly to this position when the Act was in force.[29] The vast majority of managements took the same view. Their overriding priority was to preserve the traditional framework of relations in the workplace and keep production going. In the words of Weekes *et al.*:

Employers generally refused to see their industrial relations as a problem and the 'disorder' described by others was often defended by managements because it gave them flexibility. Certainly management seemed anxious to avoid the loss of control to outsiders which they felt the use of the new legal institutions implied. In so far as any of them saw the need for change, strategies other than the use or threat of the law were generally preferred.[30]

Only in the exceptionally strike-prone sector of the docks did employers resort to the law in strength, and even they probably regretted it.[31]

The authors of the Act made an even greater error in supposing that a framework of legal *rights* could somehow be superimposed on the traditional structure of *power*. In practice, however, it is impossible to make a clear-cut distinction between rights and power, at least in the context of workplace relations. Historically trade unions and employers have only been able to claim rights (as distinct from legal *immunities*) if they have had the power to enforce them. One of the most important postwar developments in industrial relations, not only in Britain but also in Western Europe and the USA, has been the gradual growth of collective bargaining in the workplace. In other words there has been a change in the structure of power relations. Some managements

NEW PRESSURES AND PRIORITIES

have of course succeeded in hanging on to most of their traditional prerogatives, particularly where employees are still unorganized. Many others have found themselves confronted by workgroups asserting their 'right' to a higher material standard of living and to more say in decision-making on matters of substance. This 'challenge from below' has been most effective where workgroups have been able to exploit a strong labour market position and disrupt a closely integrated organization. In short, rights have been claimed and won where the structure of bargaining power has been sufficiently favourable. It is hardly surprising, therefore, that the attempt to change this power structure by imposing a body of unwanted and irrelevant rights and obligations on employers and trade unions should have failed so completely. In the aftermath of the Donovan Report the principal objective of public policy should have been to stimulate new thinking and new initiatives for change in company boardrooms and to give trade union officials and shop stewards some incentive to respond positively to these initiatives. Instead, the Industrial Relations Act pushed both sides back on the defensive. The efforts of the National Board for Prices and Incomes, the Donovan Commission and the CIR to stimulate the reform and extension of collective bargaining had begun to bear fruit by 1970. The Act, however, largely dissipated these efforts, and when it was finally repealed in 1974 the real problems of British industrial relations still awaited a solution.

It is important to note, however, that the repeal of the Act in 1974 did not bring a return to the pre-1971 situation of formal abstention by the state. By then it was generally recognized, even by the TUC, that Britain was lagging some way behind the rest of the EEC in terms of the basic floor of protective rights available to all employees. Trade union leaders also realized that the extension of collective bargaining could be promoted much more quickly with the aid of legal compulsion than by the old reliance on voluntary methods. It should also be remembered that the Labour government elected in February 1974 had committed itself to engineering a 'fundamental and irreversible shift in the balance of wealth and power in favour of working people and their families'. The introduction of a legal framework which both raised the basic floor of individual employment rights and strengthened the framework of collective regulation was therefore consistent with this overall political objective. But the current legislation, principally the Trade Union and Labour Relations Act (1974) and the Employment Protection Act (1975), also contains a fair amount of industrial logic. Firstly, it recognizes that employees and unions are increasingly concerned with 'job property rights' – a concern which has doubtless been sharpened by the steep rise in unemployment since 1974 – and seeks to improve job security. Secondly, it also recognizes that institutions such as the closed shop are an integral part of the framework of control in many workplaces and that it is therefore foolish to try to upset these arrangements. Thirdly, it accepts that collective bargaining is the best way of promoting orderly industrial relations. Finally, it recognizes that a truly independent conciliation and arbitration service can make a significant contribution to the cause of industrial peace – hence the establishment of the Advisory, Conciliation and Arbitration Service.

Nevertheless, the limitations of the law as a normative force in the day-to-day conduct of industrial relations are still apparent, though not in such an obvious way as between 1971 and 1974. If we consider first the only section of the 1971 Act which has been extended and developed by the more recent legislation – that relating to unfair dismissal – it is apparent that its general effects have been less than radical. From 1972 to 1974 the volume of applications alleging unfair dismissal was less than half the level expected and only when the qualifying period for protection was reduced to six months did the number of applications reach the 20,000 a year mark.[32] This low level of demand possibly suggests that dissatisfaction with existing disciplinary arrangements is less widespread than has often been assumed. Thus a survey carried out by the Department of Employment in 1971 and 1972 concluded that 'the overwhelming majority of employees were prepared to accept and abide by rules and standards which were set, and disciplinary action was rarely a bone of contention where it was administered fairly and consistently'.[33] It may also be that where the fairness of a managerial decision on a disciplinary matter is open to question, the instinctive reaction of most trade union members (at least in relatively well-organized establishments) is to seek the assistance of their shop steward. Thus it has been reported that industries and services where trade unionism is weak (notably construction and distribution) have regularly been over-represented in tribunal proceedings. It has also been found that manual workers in small private firms and white-collar employees generally have been disproportionately represented in unfair dismissal applications.[34] There is little evidence to suggest that the legal constraints on dismissal have given much additional impetus to the reform of procedures at plant level, particularly since formal procedures of any kind are more likely to be found in middle-size and large companies who have been under-represented in tribunal cases. Nor can it be argued that these constraints have really increased security of employment. The employee's basic right is to be compensated in cash terms if he is unfairly dismissed; reinstatement is not, and indeed cannot be compulsory. Finally the rules in the 1975 Act which compel employers to give their employees adequate warning of redundancy and to consult with unions before any final decisions are taken must, of course, be regarded as significant.[35] Yet few trade unionists should be under any illusion that these rules can somehow override the economic realities which make redundancy inevitable.

It also looks as though it may be harder to achieve certain other objectives expressed in the current legislation than was first thought. On paper at least the sections of the Employment Protection Act which deal with the extension of collective bargaining appear to be far-reaching in their intent. The job of resolving disputes over recognition has been given to the Advisory Conciliation and Arbitration Service (ACAS) which, although independent, is likely to take a generally favourable view of recognition claims. Moreover the Act contains a liberal definition of a recognition dispute, so that in practice this *could* include not only straightforward claims for negotiating rights in 'greenfield' situations but also demands from unions to extend the *scope* of collective bargaining where this already exists. ACAS is also empowered to hold secret ballots but not obliged to be bound by the majority verdict; it is certainly possible therefore that a trade union with considerably less than half the employees in a given bargaining unit may still win negotiating rights. So far, however, the results of these provisions have not matched the hopes (or fears) which were expressed at the outset. During 1976 around fifty recognition claims were submitted to ACAS every month but only a handful had been reported on by January 1977. A further point which quickly became clear was that the length of the recognition procedure, the scope which 'uncooperative' employers still had to delay the process, and the absence of an ultimate sanction which would compel employers to recognize a union were all factors likely to restrain the extension of collective bargaining. Moreover, most white-collar union leaders anticipated that the provision restricting legal rights to 'independent' trade unions would effectively destroy the staff associations which proliferated, particularly in the financial sector, in the early 1970s. In fact, however, many such associations have received certificates of independence from the certification officer and, armed with this new 'seal of respectability', now constitute an obstacle to further expansion by white-collar unions such as ASTMS, APEX and NUBE.[36]

In other areas the current legislation merely puts its stamp of approval on existing practices. One such area is the closed shop. The Donovan Commission rejected the case for prohibiting the closed shop by law on the grounds that, in the absence of widespread dissatisfaction with the closed shop, such a law was unlikely to be observed. It would also create some very difficult problems for managements if *de facto* closed shops were challenged by dissident employees. The Industrial Relations Act, by contrast, gave every employee the right to join and *not* to join a trade union – a right which theoretically struck at the heart of the closed shop. In practice, however, the vast majority of managements connived with trade union representatives to keep their closed shops in being and this section of the Act provoked nothing like the amount of trouble which many observers initially predicted. By contrast, the Employment Protection Act specifically recognizes that the closed shop, while placing certain restrictions on the freedom of individual employees, can in fact make an important contribution to stable bargaining relationships.[37] The Act also recognizes that it is impracticable to seek to regulate the relationship between a trade union and its individual members. The authors of the 1971 Act seemed to assume that many trade unions were run by small cliques of 'militants' who frequently acted irresponsibly towards both the community as a whole and some of their own members. It was thought that the individual member *needed* new and stringent safeguards against the abuse of power by shop stewards and full-time officials. This assumption, however, was based on a total ignorance of what employees expect from their unions and indeed of the reasons why they join them in the first place. One recent study of the Union of Post Office Workers, for example, suggests that the dichotomy between the 'militant' attitudes of the active minority who actually run the union and the apparently 'moderate' outlook of the silent majority is not in practice a cause for concern. It is simply that the silent majority of ordinary, non-active members belong to the union for predominantly instrumental reasons – in other words they expect it to satisfy their legitimate aspirations in terms of wages and conditions. As long as the union does this, they are quite content to let the minority pursue 'radical cultural goals' which they themselves do not necessarily share.[38] It seems hardly necessary to add, however, that an attempt by any government to restrict the freedom of the union to pursue its traditional objectives by customary methods is more likely than anything else to drive militants and moderates alike into the same defensive posture. This, of course, is precisely what happened within most unions between 1971 and 1974. It may also happen again if the restrictions on collective bargaining imposed by an incomes policy become too severe.

The growth of state regulation (2)

Incomes policy has in fact constituted the main vehicle of state intervention in industrial relations over the last fifteen years or so. The development of a new framework of collective and individual labour law has certainly been important, if only because it now constitutes a significant constraint on the traditional freedom of management to manage. Nevertheless in many workplaces the impact of the law on the day-to-day conduct of industrial relations has been less than dramatic. By contrast, few companies in recent years have escaped the much more severe constraints imposed by successive incomes policies.

At the root of all incomes policies is the belief, by no means universally shared, that collective bargaining is a factor of great significance in the process of inflation. In the postwar economic environment many workgroups and unions have been able to exploit their bargaining power and win wage increases well in excess of the rate of growth of productivity. The result has been a persistent tendency for labour costs to rise and this in turn has pushed up the general rate of inflation. From what was said in the preceding chapter about the implications of changing expectations, material and otherwise, for the management of industrial relations, it would be difficult to disagree with the view that level of pay settlements and, equally important, the structure of bargaining on matters of substance *is* a very significant factor in the inflationary process. In Jones's words, the tendency for unit labour costs to rise is attributable to 'the assertion by men of what they see as their rights in an age of nominal political equality and, judged by historical standards, of fast economic growth'.[39] These rights have frequently been asserted through collective action, not simply at an 'official' level by trade unions but also (and increasingly) by workgroups on the shop floor. The growth of unofficial strikes throughout Western Europe over the past decade or so suggests that workgroups are prepared to assert and defend what they see as their rights regardless of whether or not they are supported by their trade unions and regardless of the level of unemployment. Recent empirical investigations suggest that in recent years at least changes in unemployment, which may be regarded as a rough indicator of the level of demand in the economy, have had 'no discernible effect on the rate of wage inflation'.[40] In short, it would seem that the process of wage determination is now so highly institutionalized that aggregate demand policies aimed at reducing wage inflation via an increase in unemployment 'could produce little or no effect on the pace of wage change'.[41] Once this position is reached it is extremely difficult to deny the need for an incomes policy of some kind. The difficulty is that most of the incomes policies which British governments have devised over the last decade or so have clashed in one way or another with the long-established conventions of collective bargaining. They have also challenged most of the assumptions on which the whole system of British industrial relations (using the word 'system' in its loosest sense) has traditionally rested.

The persistent tendency for unit labour costs to rise has of course been experienced by all major industrial countries over the postwar period as a whole. Britain's inflationary problems have, however, been more acute than elsewhere, *not* because British trade unions are more aggressive and irresponsible than their foreign counterparts, but rather because British industry has failed to improve its overall efficiency to a level where cost increases can be absorbed without too much difficulty. Consequently, while incomes policies in Britain have been much more restrictive than elsewhere, the relative cheapness of British labour is still almost entirely offset by low productivity.[42] The incomes policy which ran from 1965 until 1970 specifically recognized the need for higher productivity and sought to encourage joint action in the workplace to this end. The overall framework of wage restraint was thus designed to induce managements and unions to reform their bargaining habits in the interests of efficiency. The idea itself was by no means unsound. In practice, however, it proved increasingly difficult to implement the policy. Firstly, the productivity criterion itself, while not unknown in conventional wage bargaining, had never been as popular with trade union negotiators as comparability and the cost of living. In some industries labour productivity was not too difficult to quantify and consequently the possibilities for negotiating above-the-norm pay increases were almost limitless; in other sectors the opposite was true. Some groups therefore did much better out of the policy than others, a fact which generated a growing feeling of unfairness.[43] Secondly, this feeling was reinforced by the well-known peculiarities of the structure of collective bargaining. Those groups who had plenty of scope for bargaining at workplace level obviously stood to gain much more than those who relied almost entirely on industry-wide agreements. Thirdly, in so far as some groups found that their real incomes were rising either very slowly or not at all, the policy failed to fulfil the promises which government ministers made on its behalf and thus it challenged the established pattern of wage expectations. Finally, the success of the wages side of the policy depended on the stability of the cost of living index. After the devaluation of November 1967, however, the government was obliged to 'mop up' excessive spending power by increasing both direct and indirect taxation. This strategy not only led to a more rapid rise in the cost of living but also further restricted the growth of disposable incomes. By 1969 many workgroups were blaming incomes policy for the stagnation in their living standards and, once deprived of the support of rank-and-file trade union members, no incomes policy can last for long.

The problem of persuading managements, workgroups and their national organizations to accept an incomes policy is, of course, extremely complex. An ORC poll conducted in the autumn of 1972, when the Heath government was trying to persuade the TUC to accept a new voluntary incomes policy, suggested that an overwhelming majority of the population was prepared to accept a pay rise of not more than £2 per week provided that price increases could be kept below an annual rate of 5 per cent. An equally large majority felt that it was more important to control the cost of living than that people should obtain large increases in money wages.[44] Other surveys of public opinion have also indicated that there are strong, widespread feelings against the deliberate use of unemployment to control wage inflation. To this extent one could say that in recent years there has been considerable public support for the idea of an incomes policy. Thus when the negotiations between the TUC and the Heath government broke down, the latter were confident that if they introduced an incomes policy which applied the same rules to everyone, permitted no group to claim special treatment and maintained effective control over prices, profits and dividends, the great majority of the public (including trade union members) would support them. Yet, as Daniel has pointed out, there is some ambiguity in public attitudes towards incomes policy:

> When it comes to people's feelings about their own pay and the extent to which their own employer could pay them more, quite different considerations come into effect than when they are assessing the problem of inflation from a national perspective. Wage and salary earners respond in relation to their own pay according to their particular family circumstances and workplace relations, and the facts of life from their perspective, rather than the facts of life as they appear from a perspective derived from the management of the national economy. For these reasons concern about the general problem of inflation is relatively remote and abstract. Concern about personal earnings in relation to commitments and the rising cost of living is immediate and specific.[45]

Initially the statutory policy introduced in November 1972 was reasonably effective. During the second half of 1973, however, inflationary pressures began to build up, culminating in an explosion of world energy and commodity prices. Not even the most draconic legal controls on prices could have kept the rise in the cost of living down to the 6 per cent level which the government had anticipated for the period from October 1973 to April 1974. It seems probable, therefore, that even if the miners had not challenged the policy it would have broken down sooner or later in the face of sustained pressure for large compensatory increases in money wages.

The search for an effective voluntary incomes policy has also raised the emotive question of trade union power. In the words of the *Economist*,

> Curbing inflation has become an essential political objective. As governments have reckoned that excessive pay awards have played a crucial role in accelerating inflation, they have tried to interfere with collective bargaining or to win voluntary cooperation from the unions. These developments have given the unions a new leverage over government. Simultaneously, governments have had to make large concessions to preserve industrial peace and control wage inflation.[46]

The last attempt to restrain wages without the support of the TUC and CBI was made in the year 1970–72, when the government sought to de-escalate wage inflation by taking a hard line with public sector employees and hoping that private sector employers would follow suit. The policy had some success, at the price of several major strikes, but received a fatal blow from the miners early in 1972.[47] Once the government conceded the miners' case for special treatment – and they had no choice but to do so once the full extent of the miners' bargaining power had been revealed – they had in effect taken the first step back towards a formal incomes policy. In Blackaby's words: 'Incomes policy in the long run has to be able to discriminate: to judge that this group deserves a larger increase than that.'[48] This in turn implies that there must be a high level of trade union commitment to whatever policy is decided. Towards the end of 1972 the government sought to gain the agreement of the TUC to what was, in effect, a prototype 'social contract'. The unions were offered a target growth rate of 5 per cent for the economy as a whole, a limit of 5 per cent on price inflation, protection for low-paid workers and a system of threshold payments. As a *quid pro quo* the TUC was asked to accept a general flat-rate norm of £2 per worker per week, together with the principle of annual settlements. In the TUC's view, however, it was impossible to separate a policy on prices and incomes from a wide range of other social and economic policies. At the very least they wanted the Industrial Relations Act repealed. The government, however, decided that they could not meet the TUC's demand for participation in making such a wide variety of policy decisions and at the same time retain their own political credibility. The resort to a system of comprehensive statutory controls was in this sense inevitable.

In the spring of 1974, however, the political barriers in the way of a social contract disappeared with the election of a new Labour government. Statutory wage controls were abolished but the threshold payments inherited from the previous government's incomes policy were retained; price controls were also retained; food subsidies were introduced; council house rents were frozen; increases in various social benefits were announced. The idea behind the contract (at least in its early form) was that workers might be induced to moderate their claims for higher money wages if their 'social wage' was improved. In return the TUC undertook to persuade affiliated unions not to push for increases in the *real* incomes of their members – a brave undertaking in view of all the anomalies and eroded relativities bequeathed by nearly two years of statutory control. In practice, however, the social contract could not contain the enormous inflationary pressures which had been building up within the economy for over a year. The situation was greatly aggravated by a series of major relativity adjustments in the public sector, from which groups such as miners, teachers, railwaymen, power workers, civil servants, doctors and nurses all gained increases well in advance of the cost of living. As a result average earnings in the year to July 1975 rose by 28 per cent and the retail price index increased by 25 per cent. But even those groups who received the average increase, let alone those who got less, experienced a *fall* in their real disposable income due to the effects of progressive taxation.

The absurdity of this situation prompted the TUC to take the initiative and propose a flat-rate norm, with no exceptions, of £6 per person per week for the wage bargaining round of August 1975/August 1976. The proposal was accepted by the government. But neither the £6 norm nor its even more stringent successor was sufficient to bring the inflation rate back down to single figures, due to the drastic and precipitate decline in the exchange value of sterling during 1976. Meanwhile the sharpest recession the world had experienced since the 1960s pushed unemployment in Britain beyond the 1¼ million mark. Cuts in government spending threatened the existence of many jobs in the public sector and removed any possibility of further improvements in the 'social wage'. The thinking behind the initial phase of the social contract had been stood on its head. As inflation continued to outpace earnings, real incomes fell. The real purchasing power of the worker with two children on average earnings declined by about 3 per cent between 1973 and 1976; higher income groups experienced a much greater reduction in their standards of living. In these circumstances it is hardly surprising that by the beginning of 1977 several trade union leaders were calling for a return to free collective bargaining. Yet, given the continued existence of severely progressive taxation, it was clear to most observers that the upsurge in money wage increases which would follow a return to unrestricted collective bargaining could bring only marginal and temporary improvements in real incomes. By 1975 the worker on average earnings with two children paid over 25 per cent of his income in tax and national insurance contributions; these would also absorb 40 per cent of any increase in that income. In the words of Turner and Wilkinson:

> Each year's change in workers' living standards now depends not on nominal wages and prices but on the government's tax decisions. So it is in the unions' interest now to move to an annual central agreement between the government, TUC and CBI, which would determine not just the general rates of wage and price change alone, but the general incidence and structure of taxation as well.[49]

Implications for collective bargaining

The growth of state regulation over the postwar period as a whole, but particularly in the last fifteen years, has therefore challenged the assumptions on which the primacy of free collective bargaining has traditionally rested. Governments can no longer be expected to stand aside from the conduct of industrial relations and merely 'hold the ring' while employers and unions haggle over the relative share of pay and profits in the national income. The government is now the largest single employer in Britain, accounting for over one third of total employment. Indeed it has recently been argued that many of Britain's economic problems stem from the rapid increase in non-industrial public employment which has occurred over the past fifteen years. Between 1961 and 1974 employment in the 'non-market' sector (i.e. in those services which do not produce marketable, income-generating output) increased by 45 per cent; employment in the market sector, by contrast, declined by 5 per cent.[50] This expansion in non-market employment (which has proceeded further and faster in Britain than anywhere else in Western Europe) has placed an increasingly heavy burden on those who are still employed in the market sector. The latter must produce enough goods and services to support not only themselves but also those in the non-market sector. For a variety of reasons, however, the output of the market sector has not kept pace with the growth of non-market employment, the result being an increasingly severe squeeze on resources. As the state and its employees claimed an increasing share of GNP (up to 60 per cent in 1975 from 42 per cent in 1958) so profits and investment declined. Company profits net of tax, capital consumption and stock appreciation as a proportion of total manufacturing output declined from 17·5 per cent in 1964 to a mere 3 per cent in 1973, out of which managements had to provide for further investment as well as dividends.[51] The squeeze on resources caused by the claims of the non-market sector has clearly been aggravated by the conventional processes of collective bargaining. Governments have long accepted that their own employees are entitled to make fair comparisons with appropriate groups in the private sector for the purposes of bargaining over pay. The problem is of course that this convention took root at a time when the share of the non-market sector in GNP was much smaller. In recent years only the Heath government in its early phase showed signs of rejecting this traditional obligation. Since 1972, however, the claims of non-market sector employees, aided by militant bargaining tactics, have been successfully pressed home.

In terms of macro-economic policy these trends obviously pose acute problems for any government, and the Callaghan administration has declared its intention of reversing them. The implications of these trends for collective bargaining, however, are very clear. In Phelps Brown's words:

... collective bargaining today is not between labour and capital, or employees and management, for the distribution of the products of particular industries between pay and profit; but between different groups of employees for the distribution of the national product between them one with another, and between them as a whole and the inactive population. Cost inflation appears basically as the process by which particular groups of employees enter and enforce claims to shares in the national product that add up to more than the total product; and the over-subscription comes out as a rise in prices. Hence today's inflation, and the *anomie* of pay determination. Expectations are heightened but confused: they lack norms, be it for the extent of annual betterment, or for the relativities between occupations and industries. Procedures that once adjusted costs to prices are pushing costs and prices up together, because institutions have changed comparatively little while the forces that operate them have changed greatly; here is the new wine in old bottles. The market environment, hitherto permissive of cost and price rises, has become harder of late, without the impetus of cost rises being exhausted.[52]

Once it is accepted that the determination of real take-home pay is much more dependent on the decisions of central government than on extracting more money from the boss's pocket, and that in those circumstances the real function of the trade unions is not to obtain a larger share of the national income for employees as a whole but to decide the relative amounts allocated to different workgroups, then the need for a new institutional framework becomes obvious. Thus several commentators have recently argued that a more formal and authoritative system of tripartite policy-making should be established. Every year the government, the TUC and the CBI would jointly decide how the national income should be distributed – how much should go to manufacturing investment, how much to public spending, how much to wages and salaries, and so on. Economic strategy as a whole, including incomes policy, would then be geared to these key decisions.[53]

While some observers profess to be alarmed by the 'corporatist' implications of these suggestions, it must be recognized that in a sense they would, if implemented, only formalize and strengthen a well-established trend. In Britain the run-up to the spring Budget has long been marked by extensive consultation between the Chancellor, the TUC and the CBI. In recent years these tripartite discussions have assumed an even greater significance as governments have attempted to work out a voluntary policy through the medium of a social contract. The full implications of corporate management for collective bargaining, however, will also need to be recognized and acted upon. In Daniel's words:

As long as people feel free to negotiate individually or collectively the highest level of earnings their employers are prepared to concede, or as long as the distribution of incomes is seen as the result of some mysterious economic or historic forces, then differences in earnings may be endured that become quite unacceptable when they are seen to be determined by a democratically accountable human agency.[54]

Conversely workgroups may resent the interference of this 'human agency' with long-established differentials which they regard as an indispensable support for their social and industrial status. It is now common knowledge that successive incomes policies since the late 1960s have helped to compress the structure of differentials and relativities. While this trend has been welcomed by union leaders who represent large groups of low-paid workers, it has aroused intense resentment among other groups of manual and white-collar employees (including many senior managers) who feel that their special skills are not being adequately rewarded. It is obvious, therefore, that if widespread conflict over relativities and differentials is to be avoided an attempt must be made to resolve the problem by discussion and agreement. A new tripartite institution would be a necessary first step towards achieving this objective. Several suggestions have already been put forward regarding how such an institution might operate and what criteria it should adopt. All that needs to be said here is that sooner or later – and preferably sooner – tripartite machinery for handling major relativity problems will have to be established.

When this happens it is likely that there will also be a concerted attempt to accelerate the reform of payment systems at plant and company level. The need for reform was discussed in depth by the Donovan Commission and actively promoted by the NBPI from 1966 to 1970. Donovan pointed out that in manufacturing industry basic wage rates laid down by national agreements were unrealistically low and were being increasingly supplemented by incentive schemes, bonuses, merit allowances and overtime payments at workplace level. This situation gave cause for concern because it encouraged inefficiency and conflict:

... a large proportion of overtime was worked not because it was required by the job but because it had become an established practice to supplement low basic earnings from normal working time. Pressure was exerted on piecework prices and other means of increasing earnings in a way that caused wage costs to rise without any corresponding rise in output and in a way that management could not control. Consequently disputes and dissatisfaction were widespread as workers sought to exploit the different means open to them to increase their earnings, as the earnings of different groups moved out of line according to the differential scope they had to exert pressure and as the composition of pay packets was complex and confusing.[55]

Under the stimulus of incomes policy many managements negotiated the replacement of decadent piecework schemes by job-evaluated wage structures. Even when incomes policy ceased, at least directly, to encourage the reform of payment systems, some companies (for example, British Leyland) continued to pursue this objective. Thus during the late 1960s and early 1970s there was a general decline in the number of workers covered by payment-by-results schemes, and this in turn resulted in a marked reduction in the gap between basic rates and actual earnings.[56]

Nevertheless there are still many workplaces in which earnings levels are not under control, in which a great deal of unnecessary overtime is still being worked, and in which job evaluation is unknown. As Hugh Clegg has pointed out, 'The problem of control for a British incomes policy is not how to regulate pay in two thousand plants, but how to cope with two hundred thousand or more workshops, sections and groups, each having considerable autonomy to negotiate for themselves.'[57] Some economists may well argue, of course, that it is the relatively high level of unemployment in most years since 1967 which has been responsible for damping down the rate of wage drift. Research into the working of incentive schemes, however, suggests that they have become increasingly unresponsive to changes in the level of demand for labour and that what really matters is the ability of management to control these schemes in the face of pressure from workgroups.[58] It seems likely therefore that if tripartite machinery for investigating and resolving relativity problems is established at national level, the parties involved will have to take a much greater interest in the management of industrial relations and the reform of collective bargaining in the workplace.

In summary, therefore, it may be said that the emergence of

new priorities within the broad field of economic policy has directly challenged the traditional habits, attitudes and institutions of industrial relations. Successive governments have sought to impose *controls* of some kind over the behaviour of managements, trade union representatives and workgroups in the interests of reducing inflation, avoiding strikes or increasing efficiency. Their efforts have been successful only to a limited extent because the institutional framework of British industrial relations was never designed to accommodate systematic intervention by the state. The survival of Victorian institutional arrangements is, of course, in turn attributable to the attitudes and preferences of the parties themselves, most notably their desire to settle their own disputes in their own way according to their own particular needs. But while the principles of freedom and flexibility have in theory much to commend them, in practice they have done little to encourage a climate of opinion on either side of industry favourable to change and innovation. In the 1960s the government attempted to use incomes policy in order to promote joint action to improve efficiency at plant level. Since 1970, however, successive governments have failed to develop the momentum which this policy had begun to generate. There is a great deal of evidence to suggest that the level of investment in manufacturing industry needs to be raised and, equally important, that existing resources could be used much more efficiently. Any strategy designed to remedy these weaknesses would obviously have critical implications for the management of industrial relations in the workplace. It is also clear that a more sensible method of determining relative pay will have to be devised and this again will have important implications for the institutional framework of industrial relations. Whichever way one looks, therefore, it seems self-evident that traditional habits, attitudes and institutions will come under more and more pressure over the next few years as governments seek to make fundamental changes in the structure and performance of the economy. The problem which must now be faced is how managements and unions can be encouraged to respond to these pressures from above, while simultaneously recognizing the significance of those from the shop floor itself, which were discussed in the previous chapter. The pressures from inside the organization and those from outside it are not necessarily incompatible. The extent to which they can be accommodated will depend largely on whether appropriate institutional arrangements can be devised at plant and company level and on whether intervention by the state in the future can overcome the hostility and suspicion left by intervention in the past.

CHAPTER THREE

The Role of Incomes Policy

I understand the pressures and worries that our people are feeling. I know too that pay rises have not been the primary cause of our poor economic performance over the years. We are a low-wage country. That is because our industrial performance has been low, below that of our competitors; because investment has been too low and too often in the wrong places; and because, in turn, productivity has been too low. We cannot put that right in real terms simply by paying ourselves more money . . . Trade unionists want to see Britain on its feet again. But we are tired of lectures, we are tired of appeals; we want to get involved, we want to work it out together and then get on with it.

Len Murray, TUC Annual Congress, September, 1975

The feeling of impotence against the forces of the market oppresses those who regard the income distribution as unjust and the *post factum* redistribution by the state as insufficient. The intensity of the struggle for a redistribution of income is, therefore, not only a mirror of market happenings but also the expression of an opposition to deeply felt injustices which change little. As long as these persist it has to be accepted as inevitable that trade unions are pressed by their members to fight for nominal wage increases for obtaining a more 'equitable' real wage, fruitless as this is in the end.

German Council of Economic Experts, 1971

BETWEEN 1972 and 1977 the bias of successive incomes policies in Britain favoured equity at the expense of efficiency. The principle that all groups should receive the same flat-rate increase has been supported principally on the grounds that a policy which deals out the same 'rough justice' to everyone, while it may cause some distortions here and there, is more likely to be observed than one which gives some groups the opportunity to move ahead faster than others. Those who take this view could point to the success of the policies pursued in 1972 and 1973 and again from 1975 to 1977, when almost all trade union negotiators settled within the guidelines and the level of strike activity was relatively low. Nevertheless, it must be recognized that a number of practical objections can be raised against flat-rate policies. Firstly, they tend to underestimate the importance of differentials. Trade unions and workgroups who may be prepared to accept a 'rough justice' flat-rate increase in response to a severe inflationary crisis of the kind that Britain experienced in the first half of 1975 may find the restrictions imposed on their traditional bargaining objectives increasingly unacceptable once the crisis has passed. Secondly, they encourage trade union negotiators to regard the prevailing norm for wage settlements as a basic right to which their members are entitled without any strings attached. In other words, flat-rate norms give trade unionists no incentive to offer any *quid pro quo* in terms of efficiency or to cooperate with management in the reform of collective bargaining.

At the time of writing there is a persuasive case for an incomes policy which encourages managements and trade unionists to negotiate improvements in the level of efficiency in the workplace. It is now generally accepted that the level of labour productivity in British industry is low by the standards of our major competitors. It should also be apparent that despite a rapid increase in unemployment, between 1975 and 1977 productivity virtually stagnated. While it is certainly true that productivity will increase when capital investment in manufacturing industry rises above its current, extremely low, level, the evidence suggests that there is still considerable scope for improving the level of efficiency and output *without* any major increase in investment. Since this will involve changes in the organization of work at plant level, the cooperation of trade unions and workgroups will be essential, and this means of course that – as between 1965 and 1970 – collective bargaining will play a central role in the management of change. Furthermore, there is a growing belief that through the medium of incomes policy the government should seek to reform some of the more outdated principles and structural characteristics of collective bargaining. At national level, in both the public and the private sectors, different industries and groups negotiate their wage and salary settlements at different times in the year. This, it is argued, greatly strengthens the force of comparability in wage bargaining, so that if one important group settles at some point in the first half of the annual pay round for terms which appear significantly better than the prevailing norm, those groups who follow them are likely to quote this settlement as a precedent. The same kind of competitive bargaining often tends to occur in large, multi-plant companies where there are several bargaining units involving different unions and different occupational groups. In short, there appears to be a strong *prima facie* case for moving towards a much more centralized structure of collective bargaining, both at national and company level, within which all major wage settlements would be negotiated simultaneously. This, it is said, would bring much more predictability into the movement of the national wage bill and would enable all employers to control their labour costs more effectively.

It is worth noting that the policy which the government hopes will be observed in the pay round between August 1977 and August 1978 represents a modest movement away from the principle of equity. Firstly, the norm for settlements is a percentage, not a flat rate, which should enable managements and trade union representatives to discriminate between the claims of different groups where they feel this is appropriate. Secondly, the policy specifically allows negotiators to settle beyond the 10 per cent limit *if* they can agree on a 'self-financing' productivity deal. Observers have, of course, pointed out that since the government has failed to establish any machinery to analyse and monitor these productivity agreements, many of them may in practice prove to be a convenient way of circumventing the 10 per cent limit. While this objection is almost certainly well-founded, it does not necessarily negate the *principle* of giving managements and unions a direct financial incentive to negotiate improvements in efficiency. Nor does it allow for the possibility that even if a particular agreement is not strictly self-financing, it may well have important spin-off benefits for the management of employee relations in the workplace. The purpose of this chapter, therefore, is to analyse the need for a return to some form of productivity bargaining, to identify some of the key problems involved, and to suggest how these might be overcome.

Industrial efficiency and workplace relations

It is as clear now as it was in the mid-1960s that one way of improving the standard of living in Britain would be to raise the level of labour productivity throughout the British economy, particularly in those companies and industries which trade in international markets. There is general agreement that the level of labour productivity in Britain is considerably lower than in America, Japan and most other members of the EEC. Several comparative analyses of productivity levels in a variety of manufacturing industries suggest that while some British firms are as efficient as their overseas competitors, many others are well behind.[1] Moreover, these differentials in labour productivity have been increasing in recent years. In the immediate postwar period, the level of productivity in most British industries compared favourably with that in Western Europe. Since 1973, however, Britain has had one of the lowest levels of productivity in the EEC.[2]

What factors are responsible for this situation? One school of thought emphasizes British industry's reluctance to invest in modern, cost-saving capital equipment. This hypothesis has recently received some support in the Ryder report on British Leyland (1975). The authors of this report argued that the most serious weakness in the company's productive base was that a large proportion of its plant and capital equipment was 'old, outdated and inefficient'. In terms of fixed assets per man British Leyland was far below the level of both its major UK competitor, Ford, and even further below that of European rivals such as Volkswagen, Saab, Renault, Fiat and Volvo. This deficiency meant that the company was (and still is) grossly overmanned in relation to its average output. Thus in 1973 the Japanese car firm Toyota produced 2·3 million vehicles with 43,000 employees; by contrast in 1972 British Leyland could only turn out 1·9 million vehicles with 170,000 employees. Evidence from other industries, notably electrical goods, engineering, shipbuilding, chemicals and steel also appears to confirm the point that many British workers produce less than their continental, American and Japanese counterparts because they have less capital equipment at their elbow.[3]

However, more recent research indicates that low investment is only one of the factors involved. A report by the Central Policy Review Staff on the motor-car industry (1975), for example, concluded that 'with the same power at his elbow and doing the same job, a continental car-assembly worker normally produces twice as much as his British counterpart'. The report identified several contributory causes, notably overmanning, slow pace of work, quality faults, poor maintenance, under-investment, high capital overheads and frequent stoppages of production.[4] Similarly, a recent survey of several key industries in the West Midlands has drawn a depressing picture of wide-spread inefficiency. In medium-sized batch production plants it was found that no more than 20 per cent of the time taken to process materials through the factory was spent productively. In these same factories, neither labour nor plant was employed on directly productive work for more than an average of 50 per cent of the time available. The authors emphasized that where machines were standing idle for over half of the working day, the chief responsibility lay with *management*. Their general conclusion is worth quoting: '... at a time when industrial viability is being undermined both by lack of ready cash and of capit.. investment, increases in production of up to 100 per cent can be achieved by the more efficient utilization of existing resources.'[5] Alternatively, if the worst companies could improve their performance to equal the best, output would rise by 50 per cent. Similarly, a comparative study in 1976 by the engineering construction industry's NEDC of British, American and continental projects revealed that foreign projects were finished more quickly, were less prone to delay, were mostly executed with greater technical efficiency, and required less labour. Once again, the report emphasized the relationship between poor managerial organization and the relatively high level of nonproductive time on the British sites.[6] It must be emphasized, of course, that *some* British companies have achieved levels of efficiency comparable to those of their foreign competitors, but this further underlines the significance of the quality of individual managements and their approach to the organization of work and the use of manpower.

Several researchers have commented on the casual attitude of many managements towards their manpower resources. One well-known symptom of bad management is the prevalence of unnecessary overtime. The level of overtime in British industry has remained consistently high since 1945, despite a slow reduction in the length of the 'standard working week' from forty-seven hours to forty hours. The NBPI, for example, found that in 1968 (by no means an exceptional year) overtime in Britain was running at an average of nearly six hours a week, compared with three to four hours a week in the USA and three hours in West Germany.[7] Overtime levels in Britain seem conspicuously unresponsive to fluctuations in industrial activity, which in turn indicates that much of it has become institutionalized.[8] Thus in November 1975, with unemployment at 1·2 million and rising, nearly one third of those employed in manufacturing were still doing an average of 8·3 hours overtime per week. Average figures, however, tend to hide the fact that the distribution of overtime is concentrated in certain industries and firms for reasons which have little to do with production needs but everything to do with earnings. As Whybrew argued in his survey for the Donovan Commission:

> Overtime is highest in those industries with low average increases in earnings. It grows fastest in those industries with below average increases in earnings. Within industries overtime is highest in the lowest paid occupations and among those workers not on incentive schemes which would enable them to increase their earnings in normal hours.[9]

More recent research confirms that where incentive schemes either do not operate or cannot be manipulated to yield higher earnings, workers put pressure on managements to concede more overtime.[10] Indeed, under the flat-rate incomes policies of 1975 to

1977 the only way in which employers could increase the earnings of their workers above the limit was by offering more overtime. Systematic overtime is obviously inflationary in so far as premium rates are paid for little or no increase in output. Indeed, it may well be that the regular availability of overtime encourages many workers to 'go easy' during their normal hours. It also provides management with a relatively painless way of avoiding redundancy during recessions. In Crawford's words: 'When things are slack, work gets spaced out. Not only do firms appear reluctant to lay people off, they absorb a great deal of slackening of the workload by reducing the intensity with which each man hour is used.'[11] This strategy, however, simply cocoons inefficient working practices which then become even more glaring in periods of expansion.

The manager may well reply that this kind of analysis ignores the significance of restrictive practices, imposed by workgroups and trade unions, and retained in the face of all management's efforts to change them. While it is indeed the case, however, that workgroups in industries such as newspaper printing and ship-building have long been noted for their resistance to new, labour-saving technology, it has still to be proved that restrictive *labour* practices are widespread in manufacturing industry as a whole. The few industries where they exist in strength are characterized by the presence of well-organized groups of craftsmen who enjoy considerable strategic bargaining power. But why are such groups apparently so determined to hang on to working rules which are now totally at variance with the requirements of modern technology? Flanders has convincingly explained their behaviour in terms of the continuing normative influence of craft traditions:

First, the principal goal that adherence to craft traditions is expected to promote is security for the group and for the individual; lifelong security of employment in the first instance but also security in its broadest sense of an anticipated satisfaction of any established expectations. Second, the actual patterns of behaviour that the traditions impose as obligatory all turn on defending a particular preserve of work against trespass. Lines of demarcation, the frontiers of job territory, may be matters of expediency in management's eyes, to be judged by their effects on economic performance. For craftsmen, true to their traditions, they are matters of principle.[12]

It seems reasonable to suggest, therefore, that the 'shake-out' of labour, including skilled labour, which has occurred in many manufacturing industries since the late 1960s may well have reinforced the determination of many craftsmen to preserve their jobs at all costs. It is of course debatable whether insecurity of employment has bred a reluctance to accept change, or whether reluctance to accept change has led to inefficient use of manpower and hence job insecurity.

One recent survey of engineering craftsmen, however, suggests that there are several features in the contemporary work situation, including redundancy, poor prospects for advancement and low pay, which help to explain the difficulties which managements commonly encounter when trying to introduce some change in the wage–work bargain:

Most craftsmen have invested several years in training, at considerable cost to themselves. In the past one thing skilled men possessed was relative security of tenure of what they considered to be their job property rights. Once the employer shakes them out, then they will look over the fence to see if the grass is greener there, and the other factors – pay, conditions and so on – will assume greater importance. If their skill can be considered an expendable commodity by the industry, then they could reasonably, if reluctantly, consider it expendable to themselves . . . this is probably the root cause of much bitterness among employees and former employees of the industry, which manifests itself in restrictive practices, refusal to make flexibility agreements, refusal to accept skill-centre trainees and a whole host of other factors which contribute to sub-optimal use of manpower, which in turn appears as 'labour shortages'. A necessary *quid pro quo* for increased flexibility is increased security of employment.[13]

The authors of the report also added that managements should do something to tackle the expressed frustration of many craftsmen in areas such as job satisfaction, work organization and, most important, employee involvement in major company decisions.

One potentially useful approach to these problems was adopted by some companies in the 1960s in the form of comprehensive productivity bargaining, which attempted to reconcile management's need for higher efficiency with employees' demands for greater rewards, security and influence over managerial decision-making. While it is certainly true that workgroups and their representatives have generally been reluctant to part with long-established unilateral controls over the effort bargain, the experience of productivity bargaining proved conclusively that these controls are in certain circumstances negotiable. In batch and mass-production industries, productivity bargaining typically involved some change in the payment system designed to strengthen managerial control over the movement of costs and output. In plants using process technology, agreements tended to focus on changes in working practices, on relaxing demarcation rules, and on reducing manning standards and overtime – again with the idea of strengthening managerial control over the effort bargain. In practice, however, the net result was to strengthen the framework of *joint* control over key matters of substance. In the words of one report:

The process of hard negotiation over a wide range of issues between management and trade unions at plant level had increased understanding and improved relationships. Previously the situation had often been characterized by guerrilla warfare, now it approximated more to controlled peace keeping. Procedures and mechanisms had been introduced for controlling and regulating differences and for introducing change. The *de facto*, informal power exercised by shop stewards was recognized and channelled more constructively into formal institutions ... The more substantial had been the formal content of agreements and the savings it had generated, the more the respective respondents felt that relationships and institutions had been improved.[14]

What killed productivity bargaining in the end from a trade union point of view was not a growing resistance to the idea itself but rather the high and rising level of redundancy and unemployment which accompanied the economic recession of 1969 to 1972. In these circumstances trade unions and workgroups alike 'became strongly resistant to agreements that contributed to better utilization of labour within individual companies only by creating national under-utilization through unemployment, this resistance being reinforced by their ability to succeed with high, straight wage demands'.[15] In view of the relatively high level of unemployment which has prevailed in Britain in most years since 1970 it seems unlikely that the trade unions would support a return to the kind of productivity bargaining practised in the 1960s, at least without a radical change in the prevailing framework of policy on unemployment and retraining. As long as higher efficiency is associated with redundancy and unemployment, there will be strong trade union resistance to any attempts by management to erode what they see as the 'job property rights' of their members.

In these circumstances there is a heavy burden on managements and indeed on the government itself to break down this resistance by taking new initiatives. Unfortunately British employers have typically never shown much inclination either to innovate in the field of employee relations or even to anticipate demands from the shop floor. The standard reaction to the 'challenge from below' has been fundamentally defensive, with the main casualty being efficiency. As the Donovan Commission observed: 'Full employment would in any case have increased the influence of the workgroup but British managers have augmented it by their preference for keeping many matters out of agreements, by the inadequacy of their methods of control over payment systems, by their preference for informality and by their tolerance of custom and practice.'[16]

One reason for this lack of initiative lies in the boardroom itself. One recent survey by Winkler of the role of company directors in industrial relations has pinpointed two major weaknesses. Firstly, it would seem that many directors have little or no contact or communication with shop-floor employees and trade union representatives; secondly, this lack of contact generates an ignorance of and indifference towards the aspirations, opinions and problems of ordinary employees.[17] A P E P survey in 1971 suggests that at that time less than one third of even the *major* companies in Britain had appointed a director with full-time responsibility for labour relations.[18] Indifference in the boardroom shows itself in many ways, but principally in the lack of industrial relations *policies* at plant and company level. Thus the CIR found that managements differed widely in their conception of the substance and purpose of an industrial relations policy:

In some companies we studied, the main industrial relations policy decision had been to join their employers' association and observe the basic agreements on terms and conditions ... But on many important points company policy would often be only implied in their customs and traditions which are taken as precedents for the resolution of any new problems ... Important areas not often covered by industrial relations policy included manpower use and planning, communicating and consulting with employees and various aspects of collective bargaining. In fact a dominant impression gained from many companies was that industrial relations did not receive the attention they need along with commercial and operational matters.[19]

In another report the CIR drew attention to the neglect of industrial relations training at all levels within many companies. It would appear from this survey that the vast majority of managers and shop stewards do not receive any systematic training in industrial relations and much of the training that is done is of little value.[20] Moreover, by comparison with many of their competitors in Western Europe, British managements have been backward in improving the general working environment. Many manual workers are still not covered by company pension schemes, nor do they enjoy many of the other fringe benefits which have long been standard in some continental countries.[21] In Daniel's words: 'The whole picture symbolizes a management that does not care, that has no pride in what it does and is interested only in its own comfort and profit.'[22]

But, it may be asked, are not the new environmental pressures described in the previous chapter tending to make managements more aware of their responsibilities in the field of employee relations? The answer must be a qualified affirmative. The growth of protective legislation since 1972 has undoubtedly forced many senior managers to turn a more critical eye on their internal collective bargaining arrangements. The personnel function is by no means as neglected as it used to be. The tendency, noted earlier, is for the scope of collective bargaining in the workplace to grow, and to this extent managements are becoming more aware of the value of extended joint regulation. The current debate on employee participation and the probability of government legislation on the establishment of a system of worker directors has encouraged some companies to experiment and innovate in this field. There is also a growing awareness on the part of senior managements that some of the more conspicuous differentials in status (including fringe benefits) between manual and white-collar employees are dysfunctional, and this has stimulated a marked though as yet limited movement towards the harmonization of certain terms and conditions of employment.[23] Nevertheless, even when all these hopeful signs have been taken into account, the reality of low productivity and widespread inefficiency cannot be ignored. Since exhortation alone is unlikely to change entrenched attitudes and habits on either side of the bargaining table, the next step is to consider how a climate more conducive to change and innovation can be stimulated. In the words of the West Midlands study quoted above:

... increased productivity is not a primary objective of any industrial company. More tangible incentives or immediate pressures are needed to encourage senior and middle managements to be more enterprising and progressive than many of them are. Pressures from workers, shareholders and government have built up in recent years. There is evidence, however, that unless incentives and rewards commensurate with the skills and responsibilities required are also forthcoming, manufacturing industry will neither attract nor hold the first-class brains it so urgently needs.

The authors are of course referring to the much discussed failure of British society to recognize the importance of industrial management as a profession and accord it the rewards and status customary in other European countries.[24] While there is much substance in this argument, it suggests that any changes are likely to be slow and piecemeal. Moreover, as long as British labour remains relatively cheap in international terms, it is difficult to see how managements in manufacturing industry can be induced either to invest heavily in labour-saving technology or to initiate radical improvements in the efficiency of their existing manpower resources. It follows that the state will have to devise a long-term strategy which encourages trade unions to adopt higher wages *and* higher productivity as bargaining objectives and simultaneously seeks to remove the threat of the dole queue. This point will be discussed in more detail below.

Wage determination and workplace relations

The level of efficiency in a given workplace is to some extent influenced by the kind of payment system in use. Up to the 1960s it was widely assumed that payment systems should be based on the closest possible relationship between effort and reward. The argument in favour of payment by results (PBR) has been well summarized by Lupton:

> It is said that men come to work to make money and that the more they can make while they are at work the better they like it ... Management wants high output, the worker wants more money, so both sides are satisfied. Some men are more skilled than others, some more conscientious, some more greedy. Individual piecework allows each man to work out his own pecuniary salvation ... If a man finds, under piecework, that management inefficiencies are preventing him from making money then he will put pressure on management and supervision to do something about it. Underlying all these arguments is the assumption that the operator has, under piecework, the power to control the amount of effort he puts into the job, and that he relates effort solely or mainly to monetary return.[25]

In the immediate postwar period the number of workers on some form of PBR scheme increased significantly as firms sought to increase their output, and it has been estimated that by the early 1960s the earnings of nearly three quarters of those employed in the manufacturing sector were influenced, if not always directly determined, by PBR.[26]

The case against PBR, however, is well-known and needs little repetition here. Sociologists have attacked the narrow theory of motivation on which it rests. Others have pointed out that since it gives workers a measure of control over the effort–reward relationship, they may resort to limitation of output on the job while using their bargaining strength to increase the rates for given levels of output.[27] It has also been shown that modern technology has frequently reduced the individual employee's ability to control the amount of effort which he puts into the job and that the emphasis on individual effort is therefore anachronistic. Above all, however, it has been emphasized that PBR simply does not work. By the 1960s many firms in the manufacturing sector were using PBR systems primarily in order to supplement the low basic rates embodied in national agreements. Researchers found widespread evidence of degeneration in PBR schemes. It was found, for example, that PBR systems tended to facilitate a continual upward drift in earnings levels regardless of factors such as the level of output, the efficiency of management control systems and the state of the local labour market. It was also observed that this earnings drift usually disturbed internal differentials and thereby set off compensatory claims from other workgroups.[28] As a result, conventional PBR systems were held to be incompatible with an effective incomes policy. In Daniel's words:

As long as there are sources of large-scale uncontrolled drift in earnings at the workplace which can enable workers to get annual increases in earnings of 5 to 10 per cent without any formal agreement or increase in output then any central, formal agreement on the level of wage increases is undermined and anomalies and inequities mushroom.[29]

Thus one of the primary objectives of the 1965–70 incomes policy was to encourage managements to re-establish some control over earnings drift and ensure that pay increases were matched by higher output. The policy achieved considerable success in this respect and many managements set about replacing decadent, inflationary PBR systems with measured day work under the broad umbrella of productivity bargaining. The impetus of reform continued into the 1970s, despite the difficulties posed by the statutory incomes policy introduced towards the end of 1972, and local studies have shown that changes in payment systems and bargaining structures have given managements and workforces joint control over labour costs which were once under the control of neither side.[30]

The gradual replacement of PBR by measured day work has had two broad effects. First, in many industries the gap between basic rates and actual earnings levels has narrowed significantly since the late 1960s. It will be recalled that the Donovan Commission attached great importance to the size of this gap, arguing that it was symptomatic of the growing ineffectiveness of the formal system of industry-wide agreements. However, subsequent developments have clearly modified this analysis. In some industries, notably engineering, managerial efforts to control wage drift at plant level have in effect increased the relative significance of basic rates negotiated at national level. In other industries workplace incentive schemes are now less widespread and national agreements have thus become far more important as regulatory institutions.[31]

Second, changes in payment systems have in some cases produced important changes in bargaining *behaviour*. The outstanding example is that of the coal-mining industry, where up to the late 1960s a large proportion of the average miner's pay packet was determined by piecework bargaining at pit level. The prevalence of pit-based PBR schemes produced a pattern of bargaining behaviour which focused on local anomalies and the rate for the job, supplemented by short, localized stoppages of work. The replacement of PBR by a uniform, graded wage structure for the whole industry, a process which began in 1966 and was completed in 1971, had three major effects on this pattern of behaviour. It made the miners much more reliant on national wage negotiations than before, it increased their sense of unity, and it enabled them to compare their earnings with those of other groups in other industries. Within a few years, therefore, the pattern of short, unofficial and localized disputes on local pay issues was replaced by one of occasional industry-wide stoppages called by the NUM in pursuit of claims for increases in the relative pay of all miners. Another example is that of the engineering industry, where Brown and Sisson found that the movement away from PBR in the Coventry area and the introduction of plant-wide job evaluation had 'encouraged and institutionalized the use of internal pay comparisons'. The fact that skilled production workers are no longer paid by the piece has made other groups both inside and outside the plant much more aware of differences in their relative earnings and has therefore tended to compress differentials between this key group and other skilled workers.[32]

The reform of wage payment systems, therefore, whether at national or company level, frequently has important implications for bargaining structures. In general one would say that the further a payment system moves along the continuum from piecework through measured day work to salary, the less likely it is that local factors will influence total earnings. Consequently, the *level* of bargaining may well move from the department or the plant to the company. Changing a payment system also has implications for bargaining *units*, which may in turn affect the structure of wage differentials and relativities within the establishment. Under PBR systems, bargaining units tend to be fragmented and autonomous. When introducing measured day work, however, managements have frequently followed the Donovan Commission's recommendations by rationalizing their bargaining structures and reducing the number of negotiating groups in their establishments. But while these changes have reduced the opportunities for groups to 'leap-frog' over others and have thereby strengthened management's control over earnings drift, they have also aggravated the problem of pay differentials *within* the new bargaining units. It is now generally recognized that since the late 1960s there has been a steady compression of differentials within most industries, within most occupations, and between men and women. The equalization of male and female wage rates under the Equal Pay Act of 1970 has obviously had some influence on this movement. The role of incomes policy, however, is more problematical, if only because the compression has continued during periods when incomes policy was either weak or imposed percentage (i.e. differential-widening) norms for pay settlements.

The figures in Table 4 suggest, however, that compression has proceeded at different rates in different industries. One underlying factor here, of course, may well be differential rates of technological change. However, it may also be the case that changes in bargaining structures have had some influence on

Table 4

Average hourly earnings (excluding the effects of overtime) of skilled workers* as a percentage of those for labourers in certain industries
(*The figures are calculated for June in each year*)

	1963	1965	1967	1969	1971	1972	1973	1974	1975	1976
Time-workers										
Engineering	143	143	145	144	144	141	138	137	132	128
Shipbuilding and ship-repairing	134	140	144	132	133	131	128	129	122	119
Chemical manufacturing	114	114	111	110	109	107	108	106	104	105
Payment by results workers										
Engineering	146	148	152	151	149	148	143	138	132	131
Shipbuilding and ship-repairing	138	140	146	148	148	142	136	134	131	130
Chemical manufacturing	111	109	109	110	107	108	107	108	108	108

*Full-time adult male manual workers.
Source: DE survey for full-time male manual workers in these industries in Great Britain, *Department of Employment Gazette*, June 1977.

the process. Overall, the differential between the average earnings of skilled time-workers (excluding overtime) and those of their semi-skilled colleagues narrowed from 9·9 per cent in June 1970 to 7·6 per cent in 1974, and by June 1976 the differential was a mere 3·8 per cent. In the motor industry, however, the compression was much more pronounced, with a 13·1 per cent differential between skilled and semi-skilled time-workers in 1970 falling to 1·7 per cent in 1976. This may well reflect the rationalization of payment systems and bargaining units in companies such as British Leyland, where groups of skilled workers have been induced to join negotiating groups in which semi-skilled and unskilled workers predominate, represented by the TGWU. In Fox's words:

Where the semi-skilled employees are in a majority on the union side they may be able to force through a flat-rate claim to put to the employer. On the other hand, they may agree on a percentage increase claim, but it is most unlikely that they would agree on a claim which widened differentials unless the majority of semi-skilled workers could expect a hefty increase in their own earnings.[33]

It is certainly significant in this context that the period 1975–7, in which incomes policy emphasized 'rough justice' flat-rate norms and thereby reinforced the equalizing effects of bargaining reform, also witnessed numerous stoppages by small groups of skilled men throughout the motor industry in pursuit of higher differentials and separate negotiating facilities. In electrical engineering, by contrast, unions representing skilled men (for example, the EEPTU) have retained their grip over bargaining units and in this sector the skilled/semi-skilled differential fell by only 3·5 per cent (to 15·5 per cent) between 1970 and 1976.

This evidence enables us to offer a few observations on the discontent over differentials which has gradually been growing in many sectors of British industry over the past few years and, simultaneously, to underline some of the key problems facing many managers who wish to reform their bargaining structures and payment systems. Most wage bargains are ultimately bargains over wage differentials. Differentials have a *market* function. They can either induce workers to enter a particular industry or occupation or discourage them from doing so. One point repeatedly stressed by the NUM, for example, is that the relative pay of their members has been (and to some extent still is) inadequate to attract large numbers of young men into the pits. Similar arguments have been used to explain both the steady decline in the number of school-leavers taking up engineering apprenticeships and the tendency for engineering craftsmen to leave the industry in search of better-paid employment elsewhere. But differentials also have a *social* function. In Robinson's words: 'Some differentials indicate society's assessment of the value of a particular job, and they are frequently interpreted by individuals in specific occupations as indicators of status and a general sort of esteem. Indeed, differentials and relativities are the only way in which a worker can decide whether he is fairly paid.'[34] Fairness, of course, is based on comparison. Individuals and groups decide whether they are fairly paid by comparing their earnings with those of other individuals and groups. While there may well have been a tendency in recent years for certain groups to adopt wider orbits of comparison, it is still probably true to say that 'the comparisons which people make most spontaneously and frequently in evaluating the relative fairness of their pay are with groups that are socially and spatially closest to them'.[35] In industries where a significant proportion of workers' pay packets depends on bargaining at plant level, the orbit of comparison is very often restricted to the plant itself or, even more narrowly, to specific bargaining units. Robinson, for example, has commented on the fact that 'workers in the same occupation, and presumably with the same qualifications and training, working in different plants in the same industry, in the same locality, appear satisfied with different internal wage structures and differentials', and suggests that workers in different plants 'can establish and maintain independent views of what is a fair relationship in the pay of specified occupations'.[36] Recent research has confirmed the existence of strong pressures to maintain established differentials *within* bargaining units at plant level, regardless even of changes in relativities *between* different units, and this, it has been suggested, 'reflects a general belief by members of each unit about the relative worth of each occupation'.[37] It is hardly surprising, therefore, that managerial attempts to merge and rationalize bargaining units, particularly in multi-plant companies, have caused so much resistance and disruption.

Another factor which complicates management's task is that the rationalization of pay structures and bargaining units may well conflict with the wage policies of individual trade unions. As Robinson has pointed out, trade unions 'compete either for members or for prestige'.[38] The structure of trade unionism in Britain reflects, to a greater degree than in most other industrialized countries, the continuing force of competitive norms. This does not, of course, mean that if British trade unions decided to imitate their German counterparts and reorganize themselves on purely industrial lines, all arguments over differentials would be immediately resolved. The experience of Sweden since the late 1960s clearly shows that different occupational interests can in certain circumstances break through even the strongest institutional barriers.[39] Nevertheless, it would be difficult to deny that inter-union competition for members within a given industry can produce almost insoluble problems for management. In Robinson's words:

Where there is only one trade union in the bargaining unit, there are still difficulties in the workers arriving at agreed differentials or an agreed common view of what differentials should be. However, these differences tend to be settled within the union itself. Where there is more than one organization the differences become formalized and public commitment to a position can raise problems if a compromise solution needs to be found. The adoption of public positions on differentials is not the same as taking up a public position about the size of an increase that a union is seeking from an employer. In the latter case it is generally recognized that some compromise is to be reached. In the former case, failure to secure the publicly declared differentials might be seen not as a victory for the employer but for the other union. It may be that 'losing' a differentials argument with another union is considered more serious than 'losing' a wage claim to an employer.[40]

It should not, of course, be assumed that this kind of competitive behaviour is rife throughout British industry. It is, however, particularly marked in the motor industry, where the union with the biggest membership (the TGWU) represents most of the unskilled and semi-skilled workers and has for several years been pursuing a wage policy based on the principle of 'second to none'. This policy naturally conflicts with the objectives of those unions who represent the skilled men, which emphasize the importance of maintaining differentials. The same kind of conflict is also evident within British Rail, where the train drivers' union ASLEF has long been at odds with the NUR over what the differential between drivers and other railway grades should be. Similar conflicts have also occurred between white-collar unions in both manufacturing industry and in the services sector. These unions have frequently based their appeal on the need to correct the eroded differentials of their actual or potential members and where more than one union is present in the same company the urge to adopt competitive bargaining objectives has often been overwhelming. Finally, it should be noted that the process of formalizing plant bargaining may in itself create problems where none previously existed:

With informal, unwritten bargaining, a set of relationships can be created and can survive for a considerable time, even though the trade unions concerned refuse to endorse them publicly and may even criticize them publicly. The bargainers are not formally responsible for the relationships that result from a set of fragmented bargains in the same way that they are for differentials that are included in the formal agreement. They can, therefore, avoid responsibility for the results and advocate or accept views from their rank-and-file members which advocate a change in relative wages.[41]

The negotiation of a formalized, comprehensive plant or company agreement on wages, however, compels all groups and their organizations to accept responsibility for its contents and to resolve their differences. Senior managers at British Leyland, for example, have recently declared their intention of moving towards a standardized pay structure for the entire company. This will not only reduce the autonomy of individual plants and bargaining units but will also compel all the unions involved to come to some agreement on what the structure of differentials for the whole corporation should be. It would, however, be naïve to assume that such a consensus will be forthcoming without a considerable degree of compromise on all sides. Even if the chief union representatives are able to agree among themselves, the tradition of group and workplace autonomy within the company is so long established that they may well have great difficulty in persuading some of their members to accept a compromise solution and thereby sacrifice long-established notions of 'principle'.[42]

It must therefore be emphasized that changes in payment systems frequently have important implications for bargaining structures, which in turn affect the balance of power both *between* and *within* managements and trade unions. Firstly, a move towards formalized company bargaining, accompanied and encouraged by the replacement of piecework by a time-based payment system, may well give management much greater control over the movement of earnings and labour costs within the organization. However, it may also increase the bargaining power of the unions involved by encouraging them to coordinate their negotiating strategies and tactics and enabling them to concentrate their efforts. Furthermore, it may well encourage groups to adopt new and wider comparative reference points, so that their aspirations in wage bargaining become more demanding. Secondly, research suggests that the level in the organization at which management makes agreements, whether formally or informally, is a critical determinant of the level at which decision-making power is concentrated on the union side.[43] However, these internal changes in authority relations cannot be expected to occur without friction. As two researchers have pointed out: 'Shop stewards used to negotiating will not relinquish all key decisions to national union representatives, and if the resulting agreement is to be workable at plant level it is desirable to provide for participation by plant representatives participating in them.'[44] A move towards a more centralized system of bargaining in companies such as British Leyland will certainly be resisted by shop stewards unless appropriate facilities are provided for them within the new negotiating machinery.

In general, it would be fair to say that blueprints for bargaining reform which assume that full-time union officials can somehow be brought back into the forefront of plant or company bargaining in situations where they have long since lost the initiative to shop stewards are unrealistic. The Donovan Commission, for example, argued that a more formalized system of plant and company bargaining could be reconciled to the needs of an incomes policy because a more decentralized structure would need a large number of full-time union officials. In other words, it was assumed that formalized plant and company bargaining would demand a higher level of professional expertise on the trade union side and that this would be supplied by the full-time officials. It was also envisaged that this would narrow the gap between trade union leaders on the one hand and shop stewards on the other, thereby making the latter more responsive to national union objectives and, by implication, to the requirements of an incomes policy. In practice, however, Donovan's assumption has not been validated. The increased workload arising from the growth of workplace bargaining has been taken up by shop stewards and there is little evidence that the formal influence of trade unions has grown.[45] Consequently, the acid test of an incomes policy, particularly in manufacturing industry, must be the extent to which it meets the needs and aspirations of managers, shop stewards and employees in the workplace. The problem, as was argued above, is that these needs and aspirations vary considerably from one workplace to another; indeed, there are often considerable differences of interest *within* a given workplace.

It must also be recognized that after several years in which relatively rigid guidelines have been imposed on wage bargaining at all levels, many shop stewards are probably becoming increasingly anxious to re-assert their influence over the process of wage determination in the workplace. These aspirations will undoubtedly be made more explicit by the demand that the losses in real income which were sustained between 1975 and 1977 should be recovered and that eroded differentials should be restored. By the same token, many managements have found that the flat-rate policies, while helpful in some ways, have in effect strongly discouraged both the reform of payment systems and the negotiation of improvements in the organization of work. Research suggests that the reaction against incomes policy is likely to be particularly forceful in larger establishments, in those where strikes have become an accepted part of the bargaining process, and in those which operate in expanding product markets. Furthermore, it is in these companies and plants that both managements and union representatives seem to be relatively hostile towards income policy in any circumstances.[46] Consequently, as the economy pulls out of the worst recession for forty years, the possibility of a massive pay explosion in the manufacturing sector will become increasingly obvious.

Wage determination and incomes policy

Is another pay explosion inevitable? Or, to phrase the question in a different way, is it possible to return to free collective bargaining and simultaneously avoid an unacceptable rate of inflation and even higher unemployment? At the time of writing (September 1977), it must be said that the prospects for Phase Three of the Labour government's pay policy are by no means as hopeless as at first sight they would appear. The policy lays down, firstly, that the overall increase in *national* earnings in 1977/8 should not exceed 10 per cent. But this is not a figure at which negotiators must invariably settle; it is a ceiling on aggregate earnings, not a limit on individual pay increases. As such it introduces a much-needed degree of flexibility into wage bargaining and gives individual employers more room to manoeuvre. As a ceiling on earnings, however, which is supposed to include overtime, bonus payments and all the other components of wage drift, the 10 per cent norm is manifestly unrealistic. It assumes that the average increase in basic wage *rates* will be 'well within single figures'. Yet even if the rate of price inflation falls into single figures during 1977/8 – which is by no means certain – the policy fails to allow either for the possibility that trade unions will seek to compensate their members for their loss of real earnings between 1975 and 1977 or for the usual labour market effects of economic expansion. It should be noted that even in the severe recession of 1975–7 both the £6 limit and the $4\frac{1}{2}$ per cent norm were subject to a significant degree of 'slippage'.[47] It would therefore be reasonable to expect that the average growth of earnings in 1977/8 in the private sector will be considerably in excess of 10 per cent. In the public sector, by contrast, the government intends to enforce the ceiling through the application of 'cash limits' on public expenditure, which means that some groups may get no more than 6 or 7 per cent. Strategic manual groups such as the miners may, of course, benefit from productivity agreements, whether self-financing or not, but if the policy is strictly maintained in the public sector it implies a radical change in average relativities between public and private employment. During the 1950s and 1960s public and private sector earnings tended to move together, with a slight margin in favour of the latter. From 1971 onwards, however, the public sector moved ahead, with a marked acceleration in 1974 as several large groups received major increases in their relative pay.[48] The 1977/8 policy is clearly intended to reverse this movement; it could therefore be said to be consistent with the government's overall economic strategy, which aims to regenerate the manufacturing base and draw people back into the market sector of the economy.

The second pillar of the policy, described officially as 'the keystone for an orderly return to collective bargaining', is the rule that for every negotiating group there should be a minimum of twelve months between pay settlements. If observed, the rule should play an important role in restraining the aggregate level of wage inflation in so far as it will in effect preserve all those Phase Two settlements which come up for re-negotiation during 1977/8 until the dates at which they formally lapse. Thus, while some groups will be negotiating new agreements under the 10 per cent guideline, others will observe their Phase Two settlements until their twelve-month period has expired. The twelve-month rule will probably survive as long as the general rate of inflation continues to fall. When a voluntary twelve-month rule was announced in the pay round of 1974/5, it was ignored by many groups because the general rate of inflation and the 'going rate' for pay settlements were both rising. No sensible negotiator will wish to commit himself and his members to a particular wage agreement for twelve months if he believes that the real gains from that agreement will have been eroded after only six months. Consequently the behaviour of the cost of living index in 1977/8 will play a vital role in determining the fate of the twelve-month rule.

At first glance there would seem to be so many pressures making for another pay explosion that any discussion of the prospects for the third phase of pay policy might appear academic. First and foremost, average real earnings fell by about 7 per cent in 1976/7 which, as the *Economist* has pointed out, is 'the biggest recorded fall in the average Briton's real disposable income for over a hundred years: worse than anything that happened in the 1930s'.[49] Secondly, after so many 'false dawns' on the general rate of inflation during 1975, 1976 and 1977, there is no reason why trade union negotiators should have any more confidence in government forecasts for 1977/8. Are they not more likely to do what they did in 1974/5, and seek both to compensate their members for their past loss of real income and to re-insure themselves against any acceleration in the cost of living during the life of their agreement? Thirdly, the introduction of the 'self-financing' productivity agreement could be regarded as a potentially enormous loophole through which many employers and union negotiators can and will escape. No vetting machinery of any kind has been set up to ensure that these agreements *are* self-financing. In the circumstances there is nothing to stop negotiators settling for considerably more than 10 per cent whether their productivity targets are genuine or bogus. The extent to which these productivity deals are not self-financing will eventually be reflected in the general rate of inflation and this in turn will have implications for the rest of the policy.

On closer examination, however, predictions that sooner or later there will be a massive pay explosion are rather less convincing than they might appear. While it is indeed the case that average real incomes declined at an unprecedented rate in 1976/7, the government itself could easily restore much of this loss through further cuts in both direct and indirect taxation. If appropriate action is taken at an early stage during the 1977/8 pay round, it could make an important contribution towards restraining the pressure for compensatory increases in money wages. Inflationary pressures from the public sector may be held in check through the system of cash limits, although the government will probably find itself obliged to stand firm in the face of strikes or threats of industrial action from groups of its own employees. In any case, productivity deals are not ruled out for the public sector and these may act as a safety valve. On productivity bargaining generally, the experience of 1965 to 1970 suggests that a substantial proportion of managements will at least try to obtain self-financing agreements, and even if some of them fail to achieve that objective completely they should at least be able to achieve significant increases in efficiency. After several years of incomes policies which have effectively discouraged *quid pro quo* bargaining, one could perhaps assume that in many companies there will be a considerable backlog of ideas and proposals for improving efficiency which managements will now try to implement. More fundamentally, it may be that the experience of 1974/5 has left a stronger impression on the minds of trade union negotiators than some of their public statements would imply. It is at least possible that the connection between excessive increases in money wages and the cost of living has been forcefully brought home by the reality of 30 per cent inflation and that the logic of self-restraint is correspondingly more convincing. If the government can, through further tax cuts, restore a significant proportion of the real losses sustained in 1976/7, then the case for restraint on money wage claims could be made even more convincing. .

But whether the 1977/8 pay policy is judged successful or not, there will still be several outstanding problems associated with the system of wage determination in Britain which will need to be tackled. It was argued earlier in this book that the growing importance of the government as both employer and allocator of resources has effectively consigned the traditional concept of free collective bargaining to the dustbin. Does this mean that market forces – and the exercise of market power – will become increasingly irrelevant to wage determination? Blackaby certainly appears to think so. Commenting on the introduction of statutory pay and price controls in November 1972, he argued that:

We are moving gradually towards a situation in which it is the government, or some other body to which it delegates its powers, which will be the final arbiter about how much different jobs, occupations and professions are paid . . . Incomes policy may begin as a short-term anti-inflationary device. It will end as an alternative to the present system of settling relativities.[50]

Indeed, the experience of accelerating inflation and higher unemployment during the 1970s has induced most governments in Western Europe and the USA to adopt a much more interventionist attitude to wage determination. The question which most of them have yet to resolve is the extent to which incomes policies (whether they are known by that name or not) are short-term, necessary evils, to be dispensed with as soon as pay and price movements get back to 'normal', and the extent to which they should take the form of a permanent institutional limitation on collective bargaining. In Britain it seemed as though the question had been resolved in the second half of the 1960s with the establishment of the National Board for Prices and Incomes.

Unfortunately a political consensus in favour of permanent institutional limitations on collective bargaining failed to emerge. It would also be fair to say that the Board became too closely associated with the exigencies of short-term wage restraint at the expense of its much more important role as both an investigative body and as a catalyst to the reform of bargaining principles and structures. However, if productivity bargaining is to be continued in some form, it will be necessary to re-establish the NBPI (under another name) in order to monitor agreements made in selected companies and industries and disseminate practical advice to negotiators. Such a body might also play an important role in the resolution of major relativity problems. It will be recalled that the now-defunct Pay Board recommended that a national procedure be established for investigating and settling claims for improvements in relative pay. Such a body might also take on board Daniel's suggestion that a national system of job evaluation should be established. A national job evaluation system would be based on the idea that people should be paid according to their value to the community, so that those occupations which required the greatest skill or effort would attract *and keep* the highest rating.[51] Despite the immense practical difficulties involved in developing such a system, few people would deny that it might at least represent a significant improvement on the traditional methods of settling relativities and differentials, which seem to satisfy no one.

Whether or not any progress on this particular front is made over the next few years, there is likely to be a growing demand from both sides for more freedom to make wage bargains which are more attuned to the needs and problems of the individual establishment, particularly in the manufacturing sector. The desire for greater autonomy has probably been sharpened by the effects of successive flat-rate incomes policies, particularly the £6 norm of 1975/6. Daniel, for example, reported that several managements in his sample resented the disruptive effects of the £6 limit on their internal pay structures and bonus schemes. He also observed that a substantial minority of managements 'had not been able to get any productivity *quid pro quo*, or the acceptance of a changed pay system or the introduction of job evaluation, because workers and their representatives had conceived of the flat rate increase as theirs by right'.[52] It is desirable, therefore, that incomes policies of the kind we have had since 1972 – i.e. those with a strong bias towards social equity – should be abandoned in favour of policies which encourage managements to achieve a better relationship between pay and efficiency through collective bargaining. Such policies should specify criteria which favour the reform of payment systems, the restructuring of internal differentials and the negotiation of more efficient working practices, while still leaving the parties with 'substantial scope for choice and collective bargaining over the distribution of increases within establishments and enterprises'.[53] In effect this means that incomes policy should no longer attempt to determine *individual* earnings levels – something which in any case it has never been able to achieve for all employees – and would instead focus, as the 1977/8 guidelines suggest, on the movement of *aggregate* earnings.

In this context it would be useful for policy-makers to consider a suggestion which has been floated on several occasions in recent years – namely that earnings at plant and company level should be linked directly to movements in the firm's Added Value. There appear to be relatively few technical difficulties in the way of calculating Added Value in the manufacturing sector. The reason this criterion has been so little used to date is simply that it is not necessary to calculate Added Value for the purposes of company accounts.[54] As a result the conventional accounting yardsticks such as return on capital employed and sales per employee have long been the only measures against which the performance of a company is assessed. It is arguable, however, that such ratios are largely meaningless as a measure of the firm's efficiency in the use of resources – which is, of course, the essence of productivity. A firm's efficiency can be evaluated much more accurately by relating its inputs to its own output – that is, by Added Value. The yardstick of Added Value – crudely defined as the difference between the value of the goods produced in an undertaking and the cost of materials consumed in the production process – may therefore be a generally acceptable method of measuring labour productivity.[55] It is important to note, however, that *net* output would be the key indicator of performance and as such would replace the traditional emphasis on increasing *gross* output as, for example, through PBR schemes. A small number of companies in engineering and chemicals are already using an Added Value index as the basis for 'productivity bonuses' and there is no inherent reason why the practice should not be encouraged. Proponents of Added Value have argued that it is a relatively simple device which brings home the basic economic truth that wealth has to be created before it can be shared out and emphasizes that increasing net value is more important than simply raising output. It has also been suggested that the use of Added Value would both give the work-force a strong incentive to cooperate with management in improving the efficiency of the enterprise and provide management with a criterion against which the pay claims of different groups within the enterprise could be assessed. Unless and until the Added Value yardstick is applied on a much wider scale it is impossible to say whether or not these claims are justified.

There are of course some fairly obvious objections to Added Value which must be mentioned. Firstly, it might lead to a good deal of conflict within the firm over the differential contribution of specific work groups to increases in net output. It would be difficult to measure the contribution of some groups (notably indirect workers and white-collar employees) to Added Value and those directly engaged in the production process itself might benefit at the expense of the others. Secondly, it would be almost impossible to apply the Added Value yardstick to some large sectors of employment, notably public services, distribution, banking and insurance, which in turn raises the question of devising an alternative incomes policy for employees in these sectors. Thirdly, the Added Value yardstick would almost certainly challenge some long-established internal and external pay relationships and would presumably allow much less scope for wage settlements based on equity and fair comparison. For this reason it may prove unacceptable to many trade union representatives.

From an industrial relations point of view, however, there is also much to be said for Added Value. It has been argued above that there is still considerable scope for reforming payment systems at workplace level. Research has shown that PBR systems are subject to almost continuous upward pressure from the workforce between annual increases in basic rates. The aim here is to make the payment system yield higher earnings regardless of the level of output or the financial state of the firm. It is also well known that PBR is not an adequate solution to the problem of low productivity. Indeed, under a PBR system employees may be encouraged to retain working practices which perpetuate low productivity. Consequently the introduction of the Added Value yardstick should give managements a strong inducement to consider introducing measured day work. It would encourage managements to develop systems for regulating the differential earnings of employees doing similar kinds of work within the establishment – that is, job evaluation. Furthermore, since one of management's main problems in annual wage negotiations is how to satisfy their workers' expectations in respect of the 'going rate' (whether or not this is primarily determined by incomes policy), it would be in management's interest to develop a reasonably objective criterion which would assist both sides in determining the firm's ability to pay. Added Value offers a potentially useful method, therefore, of dispelling much of the ignorance which currently surrounds the subject of company profitability. Daniel, for example, found that when presenting a given wage claim, union officers 'attached a high level of importance to the employer's ability to pay in good circumstances, but discounted it in bad'. The major reason for this apparently hypocritical stance, however, was found to be management's failure to supply union negotiators with adequate financial information on the position of the company or the plant:

In view of this it would hardly be surprising if arguments about ability to pay in negotiations proved to be a dialogue of the deaf, with management saying 'We just can't afford it' and union officers replying 'That's what you always say' and having little basis for evaluating its particular validity.[56]

In this way the Added Value yardstick might help to dispel the anachronistic notion that wage increases 'come out of the boss's pocket' and might therefore encourage a more realistic and co-operative climate around the bargaining table.

Summary – wider implications

In the course of this chapter it has been argued that there is considerable scope for improving efficiency in British industry through collective bargaining. The experience of productivity bargaining during the late 1960s proves conclusively that inefficient practices on both sides *can* be removed by negotiation and mutual agreement provided that there are adequate incentives to do so. These incentives can best be offered through the medium of incomes policy. This means, firstly, that there will have to be a major shift in the substantive objectives of incomes policy. In recent years great emphasis has been placed on the principle of equity and thus on the regulation of individual earnings. The policy running through the 1977/8 pay round moved away from this position in the sense that it sought to regulate only aggregate earnings and permitted self-financing productivity agreements. However, it seems clear that if the connection between pay and productivity is to be fully recognized and incorporated into future incomes policies, further changes will be necessary. A permanent, national institution will need to be established in order to analyse key agreements and disseminate advice and assistance to negotiators. If the Added Value concept is to be widely applied, one may safely assume that this institution will have an important role to play in providing technical information to both sides. It might also make an important contribution towards developing a less disputatious and more rational way of settling some of the major issues concerning relative pay. Disputes over relativities may well increase as incomes policy becomes less concerned with equity and more with efficiency. Above all, there is an overwhelming case for using incomes policy in order to encourage managements firstly to improve their planning and negotiating skills and secondly to involve trade union representatives more fully in making decisions which affect the success of the enterprise. The experience of 1965 to 1970 suggests that the process of planning, negotiating and implementing productivity agreements had positive effects on skills and attitudes on both sides of the bargaining table. It would be difficult to argue that the need for improvement is less insistent now than it was then.

There are, however, significant differences between the economic and social environment of the late 1960s and that of the late 1970s. Firstly, the level of unemployment is much higher now than it was then, which implies that union negotiators and workgroups are more likely to resist any 'efficiency' proposals which involve substantial redundancy. Secondly, there is now a more widespread realization that low productivity in the workplace is not simply or even primarily the result of 'restrictive practices' imposed by trade unions and workgroups, nor is the solution largely a matter of employees being prepared to accept more exacting work, more physical effort or more onerous working conditions. Inefficiency may be the result of either inadequate *investment* or poor *organization* or adverse norms of *behaviour*, or a combination of all three. Whatever the precise balance of causes in a given work situation, it seems clear that management is in practice likely to bear much of the responsibility for such inefficiencies as do exist. This implies that joint efforts to improve the level of efficiency will be directed as much at managerial weaknesses and shortcomings as at the more conventional target of 'restrictive practices'. The implications for management style and for participation in the workplace can hardly be ignored: 'Much more effort will have to be put into thinking through the consequences of general business objectives and decisions for the workforce. Mistakes will have to be accepted more readily and a management style adopted which does not rely on assumptions of infallibility.'[57] The application of the Added Value concept to wage bargaining at company and plant level may also serve to expose inefficiencies in management which might otherwise have remained under cover.

It is certainly worth noting that the 'incomes policy' productivity deals of the late 1960s tended to underline the significance of management's role in promoting the reform of workplace relations. In the words of two researchers:

Inadequate or ineffective agreements were a consequence not of trade union resistance or even lack of management will, but rather lack of management competence. The productivity criterion provided management with an enormous opportunity to introduce change and reform but in general it was far from fully exploited, largely because managements were not sufficiently professional to see what changes needed to be made nor the ways in which they could be made.[58]

This lack of professionalism emerged in at least four ways. Firstly, many managements lacked the kind of basic control information (for example, on hours, earnings, output and costs) which was essential to the task of identifying the key problems within the organization. Secondly, they frequently failed to ensure that all those affected by the terms of the agreement fully understood what was expected of them; still less did they seek to consult them when the terms were being formulated. Consequently they often did not recognize 'that an agreement with workers would have a profound effect on supervisors, or that an agreement with one section of the workforce would have direct consequences with regard to other sections'.[59] Thirdly, they frequently adopted the productivity criterion without attempting to formulate broader policy objectives in employee relations which might have reinforced the impact of the changes proposed or put them in the context of a more far-reaching attempt to improve the climate of relations in the workplace. Some managers seemed more concerned with the mechanics of productivity bargaining than with the philosophy behind it. Finally, managements as a whole seem to have made too little use of external sources of advice and expertise, particularly in view of the fact that most of them had never been involved in productivity bargaining before. This again reflected a lack of professionalism and no doubt contributed to the failure of some agreements. While it would not be unduly optimistic to suggest that the average level of managerial competence might have improved over the past ten years, it would be surprising if most of these mistakes were not repeated in a future round of productivity bargaining. The need, therefore, for a central, expert advisory service is self-evident.

It would, of course, be misleading to regard the revival of productivity bargaining as a panacea for all shop-floor problems. Indeed, it would be reasonable to assume that the growing climate of insecurity engendered by high unemployment may well make the process of negotiating changes in the effort bargain even more difficult and prolonged than it would otherwise be. As the authors of one study pointed out some years ago: 'There is nothing in the notion of planned bargaining change which necessarily supposes that the mere taking of an initiative, however well-designed, will result in agreement, let alone the recognition of an identity of interest between management and unions.'[60] Without powerful financial inducements in the form of an incomes policy, it would be idle to pretend either that most managements will take initiatives for change or that most trade union representatives will respond to those initiatives. On the other hand, the general use of wage restraint as a method of inducing bargaining reform opens up the possibility that some managements and union representatives will simply pay lip service to the *quid pro quo* principle and concentrate on the wages side of the bargain. Whatever strategy is adopted there will undoubtedly be weaknesses, since ultimately the success or failure of the policy will depend on the aspirations, commitment, and expertise of the parties concerned. Nevertheless, the general direction of the strategy cannot be in doubt. The foundations that were laid in the late 1960s must be developed and built upon. Thus Allan Flanders' comment on the work of the NBPI is worth repeating:

... if there were no policies of restraint (apart from the very inadequate restraints that may or may not be imposed by the market) there would be no reformist pressures at all on any of the parties. As long as they were able to pass on wage and price increases to the ultimate consumer, they had no cause to change their ways and tread the thorny path of reform. So-called *free* collective bargaining has too often meant freedom from effective criticism, for anything you can get away with goes. The Board's activities are the beginnings of the long, slow education of the parties to an awareness that in a modern, industrial economy ways must be found of registering the public interest in matters of income distribution, costs and prices.[61]

A resumption of this 'long, slow' process of education is now well overdue.

CHAPTER FOUR

The New Legitimacy

In our view it is no longer acceptable for companies to be run on the basis that in the last resort the shareholders' view must by right always prevail. There must in the future be a new legitimacy for the exercise of the management function within a policy framework agreed jointly by the representatives of capital and labour. We believe that this new legitimacy is essential for the long-term efficiency and profitability of the private sector and for the ultimate success of the economy itself.

The Bullock Committee, Majority Report

We were unable to satisfy ourselves that sufficient notice has been taken of the evidence and advice of those who work in industry – employers and employees alike – whose views and experience are most relevant and most valid. It would be exceedingly unwise for the nation to disregard their practical realism and accept the theories of those who see this debate as a means of changing the structure of society in this country and who would seek to bring the boards of the private sector under trade union control.

The Bullock Committee, Minority Report

THE argument presented so far has concentrated on the practical need for extended joint regulation in the workplace as an integral part of the introduction and management of change. It must be recognized, however, that the extension of collective bargaining raises wider issues for both managements and trade unions. Traditionally in Britain the scope of collective bargaining has been limited by the relatively modest aspirations of trade union representatives and their members. Managers, not unnaturally, have acquiesced in this situation – at least until the external pressures of change have compelled them to bring new substantive problems to the bargaining table. As Clarke *et al.* have pointed out:

Managerial decisions concerning wages, organization of work and discipline are seen as of immediate, crucial importance to workers; while decisions relating to the raising of capital and the basic distribution of the firm's earnings have generally been seen by management as fundamental to the longer-term existence of the firm. Traditionally, workers have been, through their unions, basically concerned about levels of pay and security of employment, and management has long recognized that collective bargaining on wages and working conditions is a legitimate constraint on its freedom of decision-making.[1]

It seems self-evident, however, that over the next few years it will become less and less realistic either for managements to insist that certain key areas of business policy should remain non-negotiable or for trade unions to wash their hands of any responsibility for the success of individual enterprises. If there is to be a serious attempt to raise the level of productivity through collective bargaining it is, on the contrary, almost certain that managements will come under heavy pressure from trade union negotiators not only to disclose more information for bargaining purposes but also to explain and justify their own decisions and practices. It is inevitable that the process of negotiating change will gradually move the frontier of joint regulation into areas of decision-making hitherto reserved for management. Once this central point is accepted, practitioners must focus their attention on devising appropriate institutional arrangements for sharing the power to make decisions on a wide range of substantive issues.

Some managers may, of course, argue that the problem of improving productivity could be solved by motivating employees to work harder, which would in turn depend on making their jobs more interesting and financially more rewarding. This strategy would not, however, mean any fundamental changes in the structure of power in industry. This approach to participation has rightly been described as 'task-centred' in the sense that it involves developing 'an organizational pattern in which workers are permitted to exercise a greater degree of control over their work environment and performance' for the purpose of raising productivity and reducing alienation in the workplace. A distinction may thus be drawn between the task-centred approach and *power*-centred participation, which aims at 'extending the bargaining power of the workers within the enterprise and at making managerial decision-makers more accountable either to the unions or more directly to the workers'.[2] Task-centred participation may be attractive to managers for several reasons, the principal one being that it appears to solve the problem of how to give workers more discretion in the performance of their work without weakening managerial control over the broad objectives of the enterprise. Managers who advocate the spread of task-centred participation – and they are as yet a minority – may well resist trade union demands for a more radical extension of joint decision-making. The CBI, for example, holds the view that 'participation should begin at the grass roots, at the shop floor, and that some agreed form of top level machinery is only likely to work if a suitable "infrastructure" has been established and is operating successfully'.[3] This view is examined below.

Management and participation

Participation has been defined as 'the upward exertion of control by subordinates over various forms of organizational activity, with that control being exercised directly by the worker himself, or indirectly through some means of representation'.[4] Managerial thought and action has typically tended to concentrate on the various forms of 'task-centred' participation – those primarily related to the job itself – because these would appear to be consistent with the objective of improving motivation and efficiency while retaining the overall control of the organization in the hands of management. Indeed, managements have long accepted the principle of direct worker participation in the effort bargain, although the behavioural assumptions involved have changed quite markedly over the years. The oldest set of assumptions – those based on the Taylorian notion of 'economic man' – have of course had a pervasive effect on managerial attitudes to participation. The key assumptions are that most people have an inherent dislike of work and that they respond only to a controlled

119

system of financial rewards and penalties. The most obvious manifestation of these assumptions in the workplace is, of course, an overt reliance on financial incentives, and the reluctance of many managers to dispense with traditional incentive payment systems indicates that the concept of 'economic man' still exerts a strong influence on managerial thinking.[5] In practice, however, PBR systems have also given workers an opportunity to exert direct *control* over the speed and intensity with which they work. As Guest and Fatchett have pointed out,

> The economic man perspective demonstrates that where the worker attaches sufficient value or importance to the outcomes and rewards, he will discover a means of exerting control. If he perceives a significantly large disparity in the effort-bargain, he will exert his control through restriction of output or through other means to put this right.[6]

It was noted in the previous chapter that in recent years the weaknesses of PBR systems have been increasingly recognized by managements and their use in British manufacturing industry now seems to be declining. Nevertheless it is important to recognize that what managers see as 'weaknesses' stem from the degree of job control which PBR has in practice given the worker – hence the reluctance of many workgroups to permit the abolition of PBR and the continued vulnerability of alternative payment systems to pressure from the workforce.

The experience of PBR systems suggests that while money is and always will be an important influence on attitudes to work, many workers do recognize other sources of satisfaction in and from their jobs. The work of the 'human relations' school of social scientists and their successors has given managers some insight into the nature of these additional sources of satisfaction. The importance of the informal social organization of the workplace has been emphasized. The level of output is said to be influenced by the composition and behaviour of individual work *groups*, whose normative framework is determined by social rather than economic factors.[7] The implications for management are firstly that workgroups should be given more discretion to set their own targets and organize their work; secondly, that participative styles of management should be adopted; and thirdly, that there should be more consultation and two-way communication on the shop floor. A more sophisticated but not radically dissimilar school of thought has focused attention on the intrinsic needs of the individual worker in relation to his job. The work of Maslow, Argyris, Herzberg and others has emphasized the need to redesign many jobs in modern industry so that they satisfy the individual worker's alleged desire for more autonomy, responsibility and control. It is argued that if jobs were restructured to meet these personal growth needs, motivation and therefore efficiency would be much higher and the level of conflict correspondingly lower.[8] The main practical result of these writings has been a growing level of interest on the part of some managers, both in Britain and abroad, in the possibilities of job enrichment, job enlargement and job rotation. Changes in the organization of work which are based on the assumption that most workers want more challenging work and more freedom to do it in their own way also have wider political implications for management. As Guest and Fatchett have pointed out, they have given managements the opportunity to show a sense of social responsibility and thereby refute the arguments of those who question the moral right of management 'to take away the meaning from work and to increase the control of the machine over the worker'.[9] It has also been argued that if managements pay more attention to their workers' need for higher intrinsic rewards from work, the latter's preoccupation with money and other extrinsic factors will become less significant. Are these hopes justified? Recent research suggests that they are not.

Workers and participation

The arguments advanced by professional job-enrichers are usually based on the assumption that the desire for intrinsic satisfaction with, or 'self-actualization' in the job is an overriding priority of most workers for most of the time. In reality, however, there is little evidence to support this assumption. Attitudes and behaviour on the shop floor seem to be influenced by a complex range of variables, some of which are specific to the work situation and some not. Among the most significant variables are the orientations and expectations which workers bring to the work situation. To illustrate this point in simple terms, one could say that if workers have been conditioned by a variety of socializing agencies *outside* the workplace to expect little from their work other than purely extrinsic rewards, the satisfactions they seek are likely to be largely instrumental; in other words, they will value work primarily for the money it brings. They may, therefore, be quite prepared to put up with jobs which many writers have long regarded as 'alienating' (for example, motor-car assembly work) provided that the extrinsic rewards are sufficiently attractive. As long as their main expectations are met they may even take a favourable view of their employment and demonstrate cooperative attitudes towards management. Workers in this category are likely to adopt an equally instrumental attitude towards their trade unions and regard collective action primarily as a means of improving extrinsic rewards.[10] This in itself, however, suggests that predominantly instrumental relationships between effort and reward may be neither easy nor stable. It has already been noted that there are several factors, both internal and external to the workplace, which can effectively erode an individual worker's satisfaction with the financial reward he gets from his work, and the recent inflation has underlined their importance. In these circumstances the behavioural consequences may be particularly unwelcome to management, for as Westergaard has observed:

One worker may be willing to accept the lack of other interests and satisfactions in the job, for the sake of the money. But should the amount and dependability of the money be threatened, his resigned toleration of the lack of discretion, control and 'meaning' attached to the job could no longer be guaranteed. The 'cash nexus' may snap just because it is *only* a cash nexus because it is single-stranded; and if it does snap, there is nothing else to bind the worker to the acceptance of his situation.[11]

In his study of workers' attitudes at Ford's, for example, Beynon noted that 'a moral commitment to the firm was almost totally absent . . .'[12]

However, other research seems to indicate that this preference for extrinsic rewards is a much more complex phenomenon than the notion of a simple trade-off between boring work and high pay would imply. Firstly, it may involve security of employment as well as pay. A study by Wedderburn and Crompton suggests that in areas with a long tradition of relatively high unemployment, many workers may attach as much value to job security as to money.[13] In certain circumstances, of course, workers in this category may find themselves obliged to moderate their wage aspirations – at least temporarily – in order to protect their security of employment. Secondly, an instrumental orientation to work does not necessarily imply *alienation* from the job itself and is not always related to technology and the division of labour. In his survey of process workers in South Wales, for example, Cotgrove found that instrumental orientations stemmed primarily from the market situation in which the workers found themselves, 'from the overriding need of men whose market situation is weak and vulnerable for a job which offers pay and security'.[14]

A third and more complex point is that an instrumental orientation does not necessarily prevent a worker from obtaining and valuing intrinsic rewards from the job itself. As Daniel and McIntosh have observed, it is too often assumed that the worker 'has an ordered and consistent set of needs or priorities in what he seeks from a job and that this set of priorities is reflected and manifested in all aspects of his work behaviour and choices'.[15] It may be more useful, therefore, to distinguish between 'primary' values in work, chiefly pay and security, and 'secondary' values such as job content and control. Alternatively, we may adopt Fox's distinction between high priority and low priority aspirations:

The former are those which are actively entertained and pursued. They are experienced as pressing and they appear realistic and within hope of realization. They may well be the aspirations which attract a man to a particular job, which cause him to stay in it, and which constitute the predominant criteria by which he evaluates it. Low priority aspirations are less strongly held or seem unrealistic and beyond hope of realization, or both. They may nevertheless profoundly affect the individual's behaviour in work. A manual worker who takes, keeps and values a given job for predominantly instrumental reasons may yet have expressive aspirations which inform his responses to the work situation and management.[16]

Daniel's own work suggests that the relative importance which workers place on these values may change according to the circumstances in which they find themselves.[17] If workers are relatively satisfied with the extrinsic rewards they get from their work, they may be receptive to managerial initiatives designed to increase their intrinsic sources of satisfaction. It should be remembered, however, that, given all the destabilizing influences in the economic environment, the satisfaction of any group with their extrinsic rewards may not last very long. Indeed, as Roberts *et al.* have pointed out, '. . . the individual does not carry out his work role in a vacuum; he is constantly judging his task, role and rewards against a number of reference points, and is more or less satisfied in relative terms only'.[18]

The individual worker's orientation to work may also be reinforced or modified by the norms and expectations of the workgroup to which he belongs. In Roberts' words:

> The workgroup does more than offer rewards of ascribed status and approval. People working in similar conditions will come to be recognized as equals or peers and will normally be regarded as colleagues. Such individuals may develop an identity arising out of their common conditions of work and shared expectations and sentiments . . . which becomes manifest under stress, such as when any one of the loosely defined expectations or aspirations, developed within their work role, has become accepted as legitimate by their group and is challenged by an outsider.[19]

The 'outsider' may be either another workgroup or management itself, or a combination of both. In the study quoted above, it was found that while many technicians still aspired as *individuals* towards personal achievement, they had also acquired a sense of *collective* dissatisfaction as a group with their work, their status and their relative pay. Moreover, the authors found that the technicians did not in fact draw a clear distinction between intrinsic and extrinsic rewards. Their pay was closely related to their position or status, and changes in their pay as a group could not be divorced from their individual advancement, or lack of it, within the firm.[20] Other studies have underlined the significance of collective norms and aspirations, particularly in relation to craftsmen. Wedderburn and Crompton, for example, found that the craftsmen in their survey, compared to the general workers, 'were far more concerned with the nature of the work they had to do and with their status. They emphasized the importance of having control over their work and took it for granted that it should be interesting'.[21] When it was *not* interesting, or when they felt that their ability to do 'a good job' was being frustrated by management, they readily took action to protect the interests of 'their' craft. The reported tendency of the craftsmen in this study to view the enterprise through a unitary frame of reference and use 'football teams' imagery might seem inconsistent with their militant behaviour. In fact, however, there was little inconsistency: 'Their efforts, however disruptive to teamwork they may have appeared at times, could be seen as directed towards ensuring that their own place in that "team" was adequately recognized.'[22]

The evidence of these and other investigations suggests, therefore, that the pattern of aspirations and behaviour in a given workplace can only be understood by relating the orientations of the workers to their experience of the work situation itself. In this sense the focal point for analysis is the extent to which workers' expectations are met by the actual rewards received from work. Yet in reality the problem is far more complex than this simple statement would imply. The pattern of expectations differs considerably from one workgroup to another. Some groups expect little more than their pay packet at the end of the week; others couple pay with job security; some, especially white-collar groups, have fairly well-defined aspirations towards a career and individual advancement; others are conscious of the status which their skills and market position have given them. Some groups attach great value to both extrinsic and intrinsic rewards; others seem to change their priorities in work according to the circumstances in which they find themselves. The problem is further complicated by the fact that in practice it is not always possible to make a clear distinction between different rewards and priorities.

A few points of substance do, however, emerge from the evidence collected to date and managers should be aware of them. Firstly, it would appear that while an instrumental orientation to work may – as long as the extrinsic rewards come up to expectations – give rise to satisfaction *with* the job, this is not the same as satisfaction *in* the job. Satisfaction is a function of the gap between expectations and experience. It was argued earlier that the traditional 'fatalism' of the manual working class has declined over the postwar period as a whole and their horizon of expectations has risen, not simply in respect of living standards but also in relation to their rights, power and status in the workplace. It was also noted that this change in expectations has shown itself primarily through the growth of collective bargaining at plant and company level. The extension of workplace bargaining to cover substantive issues other than wages and conditions of employment, though gradual and uneven, in itself refutes the argument that most workers are interested only in the size of their pay packet. Indeed, some recent research suggests that there is a considerable demand by workers for more influence over decisions affecting their own jobs and working conditions, including the organization of work, the fixing of work standards and methods of payment.[23] In other words many workers may be significantly less satisfied *in* their jobs than they are *with* their jobs. This felt lack of intrinsic satisfaction does not necessarily imply that there is a widespread alienation from work itself and a fundamental rejection of managerial priorities. The authors of a recent study of participation in the British Steel Corporation, for example, found that many workers and shop stewards regarded participation as a means of improving efficiency in the sense that workers should be given more freedom to exercise their skills and abilities, based as they were on a level of knowledge and experience which they regarded as superior to management's.[24]

The point to emphasize is that any attempt by management to enhance the intrinsic satisfactions which the worker can obtain as an *individual* must be seen in the context of the continuing importance of extrinsic rewards and *collective* aspirations. As Daniel and McIntosh have observed, most manual workers expect to remain in whatever job they have chosen for most of their working lives:

> While it may be possible to enrich the job he is doing, even substantially, it is not realistic to expect that it might be possible to create progressively more interesting, responsible, challenging and demanding jobs for him . . . any hope that he has of advancement in his status and earnings lies in the advancement of the group of which he is a member. In short his economic and social advancement is linked inextricably to collective advancement, for it is only if the wage or salary grade to which he belongs receives an improvement in earnings, fringe benefits, status or conditions that he will progress. This does not mean that job content is unimportant or that job enrichment is not practicable or desirable. What it does mean is that as far as these types of manual worker are concerned, job enrichment has to be placed in a collective bargaining context and management has to distinguish between the different attitudes, priorities and strategies that prevail in different contexts.[25]

To put the point at its simplest, it may be that while manual workers with some kind of skill or specialized knowledge would like more scope to use it to the full, they are unlikely to accept greater responsibility as an end in itself. Unless improvements in intrinsic satisfaction are linked to corresponding changes in extrinsic rewards they have little chance of gaining general acceptance.

It would seem that the same caveats are relevant to white-collar workers. Some writers have drawn a distinction between the expectations of manual and white-collar employees and have sought to show that the possibilities of improving the motivation of the latter by focusing on intrinsic rewards are relatively numerous. It is argued, firstly, that the nature of many white-collar jobs is such as to provide considerable scope for job enrichment and, secondly, that white-collar workers tend to think in terms of a long-term career based on personal achievement and advancement. The concept of a career, as opposed to that of a job, is seen as constituting 'a powerful force for job involvement (which) creates a strong link between the fortunes of the individual and those of the enterprise'.[26] In reality, however, the situation is less clear-cut. As white-collar employment has grown in recent years, several factors have combined to create – at least for some white-collar workers – a significant gap between expectations and experience. The increasing 'bureaucratization' of white-collar work, the growing size of employment units, the compression of pay differentials and fringe benefits and the increasing blockage of promotion opportunities have all been identified as significant factors in this context. The relative importance of these factors does, however, vary greatly between different work situations and occupational groups. In a recent survey of middle managers, for example, Weir found that while job content and job security were still sources of considerable satisfaction for a majority of the sample, salary and promotion prospects had fallen well below their expectations. The same writer also found significant dissatisfaction with internal systems of communications and consultation; the majority felt that they were not sufficiently consulted about matters which *directly* affected them.

The implications of this survey for top management are important: 'Practically everyone agrees that "something has to be done" and that this something would necessarily involve a move towards greater participation, more formal procedures of consultation, and more opportunities for employees to become involved in management at a policy-making rather than a merely policy-interpreting level.' A large proportion of the sample, however, showed considerable antipathy towards trade unionism and implicity expressed the hope that top management would satisfy their aspirations before a move towards 'full-blooded' trade unionism became necessary.[27] In other situations, by contrast, the relevance of collective action has long been more explicit. Many of the technicians studied by Roberts *et al.*, for example, had lost much of their faith in the concept of a career based exclusively on advancement and achievement. Consequently they associated improvements in their earnings and status with the collective strength of the group to which they belonged rather than with their own individual career progression.

To summarize, it has been argued that managerial attempts to improve employee motivation by concentrating solely on changes in job design and on other intrinsic rewards are unlikely to succeed. The response of most workgroups to these 'task-centred' initiatives is in practice likely to be determined by a complex interplay of factors, notably their own orientations to work, the nature of their collective norms and aspirations and the current level of satisfaction with their extrinsic rewards. Although there is no space here to discuss experiences of job enrichment in detail, it must be noted that it broadly confirms the reservations expressed above. Although relatively few managements either in Britain or in Western Europe as a whole have attempted to change the design of jobs in their establishments on a significant scale, some relevant conclusions have been drawn from the experience of those who have.[28] Firstly, it would seem that while workers have gained more control over their work, this has not had as much effect on motivation and output as was initially envisaged, nor has it diminished the value which the workers involved place on higher extrinsic rewards through collective bargaining. Secondly, the nature of the changes introduced seem to matter less than the *way* in which they are introduced. The critical factors here would seem to be the role of collective bargaining and the relationship between changes in job design and improvements in extrinsic rewards. Thirdly, the scope for changing the structure of jobs and the organization of work is to some extent limited by the technology of the workplace. In some industries it may be relatively easy to change the design of clerical and supervisory jobs regardless of the prevailing technology; with manual workers, however, the scope for such changes may be much more restricted, or alternatively the financial costs of change may be too high in relation to the behavioural risks and uncertainties involved.[29] Finally, the way in which a managerial initiative in this field is received will also be influenced by the traditions of the workplace, including the general climate of relations and the level of trust which the workforce has in management's intentions If the workplace has well-established collective bargaining arrangements, any attempt by management to introduce changes in job design outside this framework is likely to be rejected out of hand as 'manipulative'. If job enrichment is viewed purely as a motivational strategy and is introduced in isolation, without regard to its wider substantive and procedural implications, it is unlikely to be of much use to management or of much interest to the workforce. In short, 'task-centred' participation should be seen in the context of collective bargaining.

Participation and collective bargaining

In the Donovan Commission's view: 'Properly conducted, collective bargaining is the most effective means of giving workers the right to representation in decisions affecting their working lives, a right which is or should be the prerogative of every worker in a democratic society.'[30] In order to be conducted 'properly', Donovan argued, collective bargaining should include all those issues of substance which workers and their organizations regard as important and should be regulated by formal, written procedures. Taken to its logical conclusion, this argument implies that every strategic aspect of business policy, including the raising and allocation of financial resources, must ultimately be subject to joint regulation. As was noted earlier, public policy is now strongly biased in favour of the extension of collective bargaining in the sense that it is more difficult than it was for employers to refuse recognition and negotiating rights to independent trade unions. But although the pressure of public policy is undoubtedly an important influence on the spread of collective bargaining, the extent to which the Donovan model can become a reality depends much more on the objectives and aspirations of managements, employees and trade unions.

If we start from the proposition that the substantive and procedural norms of the enterprise (i.e. its 'normative system') have been historically determined by management, then the role of employees and their organizations may be seen as defensive and reactionary. While the well-known changes in the market environment over the past thirty years have often made the posture of trade union representatives and workgroups appear relatively aggressive, it is still true that the role which shop stewards and trade union officials tend to find most congenial is that of reacting to initiatives from management. The *way* in which they react and the amount of countervailing pressure they bring to bear on management both depend not merely on the market position of the firm and its technological characteristics but also on the aspirations of the employees they represent. In Fox's words:

> The lower the level of workers' aspirations, the less demands they make on the normative system, and this on the face of it would seem to enlarge the freedom enjoyed by management in the pursuit of their own aspirations. And so, in certain respects, it does. Certain kinds of change are easier to introduce to a docile, passive and undemanding labour force than to one that is keenly alert in pursuing an ever-enlarging set of aspirations. But in some circumstances the freedom of management may prove empty. Workers with low aspirations are weakly motivated. Yet some kinds of task, some kinds of pay system, and some kinds of group cooperation call for strong motivation if managerial purposes are to be achieved ... However, some employers may welcome low aspirations among their employees not because this frees them to introduce change but because it relieves them of some of the *need* for change. In other words, if their own aspirations are low, the absence of demands by their employees upon the normative system will spare them the challenge of reconciling these demands with the requirements of the organization's environment.[31]

It was noted earlier that the low level of productivity in large areas of the British economy may be attributed, at least in part, to low aspirations on the part of both managements and trade unionists. Low aspirations on both sides may also be responsible for the prevalence of peaceful and reasonably cooperative labour relations in many firms and for the strong mutual preference for informal, *ad hoc* methods of resolving such disputes as do arise. This preference for informality is particularly strong in smaller firms, where union membership tends to be low or non-existent and where the level of direct conflict is also low. In fact there appears to be a positive relationship between organizational size, union membership density, the existence of formal procedures and negotiating machinery, and the frequency of strikes.[32] There also seems, not surprisingly, to be a distinct tendency for employee influence over managerial decision-making to increase with both the level of unionization and the size of the establishment. Nevertheless it would appear that even in relatively large, well-organized plants there are very definite limits to the scope of collective bargaining. Clarke *et al.* found that the overwhelming majority of companies in their survey strongly believed, for example, that financial policy was exclusively a matter for management. They also found that many managements were anxious to retain their authority over work methods, discipline, the payment system and redundancy issues. Although the need to *consult* employees before introducing substantive changes was frequently recognized, there were few issues on which even the larger, highly unionized companies were prepared to concede that their workers' *agreement* was indispensable. This reluctance to countenance any further erosion of managerial prerogative may simply be a function of the low level of employee aspirations, expressed in the form of low unionization. In the words of Clarke *et al.*:

The evidence would suggest that the main reason why management has a unitary rather than a pluralistic view of the firm is not because of an ideological commitment but because the unions have frequently failed to increase their organizational strength to a level where they can insist on management accepting a wider field of joint regulation. The response of management to unions is almost entirely pragmatic; if unions are strong and determined to extend the range of their bargaining interests, as the evidence of the United States indicates, they will be able to achieve this goal.[33]

It is worth adding, however, that Clarke *et al.* carried out their survey in the late 1960s and since then there has been a major increase in trade union membership. The limited evidence we have also indicates that there has been a significant expansion in the substantive scope of workplace bargaining over the last few years.

Yet, despite the fact that collective bargaining has never been so widespread nor so strongly supported by public policy, many British managers remain apprehensive about its wider implications. Like their continental counterparts they would still prefer to maintain a distinction between collective bargaining and joint consultation. In the words of one study:

One of the most important considerations for management is that the ethos of a consultative committee is very different from that of a collective bargaining session. In collective bargaining the two sides generally approach each other as rivals bent upon securing the best deal for themselves. At its best collective bargaining can achieve positive gains for both sides, but at its worst it degenerates into a conflict situation which is frequently damaging to both sides. With consultation, management is hopeful that the discussions will be carried on in an atmosphere that is free from the threat of serious conflict if agreement is not immediately reached. Ideas and proposals can be discussed in the light of common goals rather than in terms of ends that are in conflict.[34]

In Britain both the recommendations of the Whitley Commission (1917) and the rapid growth of joint production committees at plant level between 1940 and 1945 reflected this search for a joint problem-solving approach to labour relations. In practice, however, the distinction between consultation and bargaining has proved increasingly difficult to maintain. In well-organized workplaces management has seldom been able to resist indefinitely the demand for more joint *regulation*, although in some firms traditional consultative arrangements have survived.[35] In continental Europe, the reliance on formal joint consultation has been much more pronounced and has frequently been supported by law. In the immediate postwar period most of these countries encouraged managements to establish works councils for the purpose of consulting representatives of *all* the employees (not merely trade union members) on a narrow and defined range of substantive issues. These systems appeared to work reasonably well as long as trade unionism at plant level remained weak. Since the late 1960s, however, trade union membership has been growing throughout Western Europe and the demand for bargaining at plant and company level has generally increased. As a result the unitary assumptions which lie behind formal joint consultation are by no means as influential or widely held as they used to be. In the words of one recent study: 'The trend in Europe is towards a greater role for enterprise or workplace bargaining and hence for the union. Consultative systems which do not permit any significant worker influence on important issues and deny a role for the unions appear to be becoming less important.'[36]

If some managements are fearful of the implications of extended collective bargaining for their own power and status, some trade union leaders are, paradoxically, becoming less confident that collective bargaining can ever really extend the influence of workers into the sphere of 'top-level' decision-making within companies. Even in its most sophisticated form, collective bargaining is still essentially an indirect form of participation. It is based on the assumption that the right to make policy and initiate changes lies with management and that the role of the employees' organization is to *react* to management proposals and if necessary modify them through negotiation. Some trade union leaders are, of course, quite satisfied with this division of labour. They argue that as long as they can react to and ultimately veto the policies and initiatives of management, they can preserve the independence of their organizations and ensure that the opinions and interests of their members are fully represented in whatever bargaining position they adopt. In their view the touchstone of independence is the right to *oppose*, and they are apprehensive lest a more advanced system of direct participation, for example worker directors, should involve union representatives in policy-making to such a degree that they would have to forego the right to oppose and thus lose their independence. Trade union leaders who think in this way are supported by many rank-and-file union members and shop stewards who simply do not want to become too involved in matters which they see as properly falling within the orbit of management. This view has, however, been increasingly challenged from both inside and outside the TUC in recent years. The General Council's report to the 1974 Congress, for example, argued that

there are a number of specific questions of close concern to workpeople which are not being effectively subjected to joint regulation through the present processes of collective bargaining and additional forms of joint regulation are needed, particularly as capital becomes more concentrated and the central decisions of boards of directors seem increasingly remote from any impact by workpeople through their own organizations.

The kind of policy decisions which are of greatest interest to trade union representatives are, of course, those concerning the allocation of financial resources, the profitability of the organization, and future plans for expansion or contraction. While information on some or all of these items may be extracted from management in the course of collective bargaining, the relevant policy decisions will already have been taken and are not likely to be changed fundamentally by trade union opposition, except in the most extreme circumstances.

The current debate on the need for some system of extended participation in British industry must therefore be seen in the context of increasing dissatisfaction on the part of some trade unionists and academic observers with the more traditional forms of social control on managerial power. It would be useful at this point to remind ourselves that these include control by the market, control by countervailing power, control by legal and negotiated rules, and control by accountability. Control by the *market* 'operates to the full when an individual employee can choose among employers and freely decide for whom he prefers to work'.[37] Even in the days when there was much less unemployment than there is now, however, this form of control was in practice only available to those employees who either possessed a marketable skill or lived in an area of excessive demand for labour. Control by *countervailing power* simply means that trade unions can call a strike or authorize some other form of industrial action, or alternatively that workgroups can take action of their own, in opposition to management decisions. The effectiveness of this form of control in turn depends on the vulnerability of the enterprise to stoppages and the level of financial loss which the strikers themselves can comfortably stand. While it is generally agreed that the power of the strike weapon has increased over the past thirty years, it still remains true that most trade union representatives and their members would normally prefer not to use it.[38] Control by the *rule of law* has emerged historically from the use of countervailing power. These rules are established not merely by legislation (which until recently has played little part in British industrial relations) but by collective bargaining.

The effectiveness of these rules, however, is influenced by their relevance to the work situation. In Britain and some other European countries the rules negotiated at industry/regional/district level have become increasingly meaningless for both managements and employees in the workplace. Yet the substantive and procedural coverage of workplace agreements is still extremely variable. In some companies the framework of negotiated rules has long been a powerful constraint on management, whereas in others management still has a fairly free hand.

The effectiveness of all these forms of control is therefore problematic. Even at their best they are all essentially *negative* in character:

... they impose certain limits on management's freedom of action, restrictions on how it may use its power. Provided, however, those restrictions are respected management can manage as it chooses. None of these controls offers the workers any share in deciding their industrial destiny; they are protective more than participative. No worker has any reason to feel any responsibility for the conduct of the enterprise that employs him because of their existence; nor has he any stake in its success. If by democracy is meant not only the division of power which we have in any pluralistic society but participation of the governed in government, they do not necessarily contribute to industrial democracy.[39]

Consequently in recent years there has been a marked upsurge in interest both in Britain and in western Europe as a whole in devising systems of control based on extended accountability. A distinction has thus been drawn between, on the one hand, imposing restrictions on the *way* in which management uses its power and, on the other hand, equal participation in shaping the *purposes* for which this power is used. On the assumption that the objectives of the enterprise are primarily determined at board level, much attention has recently been focused in Britain on the possibility of introducing some form of employee representation on boards of directors. Indeed, it is more than likely that either the present government or its successor will follow the example of our fellow-members of the EEC and introduce legislation for some form of direct representation on company boards. By way of introducing this controversial topic, therefore, it would be useful to discuss the lessons which have been drawn from recent experience both at home and abroad with extended account-ability involving worker directors.

Worker directors: the lessons of experience

The authors of a research report for the Bullock Committee, having surveyed the experience of several European countries with worker directors, advanced two conclusions: 'first, worker directors have generally had little effect on anything, and, second and consequently they have certainly had no catastrophic effect on anything or anybody'.[40] Why has the introduction of worker representation on company boards apparently proved to be such a non-event? The following factors would seem to be significant: (1) the normative framework on which the concept of worker representation is based; (2) the relationship between the worker director and his constituents; and (3) the significance of the board itself as a policy-making body. Each of these factors is briefly discussed below.

The most significant normative assumption which most European systems of worker representation reflect is that the presence of workers on company boards will encourage a climate of mutual confidence and cooperation throughout the enterprise. Conversely they reflect a strong determination to prevent the spread of collective bargaining into the boardroom. In most cases worker directors are elected either by works councils or by all the employees in the organization. The same kind of thinking is evident in the development of worker representation on the divisional boards of the British Steel Corporation. On the formation of BSC in 1967, senior management realized that the industry was in great need of rationalization and new investment and that if the necessary measures were to succeed the cooperation of the workforce was essential. Worker representation on the Corporation's divisional boards was seen by the directors as a potentially useful method of improving communications with the workforce, thereby encouraging a climate of cooperation: 'Understanding was the strong theme among directors; contact with the shop floor would provide better information on which to base decisions – hence it was knowledge of the shop floor which was important. Worker directors would reflect the shop floor, not represent it.'[41] Consequently, the worker directors could influence discussion in the boardroom only as *individuals* with a particular kind of experience which the other directors felt it useful to call upon from time to time. Any influence they exerted did not depend on their ability to represent the views and interests of employees on the shop floor, otherwise they would have taken on the status of *negotiators* on their behalf. The legal position of worker directors in both western Europe and BSC reflects this unitary perspective; they have the same legal responsibilities to the board and to the enterprise as the 'management' directors. Consequently they are bound by the same constraints when sensitive, confidential information is given to them, and this in turn restricts their ability to communicate to the workforce.

These obvious ambiguities in the rationale of existing schemes have in turn produced serious doubts and uncertainties about the role of worker directors in decision-making. If they are not there to represent the collective interests of their constituents and ensure that these are taken into account by their fellow board members, what else can they do? At BSC the worker directors were in fact nominated by the trade unions and all of them had extensive experience as trade union representatives and officials. Once they had been appointed, however, they were required to resign any offices they held within their unions because they were not to be seen as 'union men'. They were on the board as 'experts in their own right, (as) people who could bring to the board the authentic view of the average man on the shop floor'.[42] In practice, therefore, their role was frequently one of reporting what they felt were the views of employees on specific problems rather than representing those views. Not surprisingly this role aroused little enthusiasm on the shop floor and many employees soon felt that the whole idea was simply a managerial gimmick. The formal separation of the worker directors from their unions also meant that such credibility as they had *as directors* depended heavily on the assistance of senior management, particularly on the provision of information. The more information and advice they received and the more 'expert' they were, the more their perspective on specific problems became conditioned by management. In the words of Brannen *et al.*, 'The worker directors' fight to establish their role was a fight largely with management to work within the management structure. To legitimate their activities they had to work within specific confines.'[43] Moreover, considerable pressure has been brought to bear on worker directors, both at BSC and abroad, to ensure that they conform to the norms of board conduct:

Although the worker director is not seen by his board colleagues to qualify as a 'proper' director in terms of managerial talent or property rights, a process of 'negotiation' implicitly occurs in which he is treated as such on condition that he acts accordingly, accepting the assumptions and priorities of the board and conforming to the norms of gentlemanly conduct, unity and harmony.[44]

In short, unless worker directors are given a role and a form of institutional support which at least gives them a chance to retain an independent perspective on the problems and priorities of the enterprise, they will soon be absorbed into the existing structure of authority and their potential value will be dissipated.

Even if they were backed by a strong trade union organization, however, it could still be argued that the impact of worker directors on policy-making would be small, for the simple reason that company boards themselves are by no means as powerful as is generally assumed. It has been pointed out that power within any enterprise which operates in an economy where market forces are important tends in practice to accrue to those who are best able to deal with all the uncertainties which those forces generate. This in effect means that power follows expertise and in most business enterprises, particularly large ones, it would obviously be wrong to assume that expertise is confined to the boardroom. Indeed, many company directors do not have executive responsibility within the organization and rely to a considerable degree on the advice and information they receive from the managing director and his team of senior managers. Most boards, both in Britain and abroad, do not meet more than once a month and even then many of the decisions are purely a formality.

Policy guidelines and broad objectives may be set by the board but these are passed down the management hierarchy for implementation by executives and may in the process be modified to suit the latter's conception of what the needs of the organization are and what its priorities ought to be.[45] In many British companies the limitations of the board have been implicitly recognized by the establishment of a smaller management committee composed of those directors and senior managers who have a detailed and intimate knowledge not only of the business as a whole but also of specific operational areas. It follows that worker directors may find themselves excluded from the real sources of power within the enterprise not because of any devious conspiracy on the part of their fellow directors to shut them out but rather because the realities of business life are what they are. At BSC, for example, the divisional boards on which the workers sat were not at the centre of power, and even at this level 'formal and informal meetings of full-time directors were more significant to the decision-making process than formal board meetings'.[46] The same point has been made in relation to the two-tier board structure adopted in West Germany and apparently favoured by a minority of the Bullock Committee. It has been reported that in practice the German supervisory board merely acts as an adviser to the management board and as such has very limited influence over policy-making. As Batstone and Davies have pointed out: 'The condition for effective supervision is the ability to be involved in the network of information within the organization and in the decision-making process. Conversely, effective management requires the assurance that "supervisors" will not "disrupt" plans and courses of action.'[47] It would seem, however, that in Germany the needs of effective management have triumphed over those of effective supervision. There is no reason why the same should not happen in Britain if a two-tier structure were to be established here. In any case the same situation already applies in those British companies where a small management committee of directors reports to a unitary board.

To summarize, therefore, it has been argued that the significance of worker directors depends firstly on the role they are given as directors, secondly on the implications which this role has for their relationship with the shop floor, and thirdly on the role of the board itself in corporate decision-making. If their role is seen in unitary terms, as one of reporting rather than representing, they are unlikely to have much effect on policy decisions. Their influence will be further diminished – at least in organizations where trade unions are firmly established – if their *institutional* links with their constituents are weakened. But, above all, if the worker representative on the board 'is frequently not located on a body of great significance', he is hardly in a position to do anything which either his constituents or his fellow directors will regard as significant.[48] In addition, the worker director will encounter strong pressures from other board members and senior management generally to adopt the role and perspectives of a conventional director, and these pressures will almost certainly succeed because of the worker director's fundamental dependence on managerial advice and information. In the face of these 'socializing' tendencies, the worker director will, at least in the eyes of the workforce, become almost indistinguishable from his fellow board members. He will respect the confidentiality of information; he will not introduce controversy into the board-room; he will take an increasingly 'objective' view of emotive issues such as closures and redundancy and he will not question the overall priorities of the enterprise. Given all these tendencies, it seems clear that senior managers and directors have little to fear from workers on the board.

If, however, they have little to fear from worker directors, they have little to hope from them either. Worker directors have had little or no effect either on the structure of power and authority or on the process of decision-making inside the enterprise. They have not changed anything simply because they have not challenged or disturbed anything. Consequently, although the power of management has remained intact, so have other features of the work situation. Worker directors have not generated a greater sense of involvement with the success of the enterprise on the part of the workforce. Traditional attitudes have not been affected. There is little reason to suppose, therefore, that worker directors will have much effect on the efficiency and profitability of the enterprise. Why, then, is there such a determination on the part of some trade union leaders to introduce a system of worker directors in Britain? The key to their new-found enthusiasm lies in the fact that they now regard boardroom representation as an effective way of strengthening collective bargaining. If the substantive content of collective bargaining is to be extended, and it has been argued in the previous chapter that the overriding need for greater efficiency throughout British industry will generate considerable pressure for such an extension, then certain prior conditions will have to be met. Firstly, senior management, including board members, will have to take a policy decision in favour of widening the scope of bargaining. Secondly, the procedural implications of that decision will have to be recognized. And thirdly, the provision of information for bargaining purposes will have to be substantially increased. From a trade union point of view it may be argued that these decisions will almost certainly be taken sooner and may well be implemented more easily if union-backed worker directors are already on the board in strength. In other words, a strong *trade union* presence in the boardroom may well act as a catalyst to change and improvement in the management of the business in general and of industrial relations in particular. Those who hold this view, however, would also emphasize that the effectiveness of worker representation will depend on the worker directors being allowed to *represent* the interests of their constituents on the shop floor, as distinct from merely reporting their opinions on specific problems. This in turn raises two further issues for discussion, namely the desired balance between workers' and shareholders' representatives on the board, and the extent to which the role and election of the worker directors should be determined by the trade unions.

Legislators in one or two European countries have already addressed themselves to these problems but their response has been constrained by the unitary assumptions which are built into the existing provisions for employee membership of company boards. In Britain, by contrast, there is no such historical legacy to overcome. Consequently there is an opportunity to build on the lessons of European experience without repeating their mistakes. The report of the Bullock Committee (1977) represents one attempt to exploit this opportunity, and its recommendations are briefly discussed below.

The Bullock Report: for and against

The Bullock Committee recommended firstly that company boards should be composed of equal numbers of trade union and shareholder (i.e. management) representatives. The West German system of minority employee representation on supervisory boards was, therefore, explicitly rejected in favour of *parity* representation for *trade unionists* on the existing *unitary* boards. The possibility that this might lead to confrontation and paralysis in the boardroom was, however, clearly anticipated and the committee therefore proposed that a third but smaller group of independent directors should be coopted by the others – the $2x+y$ formula – which would hold the balance between them. Secondly, it was recommended that the selection of worker directors should take place solely through trade union channels and that the unions themselves must devise their own selection methods. This apparent discrimination against non-unionists was justified by the committee on essentially pragmatic grounds: 'Given the rapid and continuing development at the workplace of a representative structure based on trade union machinery, any attempt to bypass this structure would be seen as an attack on trade unions and collective bargaining and would be fiercely resisted.' Thirdly, it was proposed that the responsibility for initiating the appointment of worker directors in any enterprise should rest with the trade unions. A union would have the right to request board representation if it was already recognized for bargaining purposes in respect of at least 20 per cent of the company's employees. The wishes of *all* the employees in the company, union and non-union alike, would then be canvassed by means of a secret ballot. If a simple majority expressed a wish for boardroom representation through the recognized trade unions, and if that majority represented at least one third of those employees eligible to vote, then management would have no option but to accede to the request. Finally, the Committee recommended that their proposals should apply to companies with more than 2,000 employees (i.e. to 738 enterprises covering seven million people) and should have the force of law. An Industrial Democracy Commission would be set up to encourage the spread of participation, to resolve any difficulties arising from the $2x+y$ formula, and to supervise the £3 million government-funded training programme envisaged for would-be worker directors.

These recommendations were not supported by the employers' representatives on the Bullock Committee, who published their own minority report. In it they argued firstly that worker directors should always be in a minority on company boards; secondly, that they could serve on supervisory boards in a German-style two-tier system but not on unitary boards; thirdly, that they should be drawn from at least three specific categories of employee, namely shop floor workers, white-collar staff and management; fourthly, that there should be no worker directors in factories where employee councils had not already existed for at least three years; and finally, that the participation process should involve all workers, not merely trade union members. The minority report also proposed that elections for worker directors would not be valid unless there was at least a 60 per cent turnout. Candidates would have to be properly trained, have three years' experience on their employee council and have worked for the company in question for at least ten years. No board level representation would be allowed unless all the unions agreed or two thirds of the employee council asked for it. In other words, the authors were strongly opposed to an effective system of worker representation on company boards and were determined that if there had to be such representation, it should pose as little a threat as possible to the existing power structure. It was felt that the majority proposals of the Bullock Committee would 'place employee representatives in the wholly invidious position of being obliged to sit in on discussions to which they might have nothing to contribute because they were not properly equipped to contribute to this particular type of deliberation' and, in addition, 'cause a massive disruption in the membership, and therefore almost certainly in the effective working of existing company boards ...' Such fears are hardly convincing, if only because they ignore the probability that even under a system of parity representation strong socializing pressures would be brought to bear on the worker directors and to that extent the possibility that they would generate conflict within the boardroom would be remote. As the *Economist* pointed out, the patronizing tone of the minority report 'only underlines how much British bosses do need to sit round the same table with their workers to learn more about them'.[49]

What, then, can be said in favour of the Bullock majority proposals as they stand? Firstly, they recognize that in a British context any system of extended accountability must be seen as a natural outgrowth of, rather than an alternative to, the established system of collective bargaining. The minority report's enthusiasm for works councils on German lines seems wholly out of date and inappropriate - particularly in view of the fact that even on the continent these 'consultative' institutions are now becoming vehicles for *bargaining*. The fear that the $2x+y$ formula will bring conflict into the boardroom can only be justified if it is assumed that collective bargaining is an open and continuing struggle for supremacy between managements and trade unionists. Such an assumption would, however, be erroneous. In Batstone's words:

Even though negotiations may seriously affect the scope of managerial action, the very process of bargaining recognizes and legitimates the authority of management, while at the same time making the union partially dependent upon management and integrated with it. For the unions implicitly accept the right of management to agree or disagree to demands and, at the same time, by reaching an agreement often limit the scope of their own action.[50]

In other words there is no qualitative difference between the system of board membership proposed by Bullock and the extension of collective bargaining at plant and company level. Both contain elements of cooperation and conflict and both recognize that there is a strong, mutual dependence between management and trade unions. The $2x+y$ formula would simply emphasize the principle of mutuality and ensure that the worker directors did not become an isolated and ineffective minority on the board.

Secondly, if implemented, the majority proposals will force many company directors to give more time and thought to the interests of their employees. It has long been argued that the traditional definition in law of the responsibilities of company directors is manifestly out of date, and Bullock re-stated this point:

> It seems to us, as it did to some of our witnesses, that to regard the company as solely the property of the shareholders is to be out of touch with the reality of the present day company as a complex social and economic entity subject to a variety of internal and external pressures in which the powers of control have passed from the legal owners to professional management.

Once the substance of this argument is admitted, one is logically forced to conclude that the legitimacy of other interests, particularly those of the workforce, must be recognized in law as well as in fact. Recent research suggests that the changes in company law proposed by Bullock might help to bring a new and badly needed dimension into boardroom discussion – namely that of industrial relations. In a survey of the attitudes and behaviour of British directors, Winkler found that many of them deliberately isolated themselves from the workforce and showed an active disinclination to become involved in industrial relations. Directors tended to regard workers (and shareholders as well) almost exclusively as a *cost*, to be treated as any other claim on profits. They also tended to abdicate much of their responsibility for policy-making in industrial relations to personnel and line management. In view of the lack of contact between directors and shop floor workers, it is perhaps hardly surprising that their views on industrial relations problems reflected the emotive, unprofessional perspectives of television and the popular press. In Winkler's words: 'Directors' opinions were not so much a comment on the power of the media as on the void of concrete information from their immediate surroundings.'[51] It seems reasonable to suggest, therefore, that the permanent presence of a considerable number of worker representatives in the boardroom may do much to open up channels of communication with the shop floor and thereby improve the quality of the decisions made on manpower and industrial relations issues.

Thirdly, the majority proposals may also have a positive effect on the attitudes of the unions themselves towards the conventional managerial objectives of efficiency, profit and growth. It has often been said that the trade union movement in Britain has always thought far too much in terms of fundamental and irreconcilable conflict with management and has seldom been sufficiently aware of the interests which trade unionists and managers have in common. To the extent that this is true, it must be recognized that a great deal of the responsibility lies with management. If management policy, reflecting the assumption that trade unions *cause* conflict and dissension in industry, seeks to weaken their influence at every point, one should not be surprised if the unions react accordingly and adopt a conflict-based perspective. Bullock, however, based its recommendations on the assumption that trade union representatives could, given appropriate incentives, become just as concerned with the success of the enterprise as the shareholders: 'There does not seem to be any reason to believe that employee representatives will not have as clear a perception of where their constituents' best interests lie, or that the stake held by employees in the long-term health of the company is less than that of the shareholders.' The key incentive is seen in the $2x+y$ formula. The benefits of worker directors, said Bullock, may not be realized unless the principles of equal representation and equal responsibility are conceded. The majority report argued that there would be no incentive for worker representatives to become involved in the process of policy formulation if they knew that ultimately their views could be overruled by the majority of management directors and that if this happened the worker directors would lose all credibility in the eyes of their constituents on the shop floor. In short, it was argued that management could gain a new legitimacy in the eyes of the workforce only if it was prepared to share power with their elected representatives. By sharing in the management of the enterprise, the unions themselves would gain a new sense of responsibility for its success.

What are the principal objections to the Bullock strategy? Firstly, it could be argued that the majority report overestimates the likely effect of these legal and institutional changes on the structure of power within the business enterprise. It has already been noted that board meetings may not be as significant a factor in the corporate decision-making process as many outside observers have often assumed. It must also be emphasized that formal equality of status and responsibility does not necessarily mean *de facto* equality of power and influence. European experience suggests that supervisory boards, where they exist, do not and cannot exercise effective control over the management boards. Decision-making power resides with the management board largely because its members enjoy an immense advantage over their 'supervisors' in terms of information, technical skill and experience. A similar tendency for power to concentrate itself in the hands of a minority of directors on unitary boards in Britain has been reported by Winkler: 'All the boards studied were split into a decision-making cabal and the rest; membership is no guarantee of participation.'[52] Would the $2x+y$ formula ensure that power was shared more equally? European experience indicates that parity of representation between employee and shareholder directors is a double-edged weapon. In Batstone's words, 'Parity of representation appears to be an important condition to ensure that worker representatives become integrated into the informal processes of debate and information exchange. But in doing so they tend to become even more integrated into a managerial perspective.'[53] It is not immediately obvious how the appointment of a small group of independent board members as envisaged by Bullock would counteract this tendency for managerial perspectives and priorities to determine decisions. Nor are Bullock's other recommendations particularly convincing on this point. The committee proposed that in order to prevent key policy decisions from being taken unilaterally by senior management or, alternatively, overruled by the shareholders' meetings, the following functions should be legally conferred on the board alone – changing the corporate constitution, winding up the company, changing its capital structure, proposing dividends and selling a significant part of the business. Yet this provision obviously excludes a large number of strategic decisions which might be taken outside the boardroom.

Secondly, the Bullock strategy assumes that the trade unions will be as eager to accept the *responsibilities* of board representation as they will be to grasp the power it entails. It has been argued that the introduction of worker directors 'will inevitably lead trade unionists further along the road towards taking responsibility for the performance of our industrial organizations'.[54] Yet it must also be recognized that several trade union leaders have expressed outright opposition to board representation for their members. As the EETPU told the Bullock committee:

The belief that managers implementing the policies of a Board composed of 50 per cent trade union representatives will be more acceptable than the current exercise of the managerial function is a dangerous illusion. It could convey the impression that the management has captured or absorbed the trade unions. In particular situations, the workers who held that view might be driven to set up means of alternate representation at the place of work. In a world where state power and management prerogative have become more concentrated, more pervasive and yet more remote from those who are affected by the exercise of those powers, the impression that worker directors represent the absorption of trade unions into this scenario of corporate élitism is even more perilous.

The fear that board representation, particularly on a parity basis, might cost the unions their independence and thus their credibility with rank-and-file members seems widespread. But the TUC still appears to believe that worker directors will be able to look after the interests of the enterprise as a whole and simultaneously give priority to the interests of their constituents. If one adopts a pluralistic view of the enterprise then it seems inevitable that sooner or later a trade-union-appointed worker director will be faced with a choice between defending the interests of those who put him on the board and doing what his fellow directors feel is in the best interests of the organization as a whole. Given that this will happen, it would perhaps be more sensible to think in terms of the strategy advanced by Mr Nicholas Wilson, a member of the Bullock Committee who signed the majority report but dissented from the $2x+y$ formula. He simply argued that the unions should have *minority* representation on unitary boards (without an independent element) so that the worker directors as a group would not have to accept responsibility for board decisions with which they disagreed. This strategy would enable them to maintain their credibility as representatives of shop floor interests and opinions but would not give them the power to halt the decision-making process altogether.

A third objection could be made to the Bullock proposals, and indeed to any strategy which is based on *a priori* reasoning about what the worker wants and expects by way of extended participation. The assumption that workers care only about extrinsic rewards (pay and job security) and that these priorities can be adequately satisfied by collective bargaining may be as misleading as the contrary assumption that workers want much more influence over managerial decision-making through board representation. It was argued earlier in this chapter that different workgroups have different priorities and that these can and do vary according to changing circumstances. It may also be the case that conventional attitude survey techniques compel respondents to make unrealistic 'either-or' choices which they would not otherwise make. It has, for example, been noted that participation 'merely for the sake of sharing with management the responsibility of running the firm is not held in high regard as an end in itself.'[55] Opinion polls also suggest that the Bullock proposals as they stand have aroused little enthusiasm on the shop floor.[56] Yet some surveys suggest that many workers are dissatisfied with what they see as their lack of influence over managerial decisions in certain key areas such as rates of pay, methods of payment, selection for redundancy, overtime allocation, and the fixing of work standards. The level of dissatisfaction, however, seems to vary considerably from one workplace to the next. Much depends on the traditional climate of relations on the shop floor, the size of the organization, the technology in use, the quality and style of management, the scope of collective bargaining and the nature of the expectations which the employees themselves bring to the work situation. In these circumstances it could reasonably be argued that any attempt to impose a standard formula for extended participation on companies – even the relatively large firms with over 2,000 employees – is likely to cause more problems than it solves. If the formula imposed is both radical and complicated – as the $2x+y$ proposal undoubtedly is – the possibility that the whole concept of boardroom representation will be discredited must be all the greater. If there *must* be a standard formula, Mr Nicholas Wilson's seems more reasonable.

However, the most sensible strategy would probably be to adopt something on the lines of the approach recommended by the British Institute of Management. A BIM working party on participation (1976) proposed that all companies with over twenty-five employees should have three years in which to draw up joint participation agreements for registration with a government agency. A prerequisite of registration would be *joint* agreement on the most appropriate participative structure for the organization. The BIM also argued that the parties should be given some guidance on the form which these participation agreements should take, preferably in the shape of a code of practice covering issues such as disclosure of information, techniques of participation on the shop floor, training, formal participative structures and the extension of collective bargaining. Failure to reach a participation agreement, or the breach of such an agreement, would be referred to an industrial tribunal and eventually to ACAS, which could make a legally binding recommendation. The BIM strategy at least has the merit of allowing managements and union representatives to design procedures for extended participation which they feel most appropriate to their needs. Those who want to push ahead with board representation in some form could do so, just as those who reject worker directors and would prefer instead to extend collective bargaining could follow that road.

The obvious weakness of this approach is that it may be *too* permissive. If one of the principal objectives of public policy is to promote joint decision-making within the enterprise, it is at least arguable that the parties should be given clearer and more exacting guidelines to follow than those proposed by the BIM. In fact a minority of the BIM working party, while accepting that employee participation 'must not take a form that excludes professional management or prevents them from taking decisive action when the need arises', argued that there should be stronger legislative pressures on management than was envisaged by the majority. They therefore proposed that the following defined areas for participation should be included in the legal framework – (1) the closure or relocation of the enterprise or important parts of the enterprise, (2) substantial restrictions or extensions of enterprise activity, (3) significant changes in the organization of the enterprise and (4) the establishment of lasting links with other enterprises or the cancellation of those links. It is clear that in practice the extension of joint decision-making over these areas of business policy would have important implications for several other key issues of substance which in some organizations are already the subject of collective bargaining but in others are resolved unilaterally by management. These issues would obviously include redundancy policy and procedures, manning standards, payment systems and the organization of work. Within this broad legal framework, however, it would be left to the parties themselves to devise their own institutional arrangements for extending joint decision-making in these areas. Employers and unions would not be compelled to adopt a rigid system of board representation which neither of them might want.

In conclusion, one might say that the role of government should be to devise a political and legal framework which encourages trade unions to press for extended participation and at the same time does nothing to inhibit management's response. Given the traditions of British industrial relations – and in particular the strong and growing preference on both sides for workplace autonomy – it would seem that most trade union representatives will focus their attention on extending the substantive scope of collective bargaining. The government should encourage managements and unions to experiment with worker representation in the boardroom but it must be recognized that worker directors offer no panacea for the familiar problems of industrial relations. Since it is impossible to generalize about what 'the worker' wants either from his job or from the work situation as a whole, it follows that any attempt to devise a universal system of participation would hardly be practicable. All that can be said is that those who would extend the scope of joint decision-making at plant and company level must recognize two fundamental realities of industrial life. The first is that the growing complexity of economic life as a whole and the increasing professionalism of industrial management will in effect ensure that senior managers and executive directors retain a decisive advantage over ordinary employees and trade union representatives when strategic decisions affecting the conduct of the enterprise have to be taken. Most workers and their representatives accept this technical superiority as a fact of life. Moreover, it would seem that they also accept managerial priorities and values to a considerable degree. The second point is that since collective bargaining is essentially an integrative process, the wider its scope becomes the more pressure there will be on trade union negotiators to accept wider responsibility for the conduct of the enterprise. As this sense of responsibility grows, so too will the pressure for more participation in decision-making at board level. In short, the extension of participation should be allowed to evolve out of the growing pressures of technological and organizational change, aided by an appropriate legal framework, and should be consistent with the traditions of British industrial relations.

CHAPTER FIVE

The Role of Law

It is true that the trade union is in the last resort a fighting organization; its business is to be equipped to be able to make a nuisance of itself in pursuit of the interests of its members . . . But the trade union is also a regulative body: it makes rules about the way in which certain economic activities are to be conducted and about who is to be allowed to conduct them. Where these rules appear to run counter to the welfare of the community . . . they should be subjected to public scrutiny.

Andrew Shonfield, 1968

The law is likely to be a failure whenever it seeks to counteract habits of action or inaction adopted by large numbers of men and women in pursuance of established social custom . . . In a country in which statutes are deliberately couched in an esoteric language invented by lawyers for the use of lawyers it is difficult to rely on the educative role of legislation. Most legislation operates not by the lesson it teaches or the sermon it preaches but by the promise of rewards or the threat of deprivations attached to its observance or breach, that is, by the expectation of its enforcement. Legal norms have their social effect through legal sanctions and sanctions cannot be applied to counteract the spontaneous conduct of amorphous masses.

Otto Kahn-Freund, 1970

DURING the late 1960s, the public debate concerning the role of the law in industrial relations tended to focus almost exclusively on the possible use of legal sanctions to deter unofficial and unconstitutional strikes. It was frequently argued that the traditional abstention of the state from the conduct of industrial relations had allowed various antisocial habits to develop on the shop floor which 'the country' could no longer tolerate. These habits, it was felt, frequently obstructed managerial attempts to improve efficiency and introduce new technology; as such they held back the rate of economic growth and contributed to inflation. It was also argued, paradoxically, that the tradition of non-intervention had allowed trade unions too free a hand in regulating the behaviour of their members and that this frequently led to undemocratic practices and the erosion of individual rights. In the event, some of the more popular assumptions of the 1960s concerning the potential effect of the law on industrial behaviour were put to the test between 1972 and 1974, with generally disastrous results. Since then, the debate on the role of the law has found a new focus. It is still widely assumed that a framework of legal rules can have a major effect on norms of behaviour in industry. The current emphasis, however, is on the role of the law in extending the scope of joint decision-making in industry and in improving the status and rights of the individual employee. The Industrial Relations Act of 1971 certainly imposed a few rules on managerial behaviour, but its main emphasis lay on the restriction of trade union activities. The bias of the current (i.e. post-1974) framework is quite different. In Anderman's words:

In almost all cases, the new legal rights are given to employees and trade unions whilst the legal restrictions and liabilities are applied to employers and employing organizations. In part this may reflect an appreciation that legal restrictions on industrial action are not always effective. However, it may also be viewed as an indication that both elements of the [Employment Protection] Act have a common purpose, notably the creation of wider restrictions on the exercise of unilateral management prerogative and the provision of an alternative source of rule which is fairer to the ordinary employee. Neither the common law of the employment contract nor the economic forces of the labour market have ever provided an assurance that employment decisions would be jointly taken by parties with equivalent bargaining power.[1]

Any framework of labour law – even one based on the principle of formal abstention – makes certain assumptions about the balance of power in industrial relations. The Act of 1971 assumed that both workgroups and trade unions had acquired 'too much' power; the legislation of 1974 and 1975, by contrast, assumes that in many respects employees and their organizations do not have enough. It recognizes that in certain organizations and industries the growth of collective bargaining over the postwar period as a whole has enabled *some* employees to obtain new rights and benefits which, at least by historical standards, mark a significant limitation on managerial prerogative. It also recognizes, however, that for a variety of reasons many employees have not improved their position to anything like the same degree. It therefore seeks to give every employee a basic floor of employment rights which do not depend on either the bargaining power of his trade union (if he belongs to one) or the benevolence of his employers. The current legal framework also follows the Donovan Commission in assuming that collective bargaining is the most effective way of ensuring that employees and their organizations have at least some influence over the making of decisions which affect the work situation. Consequently, collective bargaining is seen as the bedrock of order and predictability in industrial relations – the basic assumption being that if employees and their organizations can participate in making decisions they are more likely to feel committed to whatever decisions are made.

The current legal framework does not, however, attract universal support. The main criticism is that it seeks to shift the balance of bargaining power too much in favour of employees and trade unions. This can be supported on both utilitarian and ideological grounds. It has been argued that the rules governing issues such as unfair dismissal, equal pay, maternity, redundancy and sex discrimination have together succeeded in making the employment of any kind of labour a much more expensive and time-consuming business than it used to be. The problems posed by legislation are particularly acute for the small employer, who frequently has neither the time nor the inclination to digest these new rules and operates on too small a scale to establish a specialist department. Many small businessmen are said to be afraid of employment legislation and are therefore becoming more and more reluctant to take on more labour. It is also argued that the various measures designed to further job security are making it more difficult for employers to get rid of inefficient employees and, consequently, are effectively discouraging the recruitment of young workers and school-leavers. In other words, by adopting an unduly protective approach to the employment of labour the current legal framework has actually made *unemployment* worse than it would otherwise have been.[2] From a more ideological standpoint, some critics have maintained that the law exerts undue pressure on employees to join a trade union. It is argued that the terms of reference given to ACAS – to encourage the spread of collective bargaining – reflect a normative assumption which is, to say the least, open to debate. Many observers take issue with the fact that while the law gives all employees the right to join an independent trade union, it does nothing to protect those who do not want to join one. Indeed, where a closed shop exists, the law governing dismissal actively discriminates against the non-conformist. In short, it is argued that the collective provisions of the Employment Protection Act place restrictions on the freedom of the individual which violate generally accepted ideas of 'natural justice'.

Unfortunately it is difficult in practice to say whether these criticisms are justified or not. It may well be the case that some small employers are reluctant to recruit more labour because of the present bias of the law. However, it could equally well be argued that a decision whether to recruit or not is more likely to be determined by the employer's *need* for labour, which in turn depends on the level of demand for his products and the degree to which he is substituting capital for labour. The most that can be said, therefore, is that while the legal framework may have made a marginal contribution to the unemployment problem, the claim that the law is a more important variable than either the level of economic activity or the rate of technological change is manifestly absurd. It should also be pointed out that other European countries, notably Sweden and West Germany, enacted similar employment legislation years ago without sustaining any noticeable damage to their industrial competitiveness or creating a serious unemployment problem. The ideological critique, however, is more difficult to refute in so far as it is based on fundamental values rather than on economic costs and benefits. The critique must be taken seriously if it can be shown that a significant number of employees are being subjected to unreasonable pressure, either by a trade union or an employer, in order to get them to accept a collective bargaining relationship. It must also be taken seriously if there is evidence that the closed shop is encouraging trade unions and workgroups to abuse their collective power and interfere with the legitimate freedoms of nonconforming individuals on a significant scale. So far there is little evidence to support either claim, although this does not remove the possibility that there may be a significant number of employees who 'suffer in silence', or that abuses may become more widespread in the future.

The writer, however, takes the view that while future governments may well try to tinker with some of the more controversial aspects of current legislation, the prospect of a radical change of emphasis seems extremely remote. Above all, it must be remembered that there is a persuasive social and political *rationale* behind this framework. It was pointed out in Chapter Two that the floor of basic rights contained in the 1975 Act specifically recognizes the substantive aspirations which have emerged through the spontaneous growth of workplace bargaining since the 1940s. In other words, it should not in general be seen as an attempt by well-meaning legislators to impose an alien code of norms on employers and employees. It contains little, if anything, which has not already been enacted in other European countries and which has not been the subject of voluntary provision in Britain. It should also be seen as an integral part of the wider framework of cooperation between the trade union movement and the government. While the 'social contract' in its 1974–5 form is plainly dead, the *principle* of cooperation will doubtless continue to occupy a very important place in the overall priorities of future governments. Cooperation, however, presupposes that there will be a degree of bargaining between the parties, and that trade union demands for further legal rights, either for themselves as collective bodies or for employees as individuals, will continue to be a matter for negotiation. Managers, therefore, will have to reconcile themselves to the fact that their freedom to manage will be circumscribed not simply by the countervailing powers of trade unions and workgroups but by an increasingly complex body of legal rules. Does this mean that the authority of managements either is being or will be significantly impaired by the law? More specifically, does the current legal framework inhibit managers from initiating improvements in the use of manpower? Is there any point in devising an incomes policy which encourages managers to raise productivity through collective bargaining if there are strong legal obstacles in the way? In order to answer these questions it is necessary to analyse the effects which the present legal framework has had on management's 'right to manage'.

Employment security and the law

The Employment Protection Act seeks to improve the job security of employees in several ways. Firstly, while the employment relationship is actually in being, it confers on employees (1) a new right to a guaranteed payment for workless days, (2) a new right to paid suspension from work on medical grounds, (3) new rights to paid maternity leave and to return to work after maternity leave, and (4) new rights to time off work. Secondly, it reinforces and develops existing statutory safeguards for employees when their employment is terminated in so far as it (1) increases the minimum periods of notice required, (2) amends the law on redundancy to provide for a trial period where the employer offers alternative employment, (3) gives all dismissed employees the right to a written statement of the reasons for dismissal, (4) strengthens the remedies for unfair dismissal, (5) provides new tests of fairness in cases of employees dismissed for pregnancy and for participating in industrial action, and (6) gives new rights to employees in the event of redundancy. Some of these rights were touched upon in Chapter Two and there is insufficient space here to discuss all of them in detail. It must be noted, however, that while practically all of them impose additional administrative burdens on employers none of them poses a radical challenge to the traditional employment relationship. The most important limitation on managerial prerogative – the right of an employee not to be unfairly dismissed – was originally introduced by the 1971 Act and the current legislation merely strengthens that right. Furthermore, the extent to which any law actually impinges on the day-to-day management of employee relations depends not merely on what rules the law lays down but also on how these rules are interpreted by Industrial Tribunals and by the higher courts. The significance of this point may be elaborated by a brief discussion of recent developments in the interpretation of the law on unfair dismissal.

The Trade Union and Labour Relations Act contains only one test of whether a dismissal is fair or unfair, namely the ability of the employer to satisfy an industrial tribunal that in the circumstances, having regard to equity and the substantial merits of the case, he acted reasonably in treating the reason he gave for the dismissal as a sufficient reason for dismissing the employee. Initially most industrial tribunals continued to work within the guidelines established in 1973 by the old NIRC, namely that they should regard themselves as a 'specialist industrial jury' and adopt 'a broad approach of common sense and common fairness'.[3] In effect, this was an open invitation to tribunals, when applying the general test of fairness, to say what *they* would have done had they been in management's shoes. Consequently, between 1973 and 1976, the general direction of case law at tribunal level was to impose more exacting requirements on employers. Tribunals frequently enunciated general principles which were intended to be taken seriously by management and as such were meant to encourage the reform of procedures and practices. The role of 'specialist jury' imperceptibly developed into that of 'disseminator of good practice'. Since 1976, however, there has been a marked change of emphasis. The High Court has declared that tribunals should *not* ask themselves what they would have done had they been management, but simply decide whether the employer acted reasonably in the circumstances.[4] In practice, this means that if management has reasonable grounds for deciding to dismiss an employee *at the time the decision is taken*, the dismissal will normally be fair. As long as management gathers as much evidence as they can reasonably be expected to do, and as long as they follow a proper procedure, it is unlikely that a dismissal will be unfair. The High Court's change of emphasis has been reinforced by the Employment Appeals Tribunal, which since 1976 has overturned several decisions by industrial tribunals on the grounds that the latter 'mis-directed' themselves when applying the general test of fairness.[5]

The higher courts have also indicated that tribunals should be more sympathetic to management's problems. In *Lesney Products* v. *Nolan* (1977), for example, Lord Denning said that 'nothing should be done to impair the ability of employers to reorganize their workforce and their times and conditions of work so as to improve efficiency'.[6] The implications of this judgement are far-reaching. Managerial attempts to improve the level of efficiency in the workplace frequently involve some change in the terms of their employees' contracts of employment. Initially tribunals tended to adopt a restrictive view of management's rights in this field. In several cases it was emphasized that an employer could in effect repudiate an employee's contract if he insisted on changing some term or condition in that contract, or on introducing a new contractual obligation, without the employee's consent.[7] More recently, however, the emphasis has shifted in favour of the employer. Decisions by both the EAT and by industrial tribunals strongly imply that an employer may fairly dismiss an employee who refuses to accept a change in hours or conditions of work provided that he has convincing economic reasons for insisting on the change in question. These decisions certainly emphasize the employer's responsibility to discuss changes with the workforce and try to obtain some general agreement. But an employee who insists on sticking to his contractual rights, particularly where his colleagues have accepted the changes or where his trade union has negotiated changes on his behalf, may well risk being fairly dismissed unless he can show good reason for his refusal to cooperate with management. Once management has proved the need for a given change in terms and conditions of work, it would appear that the onus lies with the *employee* to show that his refusal to accept the change was reasonable in the circumstances.[8]

A similar trend can be discerned in dismissal cases involving redundancy. In 1973 the NIRC ruled that dismissals by reason of redundancy were subject to the same general test of fairness as other dismissals. As was noted in Chapter One, over the next two years industrial tribunals imposed a wide range of obligations on management in redundancy situations under the general test of fairness. Management was called upon to justify their selection criteria and, in particular, to justify the timing of the redundancy, consult with redundant employees or their representatives, warn employees of impending redundancy, and search for alternative employment within the organization. Since 1976, however, the EAT has considerably loosened these constraints on management. The most important restriction which can be imposed on management's freedom in a redundancy situation is to question the need for any redundancy at all. The EAT, however, has ruled that a tribunal *cannot* investigate 'the rights and wrongs of the declared redundancy'.[9] In other words, it must be assumed that management has valid reasons for making employees redundant. Similarly the EAT has ruled that when selecting employees for redundancy, length of service is certainly one factor which should be taken into account but it is by no means the only one. The employer is now required merely to show that he applied rational selection criteria and 'acted from genuine motives'.[10] The obligation on management to try to find alternative employment has also been interpreted to mean that the former is simply expected to do 'something reasonable' in attempting to find such employment.[11] Finally, the need for management to give employees as much warning as possible of a redundancy situation has been significantly diluted. The EAT appears to have introduced a new test of fairness in this respect, namely whether the lack of warning and/or prior consultation in a particular case *would have made any difference to the final outcome*. If, in the EAT's judgement, the final result would have been the same regardless of whatever warnings and opportunities for consultation were given, then the dismissal will probably be held to be fair.[12] In summary, the EAT has recognized that managements are entitled to take a 'realistic' view of a redundancy situation and, by implication, to act in what they consider to be the best interests of the business.

These recent decisions by the EAT are significant for two reasons. Firstly, they lend no support to the popular notion that managements have been tied hand and foot by the Employment Protection Act and that it is 'virtually impossible' for an employer to discharge employees. In the words of one observer:

It is still possible for an employee to win an unfair dismissal case, but it is now a lot more difficult than it used to be. It is still possible for an employer to lose an unfair dismissal case but, for the large employer with a well-developed disciplinary procedure, the EAT's decisions have fundamentally altered priorities . . . the emphasis must now be on ensuring that procedures are carried out and observed by all those responsible rather than whether after the necessary investigation and assessment has taken place, it is fair to dismiss.[13]

Secondly, they underline yet again the fundamental problem facing all legislators – namely that of ensuring that the rules laid down by the law are consistent with the realities of life. Few would argue that one of the most important objectives of the 1975 Act is to improve the job security of the ordinary employee and that this is a legitimate, even laudable aim. Is it realistic, however, to expect this legislation to have much more than a marginal effect on security of employment at a time when the problems of unemployment and industrial efficiency are looming larger than ever? The security of tenure which an employee may reasonably expect to enjoy is not simply a function of his legal rights, but also depends on the continued need for the job he is doing. This in turn depends on a variety of different factors, notably the level of economic activity, the rate of technological change and the profitability of the organization. It may also depend on the willingness of the employee to accept changes in his contractual obligations, such as different hours and new working practices in order to help the organization respond to changing market conditions.

In general, therefore, our experience since 1972 has shown conclusively that the ability of law-makers to influence existing patterns and norms of behaviour on the shop floor is conditional on there being at least some congruence between the aspirations of the legislators and the needs of those to whom the legislation will apply. The notion that behavioural norms can be changed by the law if the sanctions provided are powerful enough has been convincingly challenged. It is certainly worth noting that the current framework of employment protection ultimately rests on *financial* sanctions. Some observers have seen this reliance on financial penalties as a hidden advantage for management: 'Only in so far as an employer has willingly abided by the legal norm or has been prompted to do so by the financial disincentive contained within the legal sanction will an individual employment protection succeed in producing a reversal of a managerial decision once taken'.[14] In short, the assumption is that most employers will respond to the *moral* pressure imposed by the law. The EAT, however, seems to have perceived that the norms expressed in the current legal framework, if interpreted without sufficient regard to the realities of industrial life, are likely to impose unreasonable constraints on those whose overriding concern is to create more wealth and thus more employment opportunities. Ultimately, of course, the question is that of how to reconcile the traditional managerial goals of growth and efficiency with employee demands for fair treatment and greater security. Where the balance between the two ought to lie will no doubt continue to be a subject for debate, but for the time being it would seem that it has moved back towards management.

Collective bargaining and the law

In Britain (and in certain other countries such as the USA and Canada) it has traditionally been assumed that the basic floor of individual employment rights would be built upon and improved by free collective bargaining, backed by the economic sanction of industrial action. The collective provisions of the current legal framework reflect this assumption, the only new feature being that the extension of collective bargaining has been given a measure of legal support. There is nothing particularly radical, however, in this provision. The idea that trade unions should be given some form of legal backing in their efforts to persuade recalcitrant employers to recognize them for bargaining purposes, though rejected by the Donovan Commission, did in fact find its way into the Industrial Relations Act. Other countries adopted the idea many years ago. Moreover, it should be remembered that the intention of the law in this field is simply to influence the *way* in which decisions are made, not determine what those decisions shall be. In Anderman's words:

The rights themselves are largely procedural in character, designed to produce a dialogue between the two parties to collective bargaining. They contain little direction as to the substantive results the parties should produce in an agreement arising out of that bargaining. As a consequence these results may vary with the relative bargaining strength of the parties.[15]

It has also been assumed that the extension and development of collective bargaining would in practice be largely dependent on voluntary effort and mutual agreement. In cases where the requisite degree of goodwill has not been present, the emphasis has been on conciliation by a third party. The *rationale* of conciliation is that the resolution of a recognition dispute 'turns to a considerable extent on finding out the facts of the situation'.[16] These facts would normally include the wishes of the employees themselves, the ability of the union claiming recognition to represent their interests, and the attitude of the employer. If the facts of the situation suggest that the union has a persuasive case for recognition then it is assumed that the employer will concede negotiating rights and proceed to bargain with the union in good faith. The resort to sanctions should seldom, if ever, be necessary. This perspective is clearly evident in the relevant provisions of the 1975 Act.

Nevertheless it would be unwise to assume that this liberal, pluralist philosophy will or indeed can produce dramatic results. Firstly, the experience of the CIR between 1969 and 1974 suggests that the process of 'fact-finding' is by no means as simple and straightforward as is often supposed. It has been pointed out that in some cases the 'facts' changed during the period in which the CIR was actually carrying on its investigation. A lengthy inquiry can give both sides ample opportunity to pursue their respective campaigns to influence the attitudes of the employees concerned. The employer for example, can award a general pay increase or improve other terms and conditions in an attempt to show his employees that trade unionism is 'irrelevant', and where this happens the level of support for the union may well decline. Similarly, the way in which the questions are phrased by the investigatory body can be crucial in determining the outcome of the inquiry.[17] Some employers have argued that an agency whose terms of reference include the encouragement of collective bargaining cannot possibly be impartial when it is investigating a dispute. It is almost bound to be looking for evidence which will justify a recommendation in favour of trade union recognition. In short, the 'fact-finding' exercise may itself become part of the dispute.[18] Secondly, it is rather naïve to assume that the mere publication of the 'facts' of a particular dispute, coupled with a recommendation in favour of collective bargaining, will in practice prove sufficient to persuade a reluctant employer to enter into a *bona fide* bargaining relationship. The decision to initiate collective bargaining

is in form a renunciation of sole management authority in respect of the matters covered in the recognition agreement . . . In any establishment where trade unions are recognized there are two authority systems consisting of all those aspects of running the business which are the normal and sole responsibility of management and those aspects which have been made by agreement the subject of joint determination.[19]

Many employers still regard trade unionism as a fundamental threat to their right to manage their businesses as they think best. Consequently it seems unlikely that exhortation and publicity will in themselves be sufficient to overcome the hostility of those employers who feel that by giving in to a trade union they are giving away a large part of their authority. Employer resistance certainly played an important role in nullifying the recommendations of the CIR in a significant number of the recognition disputes which it investigated.[20]

The basic features of recognition problems are the same now as they always have been, and the provisions in the 1975 Act for dealing with them by third party intervention are not fundamentally dissimilar from those in the 1971 Act. The current legal framework does little more than provide ACAS with those powers which it needs to resolve recognition disputes by investigation and conciliation. The sanction provided against employers who refuse to carry out ACAS recommendations, namely a legally binding arbitration award by the Central Arbitration Committee, can only be applied after a long procedure has been exhausted. Consequently, the extent to which ACAS succeeds in extending collective bargaining will in practice depend almost entirely on its ability to persuade reluctant employers to accept it. In some cases, however, the main problem facing ACAS will not be the resistance of the employer but the claims of rival organizations. The CIR investigated several cases in which one or more independent trade unions were in competition for negotiating rights with a staff association, and very often the latter was able to show substantial support among the employees. The same problem will undoubtedly confront ACAS, particularly in view of the fact that several staff associations have received certification as independent trade unions in accordance with the Trade Union and Labour Relations Act. In such cases the attitude of the employer is clearly of some importance since he has probably made it known that he would prefer his employees to join the staff association.[21] Yet it must also be recognized that some employees – particularly those in positions of responsibility – actually prefer to be represented by an organization which has its roots within the company. It is also still the case that if management deliberately sets out to create a climate of loyalty to the company, backed by appropriately generous terms and conditions of employment and by an effective system of communication, approaches from trade unions may attract relatively little support from the employees.[22] In short, despite the fact that ACAS appears to have adopted the criteria of potential *support* for collective bargaining (as opposed to actual membership of a trade union) in a given company or bargaining unit, it is by no means certain that ACAS will invariably recommend that collective bargaining should be adopted.[23]

Once the recognition provisions of current legislation are examined, therefore, it becomes abundantly clear that they are based on the assumption that the mere threat of third-party intervention will in practice induce employers and trade unions to establish a collective bargaining relationship by their own voluntary efforts. In effect this underlines the significance of management's role in shaping the development of collective bargaining at plant and company level. The attitude of senior management towards the principle of trade union recognition will generally have a crucial influence over the subsequent development of procedural relations within the organization. Some managers have seen the growth of trade union membership as a vote of 'no confidence' by their employees or, alternatively, as an outcome of a deliberate attempt by a handful of 'troublemakers' to subvert the loyalty of the silent majority of employees to the company. Managers who take this view may concede union recognition only with extreme reluctance, usually under the threat of direct action, and will probably seek to restrict the scope of collective bargaining to the absolute minimum. Experience suggests that such attitudes will almost certainly lead to further conflict with the union concerned and consequently to a much worse climate of relations than there was at the outset. What many managers in this situation fail to realize is that once a union gains recognition, it must immediately seek to establish its credibility as a representative organization both with its own members and, equally important, with those employees in the organization who are as yet uncommitted. This means that the union will want to bargain with management on those substantive issues which it feels are important to the employees as a whole and will want to be able to show tangible gains for its efforts. If senior management fail to grasp this point and persist in trying to hold the union at arm's length in the hope that they will thus be able to prove to their employees that collective organization was unnecessary in the first place, the most likely consequence will be growing disorder. The union will find itself obliged to become more militant and aggressive in its approach to management in order to compel the latter to bargain in good faith on matters of substance. If the union does not respond to the challenge, it risks losing its members to a more enterprising and aggressive competitor. In this way, management's predictions that trade unionism will *introduce* conflict into the organization can easily become self-fulfilling. By denying the legitimacy of conflict, management can in effect ensure that the level of conflict within the organization is much higher than it would otherwise have been.

If, by contrast, management makes a genuine effort to come to terms with the idea of collective bargaining before conceding recognition to a union, it stands to gain many advantages. As the CIR has pointed out:

By so doing it can avoid making hasty, ill-considered decisions, possibly as a matter of expediency, as a result of a sudden confrontation when a situation may have already developed over which it has had little or no influence and when problems are already more intractable than they might otherwise have been. Management's influence is more likely to be acceptable at any early stage.[24]

Once it is clear that union membership is growing and a claim for recognition is anticipated, senior management would be well-advised to formulate a *policy* on collective bargaining, which may well entail a fundamental reappraisal of every facet of their traditional approach to employee relations. The establishment of negotiating procedures will in practice require senior managers to ask themselves the following questions: (1) To what level in the organization should collective bargaining be extended? (2) What degree of recognition should be granted? (3) What are the most appropriate bargaining units? (4) Is the union claiming recognition the most appropriate bargaining agent for the employees concerned? (5) At what level or levels within the organization should bargaining take place? (6) What issues of substance are negotiable? (7) What institutional arrangements will need to be made in order to facilitate bargaining? (8) How formal should the bargaining be? (9) What training requirements will there be both before and after recognition has been granted? (10) What facilities should be given to trade union representatives? (11) Should consultative procedures be set up alongside the bargaining machinery? (12) What other domestic procedures will be required, e.g. on grievances, discipline and redundancy, and at what stage should they be established? (13) Does the organization have enough specialist knowledge to meet all the demands which will arise once recognition has been granted? (14) Should the company join an employers' association or, if it is already a member, will continued membership assist or hinder management in achieving its objectives? It may well be, of course, that once the union is recognized, its full-time officials and representatives will want to have a say in resolving many of these matters, but if senior management has already considered them in depth and formulated a coherent strategy they will obviously be in a much better position to negotiate procedural rules which are attuned to their own needs and objectives.

Finally, a brief word should be said about a particularly contentious area on which management would be well advised to have a policy – the closed shop. It is important to realize that the current legal framework does *not* impose an obligation on any employer to have a closed shop, nor does it provide any formal mechanism whereby a trade union can secure a closed shop as such. The decision to negotiate a closed shop, or union membership agreement, is entirely in the hands of the parties themselves, who must obviously be agreed on the need for one. Does a closed shop arrangement offer any positive advantages to management? Firstly, it ensures that in dealing with the union, the employer is in fact dealing with an organization which represents *all* the employees in a given bargaining unit. Secondly, it provides the local union leadership with some collective power over dissident minorities and may therefore help to deter unofficial, unconstitutional action by small groups. Finally it limits the development of multi-unionism, since an employee's right to join an independent trade union is limited in a closed shop situation (under S.53 of the 1974 Act) to the union(s) specified in the union membership agreement. The advantages of a closed shop to a trade union are equally clear. Firstly, it strengthens the union's bargaining power; secondly, it prevents other unions competing for membership within the grades or establishments covered by the agreement; and thirdly, it enables the union to preserve its membership in organizations where circumstances would otherwise combine to reduce it. In short, the closed shop *can* be a powerful force for order, discipline and predictability in workplace relations.

It would be fatuous, however, to pretend that the closed shop does not in practice give rise to certain problems. Prior to 1971 it was generally accepted that a trade union should build its membership up to at least 75 per cent of the employees in the bargaining unit before requesting a closed shop. It would appear, however, that since 1974 unions have considerably lowered their membership base from which to bid for a closed shop. This means that the employer may be faced with a difficult problem if he has reason to believe that a significant proportion of the employees in the bargaining unit concerned are likely to object strongly to compulsory union membership. Nevertheless, there is no legal objection to the exemption of *existing* non-members from a union membership agreement, nor is there any reason why the parties should not negotiate a 'conscience clause' broader than the statutory minimum of 'genuine religious objection'. Indeed, it would appear that several post-1974 agreements have incorporated both these provisions, indicating that trade unions may often be willing to forego the objective of 100 per cent membership in the short-term as a *quid pro quo* for the employer's willingness to concede the principle of long-term security.[25] As long as the position of existing non-members who choose to remain non-members is safeguarded, and as long as there is a fairly liberal 'conscience clause' through which the genuine objector can be exempted, it is difficult to see how a closed shop agreement can be considered inimical either to good industrial relations or to the cause of individual freedom.

Disclosure of information

It was noted above that the legal support for the extension of collective bargaining provided by the 1975 Act is essentially procedural in character. The rules do not attempt to influence the substantive outcome of collective bargaining, and therefore leave open the possibility that even in companies where recognition and procedure agreements have been negotiated without reference to ACAS, the employer will continue to exercise a considerable advantage in subsequent bargaining on terms and conditions of employment. If, therefore, the purpose of the current legal framework is to achieve a more equal distribution of bargaining power, it would be illogical for legislators to ignore the possibility of imposing some degree of uniformity on the substantive content of collective bargaining. The obvious way in which this can be done is to oblige employers to disclose information which may be regarded as essential to the trade unions for bargaining purposes. To some extent, of course, there has been a voluntary movement towards greater disclosure over the past ten years. The pressures of productivity bargaining in the late 1960s, for example, compelled some managements to disclose information to trade union representatives which had hitherto been regarded as sacrosanct. Since then senior managements in a number of companies, especially those which have 'household names', have become more aware of the debate on the wider responsibilities of business enterprises and, faced by increasingly strident attacks from their ideological opponents, have sought to demonstrate that they have 'nothing to hide'. Other companies, however, have made practically no gestures in this direction, beyond publishing information on a selective basis for public relations purposes. The limitations of voluntary effort, therefore, make disclosure a suitable subject for legislation.

Some form of compulsory disclosure has in fact been introduced in several European countries in recent years, most notably in Sweden and Belgium, and even British governments have felt obliged to establish rudimentary guidelines in this area. The Industrial Relations Act of 1971 placed a duty on employers to disclose information where it would accord with 'good industrial relations practice' to do so and/or without which trade unions would be materially impeded during collective bargaining. This provision has been continued in the Employment Protection Act of 1975 and, more recently, ACAS has issued a Code of Practice for the guidance of employers and trade unions. There is in fact a broad consensus of opinion that more disclosure of information would be in the interests of good industrial relations and it is generally anticipated that the extension of collective bargaining will increase trade union pressure for more information. The CBI has advised its member companies to formulate 'information policies', and various unions are making greater efforts to equip their officials and shop stewards with the skills they will need to understand and evaluate management information. There would seem, therefore, to be general agreement that the systematic disclosure of information for bargaining purposes is an integral part of the 'effective framework of rules for structuring and eliciting union demands and management responses' which the Donovan Commission advocated.[26]

There are reasons for doubting, however, whether many people have given a great deal of thought to some of the practical problems involved. To say that managements, trade union leaders and politicians favour more disclosure tells us nothing unless certain other questions are answered. What is the *purpose* of disclosure? What information is regarded as appropriate for bargaining purposes, and what should management be allowed to keep secret? What effects will disclosure have on the style of collective bargaining and on wider aspects of business policy? It is also important to grasp at the outset that the debate in Britain – as in most other Western countries – has tended to concentrate on the disclosure of information for *collective bargaining* purposes. Yet it is at least possible to argue that this perspective is unduly narrow in so far as it neglects the potential gains to both sides which may flow from better communication of information outside the bargaining context. It is interesting to note, for example, that when asked to suggest one way of improving industrial relations, all the respondents in the 1972 survey of workplace relations rated 'the introduction of better consultation procedures and communications' far above anything else.[27] A more recent report by the BIM also suggests that most managements prefer to disclose information relating to company performance through the medium of consultative committees rather than direct to trade union representatives.[28] There is no doubt that in many workplaces managements have hitherto been able to disclose limited information on wider aspects of company policy on a purely consultative basis because trade union representatives have had neither the inclination nor the ability to relate this to everyday collective bargaining. It may also be the case that trade union representatives have consciously ignored any information, whether released for consultative purposes or otherwise, which they believe may frustrate or modify their conventional bargaining objectives. To the extent that this is true it merely reinforces the need to see disclosure in a bargaining context. By contrast, it seems likely that in workplaces where there is a well-developed trade union organization and a tradition of relatively comprehensive collective bargaining, *all* management information will be regarded as ultimately negotiable and the consultative perspective will seem outdated and irrelevant.

What, then, is the case for disclosing more information for bargaining purposes? The answer depends largely on whether one looks at the problem from a management or a trade union point of view. As Marsh and Rosewell have argued:

> Company spokesmen tend to believe that disclosure and improved communications will produce rational and objective bargaining, prevent rumours, encourage approaches favourable to productivity improvements and job evaluation, enable workers to understand the affairs of the company and improve morale, workmanship and cost consciousness as well as creating a greater sense of involvement and identification with the firm. They argue that it will influence the behaviour of trade unions by stimulating professionalism and moderating some of their demands and attitudes.[29]

Stated in these terms, it would appear that some managements view disclosure from a unitary, harmonistic perspective. The assumption here seems to be that *ignorance* on the part of employees is at the root of bad industrial relations and that once this ignorance has been dispelled the pattern of behaviour on the shop floor will become much more 'reasonable'. This view does not seem to allow for the possibility that conflict might be based on a genuine and fundamental divergence of interests and objectives between employers and employees. If, however, the latter perspective is taken as a starting-point, the rationale of disclosure is very different. A trade union representative may well argue that extended, compulsory disclosure can only enhance his bargaining position because it will enable him to refute managerial arguments against which, lacking adequate information, he may have vainly struggled in the past. The assumption here is that management's last great prerogative is the control of information. Once managements are compelled to share that control with trade union representatives, then some major benefits will accrue to the latter. From this viewpoint, disclosure

will redress an imbalance in collective bargaining and enable (trade unionists) to negotiate as equals and bargain in good faith, arm them with valuable information about when an employer can least afford a strike, provide ideological and agitational enforcement for claims, compel companies to justify their decisions and, hence, be less autocratic and generally aid the process of improving the status of workpeople in industry.[30]

On the one hand, therefore, disclosure is seen as an effective way of reintegrating the worker with the company's objectives and, on the other hand, as a method of advancing the frontier of workers' control in industry and further limiting the power of management.

In practice, however, neither of these viewpoints seems wholly realistic. Firstly, both seem to invest 'facts' with a normative significance which in reality they do not always have. Information may be presented in the course of collective bargaining which, while accurate and apparently persuasive, will be rejected by one side or the other simply because it does not happen to support the argument they are putting forward: 'Trade unions which urge disclosure tend to expect that it will uncover hidden profits or provide the proof as to why a proposed redundancy should not proceed. Facts which reveal the opposite might well be dismissed as unacceptable.'[31] Or, as George Woodcock once remarked, 'Facts sometimes get in the way of argument.' Secondly, there is a tendency on both sides to ignore the possibility that, far from settling claims and grievances to the satisfaction of one party or the other, disclosure may well provoke more argument over how the information should be *presented*. Even if managements are compelled to disclose information on 'sensitive' issues such as pricing policy and cash flow, they will still have plenty of opportunity to ensure that the way in which the 'facts' are presented strengthens whatever point or impression they wish to make. Thirdly, it must also be anticipated that in practice there will be immense scope for both sides to interpret the same 'facts' differently. One problem which several managers have encountered in drawing up formal, written procedure agreements, for example, is that the simple act of writing a rule down, even with the agreement of trade union negotiators, does not preclude the possibility that there will be genuine differences of opinion over what it actually means once it has been implemented. It is also more than likely that both sides will use information for purely tactical purposes and will adopt whatever interpretations happen to suit their case at a particular point in time. The possibility of misinterpretation, whether accidental or otherwise, will be all the greater if the information concerned is channelled exclusively through trade union representatives to the shop floor. On the other hand, any attempt by management to give more information directly to the shop floor, bypassing union representatives, may be viewed with considerable suspicion. Finally, it should be remembered that information for bargaining purposes is not drawn exclusively from within the organization. In wage bargaining, for example, the ability of the company to meet the claim is only *one* of the criteria to which both sides customarily refer. External factors such as the rate of inflation and movements in the pay of other comparable groups in other workplaces and industries may be equally, if not more, significant.

Once these caveats are accepted, it becomes less important to argue in great detail over what information should be disclosed and what kept secret. Five key areas are mentioned in the ACAS Code of Practice – pay and fringe benefits, conditions of service, manpower, performance and financial information. But precisely how much information is disclosed in each area will depend on the needs and objectives of the parties themselves. The Code of Practice is only advisory; there neither is nor will be any compulsion on employers to disclose information which they consider should remain confidential for reasons other than the effects on collective bargaining. Moreover, if in the employer's view the compilation of a particular item of information will 'entail work or expenditure out of reasonable proportion to the value of the information in the conduct of collective bargaining', then he will not be required to provide it. These sections of the Code clearly give employers ample room for manoeuvre and it would therefore be reasonable to assume that some will quote them as often as possible in order to avoid disclosing anything of value to the trade unions. Indeed the Government itself seems to have recognized the possibility that the Code of Practice will have little effect on collective bargaining and at the time of writing has declared its intention of introducing new, obligatory rules in this area. A Green Paper published in July 1977 on *The Aims and Scope of Company Reports* indicates that the annual report and accounts of companies employing more than 500 people (or with an annual turnover exceeding £5 million) should in future be required to include (1) an *added value statement* showing the wealth created by the company and the way in which that wealth is distributed, (2) an *employment statement* indicating the manpower resources and policies of the company, (3) more comprehensive *financial accounts*, (4) more detailed *disaggregation* of the activities of the company and (5) an *international trade statement*. If these proposals become law, they will probably have some effect on the style and conduct of collective bargaining. Firstly they will enable trade union negotiators to compare the profitability indices of different companies more easily and secondly they will almost certainly encourage union representatives to ask for more information. Consequently it could be argued with some justice that if any real progress is to be made in this field over the next few years, it would be more sensible to adopt some form of mandatory disclosure (as outlined in the Green Paper) than to rely exclusively on the principle (embodied in the Employment Protection Act) that information should only be disclosed, subject to several important conditions, on request. Whatever happens to the general framework of company law, however, it seems virtually certain that trade union negotiators will demand more information from managements which they believe will be useful to them in collective bargaining. The effects which more disclosure will actually have on the substantive outcome of collective bargaining, however, are much more problematical.

Industrial action and the law

The argument that unofficial and unconstitutional strikes would be prevented if collective agreements were given the force of law was finally laid to rest with the repeal of the Industrial Relations Act. It is worth noting, however, that sanctions against industrial action are still part of the current legal framework and on odd occasions have actually been invoked. It is still perfectly legal for an employer to dismiss employees who have broken their contracts of employment by going on strike. The only caveat here is that the employer must be able to show, firstly, that the employees were dismissed for going on strike and, secondly, that *all* those who went on strike were dismissed.[32] In practical terms, of course, dismissal for strike action is very rare, although as the Grunwick dispute shows, in certain circumstances it can be a useful weapon for the employer.

The law also seeks to regulate the conduct of strikes by insisting that picketing should be peaceful. Thus S.15 of the Trade Union and Labour Relations Act 1974 provides that:

> It shall be lawful for one or more persons in contemplation or further-ance of a trade dispute to attend at or near (*a*) a place where another person works or carries on business or (*b*) any place where another person happens to be, not being a place where he resides, for the pur-pose only of peacefully obtaining or communicating information, or peacefully persuading any person to work or abstain from working.

The problem is, of course, that the *law* on picketing has not changed in essence since 1906, whereas the *nature* of picketing is far removed from what it was in the Edwardian era. On the one hand, obstructing the highway is held to be a common-law 'nuisance', yet in practice it is often impossible for pickets to communicate information to non-strikers without obstructing something or somebody.[33] On the other hand, it could well be argued that the legal conception of picketing is inherently bizarre. Pickets have a legal right to put their point of view 'peacefully' to those whom they regard as strike-breakers at the factory gates. In reality their main purpose is usually to deter non-strikers from entering the factory and the method used is not so much the force of their argument as the loudness of their abuse and the implicit threat of physical 'persuasion'. The gap between legal myth and industrial reality becomes particularly noticeable when the non-strikers turn up in motor vehicles. The law on picketing does not recognize the existence of vehicular traffic. Vehicles can only be stopped if the pickets are there in sufficient force. But if they are present in force, can it not be argued that their very numbers are a form of intimidation? And, since the real purpose of picketing is not to 'peacefully communicate information' but to deter non-strikers from coming to work, how can pickets achieve their objective without adopting intimidatory tactics?

The law on picketing has of course remained unchanged for so long firstly because in most industrial disputes where picketing occurs the letter of the law is not enforced, and secondly because no one can think of a method of updating the law which does not recognize that some form of intimidation is almost inevitable in present-day circumstances. Consequently it is legitimate to ask whether picketing should be permitted at all. Wedderburn has argued that 'the right peacefully to picket premises to persuade men not to work, or to urge them not to blackleg and break a strike, is an essential weapon on the workers' side in a trade dispute'.[34] This statement, however, should be treated with considerable reserve. The typical British strike is still short, localized and unofficial. In 1976, for example, nearly 20 per cent of the total number of stoppages lasted for not more than one day; nearly 50 per cent lasted for more than one but fewer than seven days. Since picketing tends to be confined to prolonged, official stoppages, it would seem that the vast majority of strikes are likely to be picket-free. In fact, of course, picketing is irrelevant to the conduct of most disputes. A group of workers who wish to bring a grievance forcibly to management's attention and who find that the normal negotiating machinery is not getting them anywhere can best make their point simply by walking out. Stoppages of this kind are essentially tactical – the continuation of bargaining by other means – and seldom develop into prolonged trials of strength. By contrast, picketing has played an important role in a very small number of major official stoppages – most notably the miners' strike of 1972, in which the bargaining power of the NUM was greatly enhanced by their decision to picket power stations in strength. The problem is, of course, that mass picketing tends to attract a significant number of people whose purpose is mainly to attack the police rather than further the aims of the strikers. The activities of this minority tend to destroy whatever sympathy the strikers may have among the public at large and enable the embattled employer to claim that he and his loyal workers are the victims of a sinister conspiracy by Marxists, anarchists and other assorted 'wreckers'. In short, whatever the theoretical justification for the right to picket peacefully, the way in which this right is exercised in the few stoppages where picketing actually occurs leads inescapably to the conclusion that it is rarely an 'essential weapon on the workers' side'. In the circumstances it is legitimate to ask what purpose the right to picket still serves.

A withdrawal of the right to picket, however, would immediately come up against the same problem of enforcement which confronted the authors of the Industrial Relations Act. If all picketing was declared illegal, what would happen when a large group of workers and assorted hangers-on decided to ignore the law and picket a factory *en masse*? The only remedy would be to send in a sufficiently large number of policemen who, after the customary exchange of pleasantries, would be obliged to 'move the pickets on' or cart them off to the nearest penal establishment. While this could no doubt be done, at a cost, one wonders whether it might not be counterproductive in the long run. The spectacle of *bona fide* strikers going to jail is something that no government, particularly after the experience of the dock strike in the summer of 1972, would willingly contemplate. An alternative approach would be to seek to prevent these disputes getting to the stage where mass picketing is thought to be necessary. This may mean, for example, that ACAS should be given the power firstly to investigate disputes on its own initiative or on that of the employer, without necessarily waiting for a request from the unions involved, and secondly to make a legally binding settlement. There are, of course, several difficulties inherent in this proposal, principally that of persuading the parties to cooperate with and accept the decision of a third party whose intervention might be resented by one side or the other. A system of sanctions would also have to be devised which would have sufficient credibility to deter either side from ignoring the settlement. But here again the fundamental problem would be one of enforcement. In a dispute where a trade union was seeking recognition in the face of both strong resistance from the employer and apparent hostility or indifference on the part of the majority of the employees (as at

Grunwick), would a decision in favour of the trade union carry much credibility? And if the decision was in favour of the employer, would the union and its supporters within the company accept it? It could of course be argued that the kind of situation which developed at Grunwick is exceptional and that most recognition disputes – indeed most disputes of all kinds – are settled in a much more civilized way, without the resort to strike action and certainly without mass picketing. Consequently any system of compulsory arbitration would apply only to a small minority of cases. Yet it is in precisely this minority of disputes, where feelings run high on both sides and personal reputations are at stake, that third party intervention, even if backed by the law, is least likely to be effective. It may be convenient to believe that the law can succeed in resolving industrial disputes where conciliation has failed, but it is hardly realistic.

Summary

The repeal of the Industrial Relations Act and the establishment of the current legal framework caused many observers to express the hope that a broad political and industrial consensus had at long last been achieved concerning the role of the law in employee relations. It would now appear that such hopes are premature. The closed shop still evokes distrust in some quarters. Others believe that the restrictions on management's power to dismiss have been carried too far. Some have argued that the various rights conferred on individual employees simply discourage many employers from recruiting additional labour. Others are disturbed by what they consider to be an undue bias in favour of trade unionism and collective bargaining. The Scarman report into the Grunwick dispute, for example, questioned whether the company's attitude to trade unionism, while undoubtedly lawful, was 'reasonable' in present-day circumstances. This point elicited the following response from the Grunwick management:

The underlying implication is that in 1977 trade union power is so great that one is most unwise to resist it too strenuously, or to expect it to observe the circumspection and restraints that are required from everyone else. If that is the meaning then it is the authentic voice of the corporate state ... Trade unions already enjoy vast legal immunities and in pursuing their industrial aims can do more or less as they please. If on top of this, companies are to be deemed unreasonable for exercising what rights they have left and using what little legal protection remains to them, then no society can exist in Britain, other than a collectivist one.[35]

This view is neither eccentric nor, given the circumstances of the Grunwick dispute, unreasonable. It would almost certainly attract the support of many ordinary trade union members. But does it reflect the realities of British industrial relations in general?

In the course of this chapter, an attempt has been made to remove some of the mythology surrounding the current legal framework. While the 1975 Act does indeed recognize the desirability of greater security of employment for all employees, the rules themselves can hardly be described as a crushing burden on management. Indeed, the way in which these rules have been interpreted by the EAT since 1976 should go some way towards dispelling the myth that management's power to dismiss employees or change their working conditions in the interests of the business has been decisively weakened. This does not of course mean that an employer who persistently ignores the legitimate interests of his employees in having some say in the making of decisions which affect them will not arouse any opposition. The need for employers to act reasonably, to follow agreed procedures and to consult employees and their representatives when some form of change is being contemplated has been repeatedly emphasized by successive codes of practice, by the EAT and by industrial tribunals. But it would be misleading to suggest that, at least in the field of dismissal, the employer is now bound hand and foot by ridiculous legalisms.

It would be equally misleading to assume that the current legal framework makes the spread of collective bargaining inevitable. Trade union membership and collective bargaining were firmly set on an expansionist course long before the current rules were enacted, for reasons which have little to do with the law. It is still open to any management to adopt an employee relations policy whose overriding objective is to weaken the appeal of trade unionism to the workforce. Indeed there are still a considerable number of companies, some of them large and well-known, who have successfully pursued such a policy for many years. The point is that the continued existence of non-union organizations ultimately rests with management and the employees themselves. It is worth remembering that despite the efforts of APEX, ACAS and all those who stood on the picket lines, Grunwick's management succeeded in their attempt to keep collective bargaining out of the company because ultimately the majority of the employees did not want it. In other words, there are very definite limits to the effectiveness of legal rules and third-party intervention in situations where neither the employer nor his employees are anxious to establish a collective bargaining relationship. The present law is obviously based on the supposition that in most recognition disputes, a clear majority of the workforce is either in favour of or at least not really opposed to collective bargaining, and that the major stumbling block is resistance on the part of the employer. However, this supposition may not always be valid and much in practice depends on the policy pursued by management.

Once a collective bargaining relationship has been established, the law takes relatively little interest in the substantive outcome. Pressure from trade union negotiators for the disclosure of more information will almost certainly grow over the next few years, but the extent to which their demands are met will probably continue to depend more on the balance of bargaining power and managerial attitudes towards disclosure than on the law. In any case, the argument that more disclosure will somehow lead to a transformation in the style and substance of bargaining needs to be viewed with some scepticism. While compulsory disclosure may well accelerate the existing trend towards a greater degree of professionalism in bargaining – and may in this sense continue to push plant and company bargaining into a more transatlantic mould – it would be naïve to suppose that this will somehow generate a cooperative consensus by helping to dispel ignorance, or that it will produce immense gains for the workforce by compelling the company to 'come clean'. In short, despite the fact that the framework of British labour law has become much more interventionist in recent years, the effectiveness of collective bargaining will continue to depend on the aspirations and expertise of the parties themselves. The temptation to regard the law as a method of altering the balance of bargaining power on the shop floor, or as a painless way of settling complex disputes, must be resisted by all parties, especially politicians.

CHAPTER SIX

Policy and Practice

What is necessary for the social order to prevail is that the
generality of men be content with their lot. But what is
necessary for them to be content is not that they have
more or less, but that they be convinced that they do not
have the right to have more. And for this to be it is abso-
lutely necessary that there be an authority whose superiority they acknowledge, and which lays down the law. For
never will the individual left to the pressure of his needs
acknowledge that he has reached the extreme limit of his
right.

Émile Durkheim

We are a job-orientated society; people still think of
themselves as miners or shipbuilders or whatever. If this
is taken away, a basis of their existence will be removed.
When I see a ship going down the slipway in Barrow, and
hear the workers cheer, I can understand that.

Albert Booth,
Secretary of State for Employment, 1976

THIS final chapter will seek to draw together the main threads of
the argument presented in this book and spell out the implications for managements, trade unions and governments. One
of the most important themes discussed has been the growing
divergence between employee expectations and economic reality.
Over the past decade or so, the general expectation that real
incomes should increase from one year to the next has been
increasingly frustrated by accelerating inflation and the growing
burden of direct taxation. This is not a phenomenon peculiar to
Britain; practically every Western industrialized country has experienced the same problem to a greater or lesser degree.
Another important theme – which is probably of greater significance in a British than in a European or American context – is the
need for a much more efficient use of manpower in industry. Low

pay and low productivity are clearly linked, and there seems little doubt that one of the main reasons why British labour is probably the most inefficiently used within the EEC is simply that it is now the cheapest. Yet the key to reconciling these two conflicting pressures does not lie in the kind of strategy advocated by certain trade union leaders – namely that the unions should become more 'aggressive' and push wages up far faster than they have been doing in the past. It has, of course, been argued earlier in this book that a more ambitious and professional approach to collective bargaining on the part of the trade union movement might well have provided a valuable source of pressure for greater efficiency during the relatively easy climate of the 1950s. In the circumstances of the late 1970s, however, it must be recognized that if the parties are to be left to bargain their way to higher efficiency, certain other things must follow.

Firstly, both the unions and the government must realize that managements cannot afford to pay considerably higher wages *and* preserve levels of manning which were viable only when labour costs were lower. To encourage managements and trade unions to negotiate high wage settlements in return for higher efficiency would be eminently sensible, yet it must be recognized that the level of unemployment would rise sharply, at least in the short term, thereby making it imperative for the government to invest more resources in seeking to improve the effectiveness of the labour market. Secondly, if wage bargaining is to be freed from all controls then it should be recognized that the parallel controls on prices, profits and dividends must also be abolished. The complete restoration of free collective bargaining will thus be nothing more than a formula for rapid inflation and even higher unemployment unless the government succeeds in creating a climate of confidence which will encourage managements to invest and, equally important, removes all obstacles to achieving a higher rate of return on capital employed. Thirdly, trade union negotiators will have to accept that if the *quid pro quo* principle is to dominate wage bargaining, the claims of equity will have to take a back seat. It will have to be accepted that different groups make different relative contributions to total output and that therefore they are entitled to expect higher relative pay. Finally, managements must accept that if wage determination is to be based predominantly on the effort bargain, workgroups and their organizations will expect to have more influence over the rule-making process, which will in turn have important procedural implications. Taken together, the changes indicated above amount to a thorough-going transformation in the way in which industrial relations have traditionally been conducted in Britain. Each one is fraught with difficulties and objections and progress towards them can only be gradual, halting and punctuated with outbreaks of conflict. Nevertheless, these are the real issues which now confront policy-makers at all levels in the industrial relations system. Politicians who continue to indulge in the rhetoric of the late 1960s and early 1970s and infer that 'excessive' trade union power is still the overriding issue are not only misleading the electorate but are also misleading themselves.

The complex of pressures which are making for the kind of changes outlined above should by now be reasonably clear. It is also beyond dispute that these changes have profound implications for the management of industrial relations in the workplace. Some of these implications have already been discussed. In this concluding chapter, however, it is necessary to focus more clearly on the kind of action which managements, trade unions and governments will need to take if the disruptive impact of the process of change is to be contained within reasonable bounds. All change worthy of the name generates conflict in one form or another. Conflict need not, however, reach unmanageable proportions *if* it is anticipated and *if* an appropriate framework of procedural rules is present to help resolve it.

Developing an industrial relations policy

Commenting on the growth of workplace bargaining in the post-war period, Allan Flanders maintained that it was the product of drift rather than design: 'It has developed haphazardly as the result of the pressure of the moment because managements, in yielding to the pressure of shop stewards and the workgroups they represent, have had no long-term objectives in mind, no clearly defined policies in labour relations beyond avoiding trouble and a stoppage of work.[1] The general absence of strategic planning in industrial relations was rightly seen as symptomatic of a more fundamental neglect of the personnel function as a whole. The Donovan Commission touched on this theme, arguing that a move towards formalized plant bargaining would force top management to face up to their responsibilities in this field:

> If the change is made, boards of directors will lose the protection provided by the existing system against their being held fully responsible for their own personnel policies. At present boards can leave industry-wide agreements to their employers' associations, and the task of dealing with workers within those agreements to their subordinate managers. Removing this protection will direct the attention of companies to the need to develop their own personnel policies.[2]

In other words, the peculiar institutional framework of British industrial relations was held to be largely responsible for the neglect of policy-making at plant and company level. Once that framework was reformed, managements would have no choice but to start thinking systematically about their industrial relations problems and objectives.

With the wisdom of hindsight, one can see that the Donovan approach betrayed little understanding of the real problems involved in developing industrial relations policies at company level. Firstly, it must be recognized that in many companies the responsibility for industrial relations still rests with line management, who often tend to be at least sceptical and at worst hostile towards what they regard as 'ivory tower' personnel techniques and ideas. Line managers frequently reject the concept of an industrial relations policy on the grounds that it would deprive them of the 'flexibility' which they see as a vital ingredient of good industrial relations. Flexibility allows managements to consider each grievance or claim on its merits, enabling them to avoid the stoppages which might occur if their response was inhibited by rigid guidelines and directives imposed from above. Flexibility also requires *informality*, and a formal industrial relations policy, accompanied by a battery of formal, written procedures and substantive agreements, is often seen by line management as an implied criticism of their own tried and trusted methods. They also tend to see formalization as a threat to their own status and authority. One researcher has recently confirmed that many middle and first-line managers are apprehensive lest formalization should establish *de jure* rights for workers where only *de facto* rights have existed hitherto:

One point often made in this context was that it is much more difficult to challenge or bargain over a formal (written) rule than over an informal one. For these managers, formalization would lead to the establishment of greater, and unchallengeable, worker rights, thus reducing the ability of these managers to bargain over work practices in ways they considered necessary to maintain production levels.[3]

Secondly, Donovan's emphasis on the importance of policy initiatives at board level was in a sense rather naïve. The same strategy was reiterated by the CIR, which argued that:

The first requirement for the formulation of a company's industrial relations policy must be that the board and top level managers themselves give proper attention to the task. They have the final responsibility for such policy and it is they who can exert a major influence and ensure its integration with policies in other areas which interact with industrial relations.[4]

In theory one could hardly quarrel with these sentiments. In practice, however, one must bear in mind the points already made about the diffuseness of power within the organization and the dependence of many directors on the advice and expertise of senior management *below* board level. If Winkler's 'no contact, anti-concern' syndrome is at all representative of boardroom attitudes towards industrial relations, then it is hardly surprising that the responsibility for decision-making in this field should in practice have remained with line management. The Donovan model assumes a much higher level of involvement by company boards in policy-making than has usually been the case, but this in turn depends on a greater upward flow of information from line management. In practice, however, it seems that frequently the reverse happens:

... given that directors' concern is only with costs and order, subordinate managers have a strong incentive *not* to communicate upwards information on emergent disorder. They are under pressure to hide problems, in the hope that they can reach covert accommodations with workers before the director finds out . . . Normal management reporting systems are, in the industrial relations context, systems of concealment. What effectively is happening is the covert decentralization of industrial relations policy-making.[5]

In these circumstances it is hardly surprising that the development of company industrial relations policies has proved to be a slower and more difficult process than Donovan and other likeminded reformers envisaged. It would seem to the present writer, however, that there is widespread misunderstanding of the purpose and nature of an industrial relations policy. The Donovan Commission's approach to this matter was decidedly unsatisfactory in so far as it laid great emphasis on the need for formal, comprehensive plant agreements and mentioned policy only, apparently, as an afterthought. The essential point for managers to grasp, however, is that an industrial relations policy is not *necessarily* a restrictive influence on day-to-day decision-making. The main purpose of a policy is to define the industrial relations *objectives* of the organization. Thus one test of the effectiveness of a policy is the extent to which it provides managers who are responsible for the conduct of industrial relations with a framework of general principles which they regard as helpful and within which they are able to act decisively on day-to-day problems. Without guidelines of some kind, managers may find it difficult to make decisions which are broadly consistent with each other, unless of course they are tightly controlled from the top. In many organizations, however, rigid centralization would be both structurally impracticable and, given the general preference for workplace autonomy, politically impossible. Clearly there are some substantive and procedural issues, notably those affected by the current framework of labour law, on which it is appropriate for personnel specialists to provide line managers with a code of practice and insist that this be observed throughout the organization. There are many other problems, however, on which the role of the specialist must be essentially advisory and where it would be inappropriate to impose rigid standardization.

Although there is not at present a great deal of empirical evidence which can be used to illustrate how some companies have overcome these problems, one or two relevant points can be made. The form and content of an industrial relations policy depends firstly on the size and structure of the organization. There would seem to be a rough rule of thumb which indicates that the bigger the firm, the more likely it is to be unionized, the more formal its collective bargaining arrangements will be, and the more detailed will be the content of its industrial relations policy. In the case of a multi-plant company, however, much depends on whether the plants themselves are geographically dispersed or concentrated. Secondly, the structure of collective bargaining within the organization is normally an important influence. As the CIR has pointed out:

> ... the level at which collective bargaining takes place may not only be different for different subjects but may not necessarily coincide with the level at which effective management decisions are made in that a company with well-developed plant bargaining may not only restrict the scope of bargaining at plant level but may impose limitations from the group, e.g. on the amount of pay increases which can be negotiated by plant management. [6]

Thirdly, and perhaps most important of all, any policy is strongly influenced by the preferences of the parties themselves. The traditional desire on both sides for as much freedom as possible from interference by outsiders has already been underlined as a powerful normative influence on British industrial relations, and the increasing complexity of the field as a whole may well have strengthened this preference rather than weakened it. Gill, for example, studied industrial relations policies in a variety of enterprises and concluded that:

> With the exception of the geographically clustered firms, all establishments manifested a clear trend towards more and more decentralization in industrial relations decision-making, regardless of whether they were autonomous or part of a larger company. There appeared to be a recognition that industrial relations problems were best settled closer to their source. The advice and instruction given to establishments by headquarters or from group level was rarely imposed on the firm concerned. Rather, a very broad set of guidelines were laid down, which were more often than not sought by the establishments themselves. [7]

Other researchers have noted a similar determination on both sides to settle disputes at the lowest possible level and under no circumstances to let them go out of the plant and fall within the jurisdiction of 'outsiders'.[8]

In a multi-plant company it may of course be totally inappropriate for senior management at the centre to impose rigid constraints on decision-making in the various operational units. By the same token, however, the policy guidelines issued to line management may be so bland as to be meaningless. A policy document which is little more than a series of well-intentioned platitudes is hardly likely to have much influence on attitudes and behaviour. The significance of a policy in this context needs to be underlined. The development of a policy where none previously existed is usually the result of a change in the attitudes of senior management, yet the policy must also help to change habits and ideas throughout the management hierarchy, and unless it says something fairly radical it is unlikely to have much effect. As Gill has observed:

All too often managers have neither the knowledge nor the confidence to change their approach to industrial relations. Their reluctance to recognize the need to change their approach is a product of their earlier training. Technical and commercial problems lend themselves more to calculation than do industrial relations problems. The outcome of a new departure in industrial relations is far from predictable once the existing *status quo* has been deliberately disturbed.[9]

It has often been remarked that line management's characteristic insistence on retaining their traditional freedom and flexibility in essence reflects a preference for 'fire-fighting' as opposed to 'fire-prevention'. In its simplest terms, however, policy is essentially concerned with 'fire-prevention'. It demands that managers should analyse their industrial relations problems, define what it is they wish to achieve, and then devise strategies for realizing their objectives. In practice, however, the task of achieving a consensus throughout the management hierarchy at all the various stages of developing a policy is usually very difficult. At one level there may be a clash of ideologies, as managers with a unitary view of the organization encounter those whose approach to industrial relations reflects a pluralist standpoint. This may lead to a profound divergence of opinion on issues such as the role of shop stewards, the scope of collective bargaining and the relevance of existing arrangements for joint consultation. At another level there may be an equally pronounced conflict between different departments within the organization. The production director and his subordinates may well regard the development of an industrial relations policy as a transparent piece of empire-building on the part of the personnel department and may therefore resist it strongly. It is hardly surprising, therefore, that, anticipating all the problems of change, many senior managers prefer to leave things as they are. As long as existing methods are working well, why, they ask, should they change them?

In reality, however, there is a constant process of change in collective bargaining, although some managers (and, for that matter, trade union officials) may prefer not to recognize this fact. The gradual growth of bargaining at plant and company level underlines the simple fact that the expectations and objectives of neither managements nor employees remain static for very long. It was argued earlier in this book that over the past decade or so, more and more managements have found themselves under growing pressure to improve both the profitability and productivity of their companies. This has frequently led them to question the appropriateness of existing payment systems and manning standards, with the result that many have taken initiatives to change the structure, principles and form of collective bargaining in their establishments. Simultaneously, a general increase in trade union membership has encouraged many full-time officials and shop stewards to press for more influence over managerial decision-making on a wider range of substantive issues. These two pressures have, of course, interacted to some degree. The relatively poor performance of large sectors of British industry lies at the root of the near-stagnation in real incomes and the growing insecurity of employment which have together enhanced the appeal of collective bargaining for many employees. Conversely, the way in which managements have reacted to an increasingly difficult economic environment, for example through productivity bargaining, has widened the scope of joint regulation at workplace level. Furthermore it is equally clear that the changing framework of labour law has had *some* impact on both procedural and substantive rules in the workplace. To reiterate a point that was made earlier, the current legal framework encourages the spread of collective bargaining and strengthens the floor of basic rights to which all employees, union members and non-members alike, are entitled. Although empirical evidence on this point is at present rather thin, it seems probable that this legal framework will help to accelerate the changes in collective bargaining which have been noted above.[10]

It is, of course, impossible to lay down a standard blueprint for the substantive content of an industrial relations policy. This will in practice be determined by the factors noted above, chiefly the size and structure of the organization, the nature of existing industrial relations practices, the character of the technology involved, the financial state of the company, and so on. Some issues lend themselves to clear, specific guidelines for action; others do not. The needs of every organization are in some respects different and the order of priorities on which an industrial relations policy should be based will differ accordingly. Clearly, however, any policy worthy of the name should address itself to certain key issues, notably pay and productivity, the role of trade unionism and collective bargaining, security of employment, job satisfaction, and other matters related to the quality of life in the work situation. It should be emphasized, however, that in many cases the shape and content of the policy will be strongly influenced by whatever philosophy senior management brings to the management of industrial relations. Philosophies also differ greatly, but in the present climate of opinion it would probably be true to say that their most important distinguishing feature 'is the extent to which companies agree to enlarge the area of joint regulation of their affairs by management and employee representatives'.[11] Many companies, of course, either seek to restrict the scope of collective bargaining to the most basic 'bread and butter' issues or do not recognize the need for joint regulation in any shape or form. As was noted in the previous chapter, the current framework of law does not really compel managements to engage in collective bargaining if they are determined not to do so. The point is, however, that senior managers who are resolved to keep trade unions out of their organization at any price *must* have a comprehensive employee relations policy geared to that end. They must also be aware that the cost of resisting collective bargaining is likely to increase within the foreseeable future.

A philosophy of benevolent paternalism which was highly acceptable to the workforce of twenty or thirty years ago may not be regarded with uncritical admiration in the circumstances of today. Such philosophies tend to work best in small units, particularly where management can offer relatively generous terms and conditions and where either the market environment or the efficiency of the firm are such that a high degree of job security has been achieved. In recent years, however, the relevance of this approach has been challenged by the same combination of external and internal pressures which has affected most other business organizations. The squeeze on profit margins has compelled even paternalistic employers to look more carefully at their labour costs and to try and improve the level of efficiency. Faced with changes in the wage–work relationship, employees have become more aware of their lack of influence over the making of decisions which affect their jobs. They may also have come to realize that their pay and conditions are being equalled or even exceeded in other comparable organizations where trade unions are present. In these circumstances senior management may suddenly wake up one day to find themselves facing a claim for trade union recognition – a claim which, because of their traditional ideology, they may be ill-equipped to handle. Alternatively management may seek to absorb at least some of these pressures by establishing some kind of formal joint consultation with their employees. The indications are, however, that such a strategy may be effective only in the short term. The experience of other countries within the EEC suggests that consultative bodies in the workplace sooner or later develop into bargaining institutions. Once employees recognize that their substantive gains flow more from their own collective power than from the benevolence of management, the chances of their settling for anything less than collective bargaining become increasingly remote. The problem facing management in a non-union environment – particularly if the organization is relatively large and cannot be insulated from external pressures – is, therefore, that of ensuring that employees receive the benefits of collective bargaining without any bargaining taking place. A solution to this problem will call for a prodigious investment of time, resources and ingenuity, based on a comprehensive employee relations policy devised and administered by specialists.

Employee aspirations and procedural change

Is the growth of collective bargaining therefore inevitable? Must managers come to terms with the fact that sooner or later their authority – their power to make decisions in the interests of the business – will be conditional on the support of employee representatives? The argument presented in this book suggests that there are several factors operating at both national level and in the workplace which will tend to increase the significance of joint regulation. The manager who believes that he has a 'natural' right to manage, which all his subordinates must accept without question, will not find this argument to his taste. Yet he will be able to dismiss it only by consciously closing his eyes to everything that has happened in industrial relations in both Britain and Western Europe as a whole over the past two or three decades.

It would be useful at this point to refer briefly to Alan Fox's analysis of trust relations in industry since it throws further light on the growth of collective bargaining in recent years. Fox has challenged the conventional pluralist notion that organized labour has been able to achieve a rough balance of power with management through collective bargaining. Instead he suggests that power has remained concentrated in the hands of a privileged minority:

People do not come together freely and spontaneously to set up work organizations; the propertyless many are forced by their need for a livelihood to seek access to resources owned or controlled by the few, who derive therefrom very great power. The few can use this power to determine the behaviour of the many, not only directly, but also indirectly through the many agencies of socialization, communication and attitude-forming.[12]

One of these agencies is the trade union movement which, by bargaining with management, helps to confer legitimacy on managerial authority and thereby reinforces the traditional structure of power in industry. It is argued, however, that in recent years the normative influence of managerial values has been declining. Managements are now confronted by a generation of employees, including a large proportion of those in rapidly expanding white-collar occupations, who are prepared to question the old inequalities of wealth and power. These 'radically minded' employees are said to be increasingly frustrated by the progressive division of labour in the workplace, by work which permits them less and less discretion and scope for personal development, and by procedural arrangements which merely seem to buttress management's authority. The most obvious behavioural symptoms of this frustration are normally regarded as 'problems' by managements, politicians and trade union leaders alike. They include an increasing willingness to strike in breach of procedure, a growing preoccupation with their obligations under the work side of the employment contract, and a diminishing respect for at least some of the traditional rights of management.

Fox has conceptualized these behavioural tendencies as the 'low-trust syndrome' and argues that low-trust relations are spreading:

> Against the combination of, on the one hand, pyramidal hierarchies incorporating great inequalities of decision-making about rewards, status and function and, on the other, social values which stress the competitive pursuit of rising material standards and individual self-development, the managerial ideology of common purpose and high-trust relations struggles increasingly in vain as far as low discretion rank-and-file members are concerned. More and more they have tended to see management's structural organization and conduct of the work process as embodying a distinction between those who are, and those who are not, trusted, and to see themselves as among the latter. Low-trust reciprocation has followed.[13]

This reciprocation has shown itself in the recent growth of trade union membership, particularly in middle management and supervisory grades, and in the increasing formalization of workplace relations. Behavioural norms which have long been observed informally, as a matter of custom and practice, are now being written down. The formal, written collective agreement covering a wide range of substantive issues, regulating the effort bargain in considerable detail, and specifying the rights and responsibilities of the parties concerned, is now generally held to be the best foundation of industrial order. Yet, as Fox has pointed out, 'What we have here is a process by which the mutual expectations of the parties become increasingly specified . . . Here is the low-trust dynamic at work which impels both parties to seek to bind each other ever more tightly within prescriptive rules.'[14]

While there is no space here to comment on Fox's analysis in detail, it would be difficult to deny that there might be at least some trade union members and shop stewards who accept his 'radical' perspective on industrial society. It seems equally certain, however, that the vast majority of employees, even those who are active union members, do not articulate their grievances in this way. As Fox himself admits:

Among the rank and file there are a few who universalize and conceptualize these perceptions into a systematic principled rejection of the existing social structure and its values, but the majority take a particularistic view in focusing only upon their own deprivations and demanding only changes in their immediate situation which will improve their own position within it.[15]

A more realistic interpretation of current trends might be to emphasize the increasing uncertainty and insecurity which the combination of rapid inflation and industrial change have generated both on the shop floor and in the lower half of the management hierarchy. Uncertainty of any kind may well act as a powerful inducement to the formalization of rules and obligations. There is, however, an additional and more positive factor which must be mentioned in this context. It has often been pointed out that managements have traditionally preferred to leave many of the rules agreed at workplace level in the form of unwritten understandings so that their own *formal* rights are not abrogated or eroded in any way. Many trade union negotiators have also tended to share this preference for informality, and for a very practical reason: '*De facto* rights confirm again and again the function of trade unions as strugglers against capitalism, wresting rights from an unwilling employer on behalf of the lads.'[16] It follows therefore that the increasing emphasis of formal rights and obligations may reflect the development of a sense of mutual responsibility and interdependence in a period of industrial change and economic uncertainy. As was argued in Chapter One, sweeping generalizations about a 'crisis of authority' in Western industrial society must be treated with considerable scepticism. The normative force of tradition is still very much in evidence. Wage bargaining is *not* a no-holds-barred struggle between the haves and the have-nots. The authority of management is still generally accepted as long as it is exercised within the current notions of fairness and rationality. Much depends, therefore, on the effectiveness of the procedural norms which govern industrial relations.

It will be recalled that the Donovan Commission attached great importance to the reform of procedural rules as a means of discouraging unofficial, unconstitutional strikes. The role of procedures must now, however, be considered in a wider context. As one observer has recently pointed out:

It is because of the need in a working community to provide orderly, consistent, known methods for dealing with working relationships, considering problems arising from them and resolving differences, that procedures are of such central importance in industrial relations. In this context procedures are commonly thought of as those procedures which have been jointly agreed between managements and the representatives of their employees . . . But the basic needs for order, consistency and a general understanding of accepted ways of proceeding existed before the evolution of jointly agreed procedures and indeed exist today in establishments where trade unions are not recognized and procedures are determined solely by managements.[17]

In essence, procedures impose restraints on the use of power. They may be entirely voluntary in the sense that they are established by the parties themselves without any kind of external compulsion, or they may be influenced by the general view of what is, and what is not, good practice. Fundamentally, however, they reflect an agreement by both sides to be bound by a code of

'Queensberry rules' in their day-to-day relationships. In this sense it is possible to regard a system of procedures as a distinct social organization within the enterprise based on shared values and norms:

The desirability of peaceful settlement; the importance of observing the other party's expectations in respect of procedure; the restraints and conventions of social interaction which maintain an environment favourable to compromise; there are at once the preconditions and the consequences of successful conflict-regulation. In so far as there is normative agreement about these behaviours, it embodies a recognition by both sides that any immediate tactical advantage resulting from violation of shared expectations would be outweighed by damage to the system within which they had hitherto accomplished satisfactory results.[18]

This means that the essential prerequisite of effective procedural relations is a recognition by both sides that their power to take action unilaterally must be held in check. In other words there must be a moral commitment to a shared system of authority. For management this means an abrogation of the right to take decisions unilaterally, without reference to trade union representatives, and this must obviously create tensions between those managers who feel that this is a severe handicap on their power to act and those who believe that joint action is more effective. The need for a moral commitment to procedural rules also presents problems for the trade unions. Workgroups and their representatives may regard procedure as a device for 'drawing their teeth' and preventing them from exerting immediate and direct pressure on management. Who else but management, they may ask, derives a tactical advantage if all disputes go into procedure? Two important influences on employee attitudes to procedure, however, are firstly the *level* at which the rules are decided and secondly the degree of *involvement* which employee representatives are allowed in deciding them. Thus the Donovan Commission argued that the moral commitment of trade unionists to procedure would be greatly strengthened if the rules were agreed through collective bargaining at plant and company level. As a general proposition this is undoubtedly true. However, it must also be recognized that even a framework of formal procedures agreed at workplace level do not guarantee industrial peace.

In order to understand why this is so, one must recognize that procedural rules – no matter how clear and comprehensive they may be – have certain inherent limitations. As Fox has pointed out, a procedural system at any level is a social organization which, like any other, can develop its own values and loyalties: 'The norms and values shared by the representatives of both sides in this social organization may become almost as important in moulding their thought and behaviour as the requirements of their managerial or collectivity role.'[19] In other words, even where the main parties to a procedure are managers and shop stewards, rather than employers' association representatives and full-time trade union officials, there is an inherent tendency for them to become immersed in the conventions and rituals of their procedural relations, perhaps to the exclusion of their respective constituents. The most recent (1972) survey of workplace relations, for example, indicates that fewer union members saw their shop steward as representing an *exclusively* workers' point of view and that more managers accepted the role and functions of stewards than had been the case at the time of the previous survey (1966).[20] This may be an indication that both sides are gradually being 'socialized' by the developing framework of procedural relations at plant level. By the same token, however, the survey also noted a rising level of dissatisfaction on the part of some union members with the achievements of their organization. It is at least possible that these two developments are not unconnected.

It may, therefore, be misleading to suggest that the negotiation of formal, comprehensive plant procedures will in itself prevent workgroups from taking direct action in breach of the agreed rules. Any assessment of the effectiveness of plant procedures must take account of the following factors. Firstly, the role of the shop steward has become less and less that of a mere mouthpiece for his workgroup. The 'socializing' tendencies noted above and the growing complexity of workplace bargaining have conferred quasi-managerial responsibilities on many stewards, and these have occasionally strained the relationship between stewards and members: 'a shop-floor leader who is expected by the managerial and union hierarchies alike to observe the full protocol of the agreed procedure may be ignored by an impatient workgroup when he urges the appropriate restraints or considers their grievance insufficiently well-grounded to justify action'.[21] Secondly, the requirement that employees should have some involvement in the formulation of procedural rules is not always fulfilled, particularly in large organizations. Shop stewards may negotiate agreements which they believe are acceptable to the majority of their members and subsequently discover that the latter's commitment to the rules agreed on their behalf is much more tenuous than they assumed. In Fox's words: 'Many instances of employees "dishonouring" agreements can be explained by their never having "honoured" them in the first place, as a result of leaders failing to understand, or choosing to ignore, the process of winning consent.'[22] Thirdly, it may be that in some work situations, where production arrangements are conducive to a relatively high level of latent dissatisfaction, occasional outbursts of direct action are an inescapable fact of life. Beynon's study of relations in a car assembly plant, for example, suggests that strikes are inherent in the work situation: 'Trade unionism is about work and sometimes the lads just don't want to work. All talk of procedures and negotiations tend to break down here.'[23]

The problem of gaining the commitment of the workforce to procedures has another dimension, namely the degree of *formality* with which the parties wish to express their rules. Should all procedures be worked out in detail and committed to writing? The Donovan Commission urged that they should, on the grounds that formalization would help to remove uncertainty about the rights and obligations of both sides. However, as Terry has pointed out, the argument for greater formalization tends to assume firstly that 'changes in the form of agreements (unwritten or written), or in the locus of their authorship or guardianship, do not greatly affect the way in which the contents of those agreements are perceived, acted upon, or enforced', and secondly that 'there are no insurmountable obstacles to prevent the drawing-up of tighter, more precise, formal rules than had existed hitherto'.[24] In reality neither of these assumptions seems justified. Most workgroups have gradually evolved their own network of unwritten rules, customs and practices which exert a powerful normative influence over their behaviour. A decision by management to formalize some or all of these rules, albeit after negotiation with shop stewards, may be viewed by the workgroup concerned as a threat to the various informal controls which they have imposed on their immediate work situation. If formalization takes place, although the rules themselves may not have changed very much, the locus of their authorship will have moved away from the workgroup. They will be seen henceforward as 'management/shop steward rules' and the allegiance of the workgroup to them will be correspondingly weaker. If the relationship between the group and its shop steward breaks down, the rules may lose all their authority. Furthermore, as Terry has pointed out, the process of formalization is itself a *bargaining* process:

The new rules and procedures which regulate work behaviour will have been negotiated, every bit as much as any substantive agreement. In so far as that is true, the procedures and agreements will be compromises, reflecting in some way the interests of the parties to the agreements, and limited by the power which each side can exert on the other to contain their discretion to act. Almost inevitably, therefore, there will be aspects of such agreements which one side or the other does not want, or strongly resents. It is unlikely that a commitment to the preservation of such aspects of the agreements will be all that strong.[25]

This is not necessarily an argument against formalization as such. All it suggests is that in seeking to formalize procedural rules, managements must be aware of the possibility that workgroups may not feel the same sense of being morally obliged to observe them, however much their representatives may have been involved in the formalization process. If they feel that their interests have in some way been damaged by formalization, or their bargaining power threatened, they may seek to bend the rules in their own favour. In other words, managements should not make the assumption – as Donovan appeared to do – that from the perspective of workers on the shop floor, all that matters is that procedures should be negotiated and agreed by their own representatives. The norms and values of shop stewards are not always wholly congruent with those of their constituents. Consequently, even in workplaces where the framework of joint regulation is fairly comprehensive, there will still be considerable scope for dissent and direct action by individual workgroups. Moreover, there is some evidence to suggest that in those workplaces where formalization has taken place, informal rules have either never really disappeared or else have quickly returned.[26] While the normative force of custom and practice naturally varies from one workplace to another, depending on factors such as technology, organization structure, the kind of payment system in use and so on, it seems that *some* degree of procedural informality is characteristic of all work situations. While it is certainly true that written procedures 'limit the area of uncertainty' and 'strengthen the defences of management, unions and employees against arbitrary and unpredictable action', there is no certainty that any procedure – no matter how formal, precise and well-written it may be – will always be observed by both sides.[27] In many workplaces, management, unions and workgroups are in a continual bargaining situation and it would be naïve to assume that neither side will ever ignore or violate procedural rules if a tactical advantage can thereby be secured.

This brings us to the most fundamental point about procedural change – namely that it usually affects the balance of *power* in the workplace. Whether it is a matter of establishing joint procedures where none previously existed or of formalizing custom and practice, management must recognize that in some way the structure of power and authority will change. It may change to the advantage of one side or the other, depending on what kind of procedure is involved. In the case of disciplinary procedures, for example, many trade union representatives have not been over-anxious to become involved in formulating the rules and ensuring that employees observe them: 'A commonly held view is that the maintenance of discipline is a management concern and that a union's function in representing the interests of its members should not be compromised by association with the disciplinary system.'[28] In recent years, however, there has been a tendency for managements to formalize disciplinary procedures (an almost inevitable outcome of the introduction of legal rules in this area) and to seek trade union involvement in the process. Where this has happened, shop stewards may well have lost some of their old freedom to challenge management decisions. By contrast, in the broader area of initiating some kind of *change* in working practices, payment systems and other substantive rules, the tendency has been for trade unions to impose procedural constraints on managerial freedom, occasionally by insisting that a *status quo* clause be included in the negotiating procedure. Broadly, a *status quo* clause lays down that changes in matters of substance which affect the interests of employees will not, if challenged, be put into effect until agreement has been reached between the parties or the full negotiating/disputes procedure, whether at company or industry level or both, has been exhausted. These clauses are not particularly common in Britain, although if the trends discussed in this book continue one would expect that pressure to extend them will increase.[29] As an interim report by the TUC General Council on industrial democracy (1973) observed:

A major extension of collective bargaining to matters involving work organization would need to be accompanied by the widespread adoption of procedural arrangements which incorporate some form of mutual *status quo* arrangements. This restricts the ability of management to introduce changes outside negotiated or customary practice.

In practice, of course, the extent to which a *status quo* clause actually restricts the power of management to act depends on the precise wording of the clause. If management are merely required to exhaust the disputes procedure before implementing a substantive change then the only obstacle which they still have to face at the end of the day is strike action, which may or may not be successful. If, however, management undertake to reach *agreement* with trade union representatives before trying to change an established practice or rule, then clearly the pace of change and innovation may be much slower than it would otherwise have been. For this reason many employers view a major extension of *status quo* clauses with apprehension. Some would argue that if there is adequate opportunity for consultation and negotiation before a new practice or rule is introduced, the need for *status quo* clauses becomes less obvious. While this may well be true, the fact remains that not all managements devote as much effort as they should to the task of winning the agreement of the workforce when change of some kind is necessary. The insertion of a *status quo* clause into the appropriate procedure would express a clear normative standard to which management would have to commit themselves. It is interesting to note that the Swedes have felt it necessary to legislate on this issue. The Democracy at Work Act of 1976 requires employers to 'initiate negotiations' with the appropriate trade union representatives *before* deciding on any major change in working conditions, business operations, or conditions of employment. The Act gives employees' organizations the right to demand that joint regulation be extended to cover 'the making and termination of contracts of employment; management and distribution of work; and the operation of the business in other respects'. It also lays down that where there is a dispute over the interpretation of a collective agreement, the *employees'* interpretation and not simply the *status quo* will prevail until the dispute is finally resolved.[30] Taken together these provisions constitute, on paper at least, a much more radical limitation on management's freedom to introduce changes than anything so far envisaged in Britain. It would not be surprising, however, if the T U C were eventually to press for similar rights.

The final point which must be made concerning procedures and procedural change may sound like a platitude, but it should nevertheless be stated. Since it is indeed the case that 'for both management and unions jointly agreed procedures betoken a renunciation of unilateral authority', a considerable degree of mutual trust and goodwill is required to make them work:

Where they have been conceded reluctantly by a management unreconciled to the union's role, or accepted as providing useful tactical dispositions by employee representatives ideologically opposed to the concept of cooperation, jointly agreed procedures can provide frequent occasions for disputes over interpretation and accusations of breaches of agreed arrangements. The wording and formal requirements of procedures rarely give a closely accurate indication of actual behaviour.[31]

In the relatively small number of workplaces where the level of trust between the parties is very low and the strike habit has become well-established, even the most sophisticated procedural rules may make no more than a marginal contribution to the reduction of conflict and disorder. However, the general impression one gets is that in most workplaces procedural rules *are* effective, which presumably implies that the requisite amount of goodwill is usually present. This in turn suggests, and empirical evidence confirms, that there is still a strong attachment on both sides to informal, customary norms and practices. It seems likely, therefore, that – given the acute need for higher productivity in British industry – the parties will find themselves under increasing pressure to negotiate changes in the effort bargain which will then be formalized in written substantive rules, and this process may well generate direct conflict in workplaces which have hitherto been entirely free of strikes. Consequently the pressures of change will also reinforce the need for procedural restraints on both sides and the negotiation of *status quo* clauses may become more widespread. In short, the role of procedures in regulating industrial conflict and restraining behaviour on both sides of the bargaining table will become even more important as the substantive scope of bargaining increases.

International perspectives

In the course of this book references have been made to industrial relations in several continental countries which, taken together, infer that the various pressures for change noted above are by no means peculiar to Britain. Over the past decade or so many European managers have found themselves confronted by the same kind of problems as their British counterparts. Employee aspirations have become more demanding and in most countries governments have recognized their legitimacy in the form of legislation. The basic framework of individual employment rights has been extended and management has less freedom to manage than it once had. Trade unions have pressed for increases in the substantive scope of collective bargaining, with the result that established institutional arrangements at plant and company level have become more and more inadequate. Since the early 1970s the problem of adjustment has been aggravated by the slow-down in economic growth, coupled with a faster rate of inflation and a higher level of unemployment. Trade union membership has increased, particularly in the public sector, and bargaining structures have become more complex. The strike habit also seems to have spread. Government intervention in the bargaining process is now a fact of life in almost every Western country. In short, almost every major development in British industrial relations has a parallel somewhere abroad.

The change in employee aspirations has been particularly marked. Numerous observers have noted the growth of a much more critical attitude on the part of workers and their organizations towards the normative standards and institutional ar-rangements which emerged in the immediate postwar period. In those days the emphasis was on cooperation and consensus, which in effect gave management considerable freedom to manage. Since the late 1960s, however, there has been a general upsurge of interest in power-sharing. Commenting on developments in Holland, for example, Andriessen has written that

> The increasing consciousness of workers concerning the distribution of power and the differences in interests implies that very outspoken attitudes towards participation structures can be found. Some of the more militant workers feel themselves to be quite alienated from the interests of the company. This might imply a decreasing faith in bodies like the works council. This could also mean that they consider that participation procedures do not give them any real influence.[32]

As was noted in Chapter Four, in most European countries works councils have developed into bargaining institutions and in doing so have increased their regulatory power. In Barkin's words:

> Councils acquired the right to deal with many issues formerly re-served to management, including distribution and organization of work and working hours as well as the operations of the assembly lines ... (they) have to be furnished regularly with more adequate economic and financial data about the enterprise, and in some countries (Belgium, France and Sweden) they even obtained the formal right to have their own auditor examine the data. Areas for bilateral decision-making

have been enlarged, and prior notices of change in operations by management are now more widely required.[33]

Since January 1977 worker-management committees in Sweden have had a legal right to negotiate the power to veto management decisions. Finally, some countries have, as noted above, introduced formal systems for worker participation in decision-making at board level.

Attitudes to work itself have also changed. Managements have become increasingly concerned to reverse the growing dislike of mass production technology. Protests against the 'inhuman slavery of the production line' have taken the form of strikes in Italy and of mass absenteeism in Sweden.[34] A survey of West German workers in 1972 found that three quarters of those in the sample who were between sixteen and twenty years of age had negative attitudes towards work. Indeed, it was found that 39 per cent of workers under thirty 'would rather not work at all'. The proportion of those who admitted they disliked work doubled between 1962 and 1972.[35] There is also evidence to suggest that in West Germany the level of unemployment benefit is now high enough to deter some workers from seeking a job even though jobs are available: 'After being pampered for years by an army of *Gastarbeiter* doing the chores, the average German has no intention now of joining the Turks on the dustcart or indeed, if he can help it, on the assembly line. Meanwhile his own holidays get longer, the working week shorter and coffee breaks more frequent.'[36] Labour mobility also seems to have declined sharply, particularly in Sweden and Germany, and absenteeism has increased, implying that workers who find their jobs monotonous or unpleasant simply compensate themselves by taking more time off.[37] It may well be, therefore, that absenteeism performs the same kind of 'safety-valve' role in continental mass-production industries as short, localized stoppages do in Britain.

Changes in employee aspirations have had important institutional repercussions in almost every continental country. In order to appreciate their significance it must be remembered that up to the late 1960s industrial relations in the EEC and Scandinavia were strongly influenced by the postwar social consensus which emphasized the need for cooperation between management and unions in the interests of faster economic growth. This consensus was much stronger and more durable on the continent than it was in Britain. In practical terms it meant that most wage bargaining was confined to national, district or industry level, where it was conducted by trade union officials who were amenable to the influence of employers, governments and the 'social consensus'. Trade union membership stagnated and trade union activity in the workplace was often non-existent. Legal systems helped to circumscribe bargaining activity by placing restrictions on the right to strike and by buttressing the role of the 'cooperative' works councils. In short, the conduct of industrial relations usually reflected a broad agreement on national priorities which, up to the late 1960s, favoured industrial growth, efficiency and profitability. Since the late 1960s, however, the consensus seems to have lost much of its normative force. The experience of continuous economic growth, full employment and rising standards of living has encouraged workgroups to consider the fundamental question of how the benefits of growth should be shared out. Many seem to have concluded that business has done well at their expense. The demand for a fairer distribution of rewards has resulted in the development of bargaining over wages at plant and company level, particularly in manufacturing industry. National agreements negotiated by full-time officials are often regarded as inadequate and are thus subject to 'topping up' in the workplace. The key figure in the growth of workplace bargaining has been the shop steward, who has been able to represent aspirations of the ordinary employees much more effectively than union officials have done. Works councils have been by-passed, prompting governments to give them additional legal rights in the hope that this will restore their credibility in the eyes of the workforce. Unofficial strikes, however, have become increasingly common and in most continental countries these now represent the typical form of direct action. Much of this has a decidedly familiar ring to British ears. Indeed, one could say that since the late 1960s most of these countries have been experiencing their own versions of the Donovan Commission's 'two systems in conflict' hypothesis.

The recent experience of West Germany illustrates most of the broad trends outlined above. The legal and institutional framework of the industrial relations system in West Germany is geared almost exclusively to macro-economic objectives and priorities. From the 1950s onwards this framework was cemented by the government's pursuit of a 'cooperative' wage policy, under which 'the employers accepted the necessity of providing annual wage increases and the unions renounced the claim of effecting a redistribution of incomes by way of wage policy, agreeing to the necessity of a productivity-oriented wage policy'.[38] The 'cooperative' approach to collective bargaining undoubtedly played an important part in Germany's economic success and helped to give the German trade union movement its international reputation for responsibility and moderation. However, it left certain gaps in the bargaining system. Industry-wide and regional agreements on wages 'did not fully capture the individual enterprise's potential for granting wage increases, particularly in the case of the larger ones'.[39] To workgroups on the shop floor these agreements also seemed increasingly remote from reality. The works councils might have filled this gap if they had been allowed to do so by law, but the legal framework frowned on bargaining at plant level. The councils 'could not effectively take the initiative to enforce or defend wage additions, secure improvements in working conditions, or prevent their deterioration. Active and militant groups developed to fill the gap left by the inability of the works councils to satisfy local expectations. They responded by organizing spontaneous strikes.'[40] Waves of unofficial stoppages occurred in several manufacturing industries in the autumn of 1969, and were repeated in 1970 and 1973. They were essentially a protest against the involvement of trade union leaders in the 'cooperative' wage policy and as such they underlined the growing significance of the shop steward as an alternative focus of authority. They also reflected a decline in the normative influence of postwar macro-economic goals – notably price stability and full employment. Where foreign *Gastarbeiter* were involved, other themes emerged from these stoppages, notably demands for a slow-down in the pace of work and longer rest periods. There is no doubt that these developments pose a threat to the assumptions on which the West German industrial relations system has

211

been based since the late 1940s. West Germany's prospects for economic growth now depend on higher labour productivity and on investment in advanced technology industries. West German labour costs are now the highest in the Western world and unless major increases in productivity can be achieved, labour-intensive industries will become increasingly uncompetitive. This will almost certainly generate additional frictions at plant level and the demand for extended joint regulation will grow. If the trade unions are to retain any authority in the workplace they will have to abandon their traditional role as guardians of a 'cooperative' wage policy and begin to represent the needs and aspirations of their members.

Trade union leaders throughout the Western world are now facing an increasingly complex problem of authority. The norms and aspirations of their members on the shop floor are less and less receptive to the needs of the national economy as defined in broad understandings at national level. The increasing involvement of trade union leaders in government policy-making, which in Britain has taken the form of the 'social contract', is in fact a European-wide development. As governments have become more and more preoccupied with the problems of rising inflation, slow growth and increasing unemployment, so they have sought to involve trade union leaders in the shaping of macro-economic policies. But the growth of workplace bargaining and the rise of the shop steward have compelled most trade union leaders to come to terms with the fact that their authority – and thus their credibility with governments and employers – ultimately rests on the consent of the rank-and-file membership. Consequently it has proved impossible to revive the consensus which prevailed during the postwar period. Trade union leaders may well be prepared to cooperate with governments in helping to restrain inflation and promote economic growth, but they are no longer in a position to offer their help unconditionally. They are now only too well aware that if they put the full weight of their moral authority behind government policies which materially damage the interests of their members, they will lose even more credibility on the shop floor. Consequently in most countires they have demanded and usually received a *quid pro quo* from the government in terms of social policies and employment legislation which they believe will help them sell an otherwise unpalatable economic policy to their members. Perhaps the classic example of *quid pro quo* bargaining at national level is the developing relationship between the trade union confederations and the government in Sweden. During the 1950s and 1960s the unions, in return for their cooperation on wages policy, successfully pushed for massive increases in social security provisions and public housing. By the early 1970s, however, the unions' legislative objectives had begun to encompass employment rights hitherto reserved for free collective bargaining. In recent years legislation has been enacted which gives employees greater job security and a bigger say in management decision-making, including representation on company boards.

The 'social contract' strategy, however, both in Sweden and elsewhere, is by no means without problems. Trade union aspirations in bargaining with governments usually involve substantial increases in public spending which, in a period of relatively high inflation and slow growth, have to be paid for by higher taxation. When the burden of direct taxation increases, however, the effect is to erode the disposable income of all employees, although of course the higher paid groups naturally suffer most. It must be obvious that organized groups who are being exhorted to moderate their wage claims at a time when the cost of living is rising rapidly are hardly likely to be impelled towards moderation if direct taxation is eating away more and more of their earnings. In both Sweden and Britain, governments have recently recognized that the burden of direct taxation is too heavy and must be reduced in the interests of restraining wage inflation. In practical terms this implies either a shift in the distribution of the tax burden towards indirect taxation or a reduction in the total volume of public spending or a combination of both. The difficulties experienced with social-contract-type agreements, however, also call into question the logic behind them. Is it realistic to assume that when real incomes are either stagnant or rising more slowly than the rate of growth to which employees have become accustomed, the latter will accept increases in various social benefits as a palatable alternative to higher money wages? Do legislative gains for employees, even including the right to representation on company boards, really carry as much weight in the scales as the opportunity to bargain freely on money wages? In short, can one always assume that the aspirations conveyed to governments by trade union leaders are in fact the same as those which influence the behaviour of their rank-and-file members? Clearly not. This does not mean of course that employees attach no value to higher social benefits or to opportunities for improving the intrinsic rewards which they receive from their work; nor does it mean that they are indifferent to proposals for 'power-sharing' in the workplace. The point is that neither governments, nor employers, nor trade union leaders should assume that employees will regard these gains as an adequate *substitute* for increases in real incomes. Consequently the normative influence of 'social contract' strategies must be regarded as limited, at least in periods of recession.

This brief discussion of European trends suggests, therefore, that many of the problems which policy-makers have encountered at all levels within the British industrial relations system are by no means peculiar to Britain. Clearly, comparisons cannot be pushed too far since every national system of industrial relations has legal, institutional and behavioural characteristics which are not replicated elsewhere. There are several important differences between British and continental industrial relations which cannot be overlooked. The postwar social consensus, for example, was weaker in Britain and had virtually disappeared by the early 1950s. The emphasis on voluntarism has always been stronger in Britain and the development of an interventionist framework of labour law is of relatively recent origin. The structure of trade unionism in Britain is much more fragmented and asymmetrical than in some continental countries. The formal authority of the central organizations of both trade unions and employers in Britain is generally weaker. Macro-economic differences are also important. Real incomes in Britain have increased more slowly than on the continent and the level of labour productivity is relatively low. Other differences, however, are more problematic.

It is generally believed that the British trade unions are more powerful and more militant than those elsewhere in Western Europe. This is, however, questionable. The obvious measure of strength is the density of union membership and using this index trade unionism in Britain appears stronger than it is in France, Germany and the Netherlands, as strong as in Ireland, Italy and Luxembourg, but weaker than in Sweden, Belgium, Denmark and Norway. In terms of militancy, the most obvious index is the number of strikes. Taking the period 1965–74, and using the measure of stoppages per 1,000 employees, Britain emerges as considerably more strike-prone than Belgium, Denmark, France, Germany, the Netherlands and Sweden, but less strike prone than Italy and Ireland. Outside Western Europe, it should be noted that Canada, the USA, Australia and Finland all show a greater liability to stoppages than Britain, while Japan and New Zealand show less. However, the validity of this index as a measure of *trade union* militancy could be challenged on the grounds that most stoppages in Western Europe (including Britain) are not officially supported by the unions. Furthermore it could be argued that if certain workgroups have been readier to take strike action in Britain than in most other EEC countries it may be that, because of the slow growth of real incomes, they have had more reason to do so. Finally it has occasionally been argued that British workers are more hostile to change and innovation than their continental counterparts. This allegation has never been supported by much evidence and even if it may have had some validity in the postwar period it is doubtful if there are significant differences at the present time. In any case it must be recognized that employee attitudes towards change are shaped by a variety of factors. Much depends on the way in which change is introduced and on the extent to which the economic, social and legal environment encourages employees to accept change. Explanations which rely exclusively on the alleged moral and psychological characteristics of the employees concerned are of little validity.

A strategy for government

The changing role of the state within the British system of industrial relations has already been outlined. At the time of writing this role has two potentially divergent aspects. On the one hand, the government has enacted legislation which strengthens the employment rights of the individual and encourages the spread of collective bargaining. The intention here is presumably to help create a more equal distribution of bargaining power in industry and to increase the influence of trade unions over management decision-making. On the other hand, the government is still committed to restraining the level of wage settlements, and while its influence over wage bargaining in the private sector ultimately depends on voluntary cooperation, neither the present government nor its successor can be expected to refrain from playing a dominant role in public sector negotiations. Thus, while the present framework of labour law seeks to encourage employers and trade unions to establish collective bargaining relationships and refine their procedural rules, the substantive outcome of collective bargaining has been, is now and will continue to be influenced in some way or other by the government acting through the medium of incomes policy. What may appear to be a contradiction or at least an ambiguity in the role of the state, however, becomes less significant if one regards collective bargaining as a political as well as an economic institution. As Flanders has pointed out, white-collar and manual employees alike can gain certain non-economic advantages from collective bargaining:

They are interested in the regulation of labour markets and of labour management because such regulation defines their rights, and consequently their status and security, and so liberates them from dependence on chance and the arbitrary will of others. Equally they are interested in participating as directly as possible in the making and administration of these rules in order to have a voice in shaping their own destiny and the decisions on which it most depends.[41]

But while this is no doubt true of many employees for at least some of the time, it must also be recognized that many rank-and-file union members take a predominantly instrumental view of collective bargaining, or in other words they evaluate its usefulness primarily by the material benefits it brings them.[42] Indeed, one could reasonably argue that in the eyes of many employees the purely economic functions of trade unionism may well be even more important at the present time, after two or three years in which incomes have declined in real terms, than they have ever been before. Consequently it may be that the ambiguity inherent in a policy which seeks on the one hand to encourage the spread of collective bargaining and on the other to regulate its substantive outcome will become more pronounced.

Here indeed is the dilemma facing trade union leaders and activists at the present time. Rank-and-file members expect their union to negotiate increases in their real incomes every year and union leaders are under considerable pressure to meet this expectation. Yet their ability to do so is severely limited by a number of economic and institutional factors, all of which have been discussed earlier in this book. It is worth emphasizing, however, that incomes policy is only one of the constraints which employers and trade union negotiators have to take into account, and the removal of this particular constraint does not make collective bargaining 'free'. Other constraints are still likely to have some effect on the final wage settlement, notably the firm's ability to pay, the going rate for comparable workgroups elsewhere, the rate of inflation experienced since the last settlement and the rate anticipated before the next one, and the extent to which the government is prepared to allow inflationary settlements to work through to the level of employment (i.e. its monetary policy). In the public sector, of course, the notion of free collective bargaining has been illusory for many years, whether the government of the day has been pursuing a formal incomes policy or not. If the present government's strategy of regenerating the manufacturing base and curtailing the growth of the non-market sector remains intact, then trade union leaders will have to come to terms with the reality of permanent controls on public sector wage bargaining. Conversely, this strategy implies that employers and unions in the private sector will have to be given more discretion than they have had in recent years to negotiate agreements which meet both their own aspirations as well as the overall need for higher productivity. Consequently trade union leaders and members alike will have to accept that if the criterion of efficiency is to play a prominent part in wage bargaining once again, some groups will inevitably do better than others.

Their acceptance is unlikely to be forthcoming, however, if the government simply uses its control over public spending and the money supply in order to 'discipline' unduly ambitious negotiators. As Thomas Balogh has pointed out, 'Free collective bargaining without a social contract limiting the rise in incomes is incompatible with full employment even in a closed economy. Its effects on relative wages – which depend on the strength of union monopoly – are as artifical and distorting as even a rigidly egalitarian incomes policy would produce.'[43] Trade union officials who represent workgroups with little market power are only too well aware that in the absence of an effective incomes policy their members lose out in relative terms to those groups with more bargaining strength. This realization partly explains the groundswell of support within the trade union movement for the flat-rate incomes policies of 1975/6 and 1976/7 after the experience of relatively free bargaining in 1974/5. However, the combination of flat-rate wage norms and 'egalitarian' social policies (which have in any case been largely abandoned since 1975) has not found favour with every workgroup. Flat-rate norms dispense rough justice, but the longer they last the rougher the justice becomes. Moreover, by effectively ruling out *quid pro quo* bargaining, they also discourage initiatives to improve efficiency and reform bargaining structures. Consequently, incomes policy must now be directed towards two objectives. First, employers and unions must be given some incentive to negotiate increases in efficiency. Second, an institutional framework must be devised through which the implementation of the policy guidelines can be monitored and major relativity problems analysed. In other words the strategy pursued between 1965 and 1970, in which wage *restraint* was used as a means of promoting bargaining *reform*, must be built upon. This would, of course, give rise to considerable opposition. The CBI is known to be hostile to a revival of productivity bargaining at least in the form it took between 1967 and 1970, while the TUC has always disliked having to deal with institutions like the NBPI and the Pay Board. Neither of these obstacles, however, is insuperable. An efficiency-biased incomes policy need not be cast in the same mould as its predecessor of the late 1960s, and the machinery for monitoring its implementation at plant level could be made more effective.

Ultimately, however, the success of any incomes policy depends less on the effectiveness of the machinery for enforcing it than on a widespread acceptance on both sides of industry that the policy itself is necessary. After several years of rigid, statutory or quasi-statutory policies it is reasonable to assume that employers and trade union representatives want much more freedom to negotiate agreements which meet their own needs. The government's priority is to ensure that this freedom does not result in another round of beggar-my-neighbour bargaining which drives up the rate of inflation and leaves the weaker groups worse off than when they started. At the very least this means that there cannot be, as there was under the policy of 1965 to 1970, scope for virtually un-limited pay increases in the name of productivity, if only because the source of any increase in productivity is not always easy to identify. The fundamental point which the next incomes policy must help to drive home is that a low level of efficiency is in many cases the principal cause of low pay. The problem, therefore, is to identify those obstacles which stand in the way of higher efficiency and to assist employers and union representatives to remove them. The work of the NBPI suggests that an expert, independent agency can make a valuable contribution in this field. As Aubrey Jones has pointed out, in its later days

the width of the Board's inquiries was beginning to elicit the coopera-tion of trade unions. In so far as the reference allowed it to, the Board could inquire, not only into the utilization of labour, but also into efficiency in distribution, the purchasing and use of materials, or the level and comparison of overheads. These non-labour matters were often of great interest to trade unions, for they were relevant to the costs per unit of output, to the future of an industry or firm and therefore to the context within which wage negotiations took place.[44]

The adoption of the Added Value criterion (as suggested in Chap-ter Three) would also further this objective. Clearly, an agency with the necessary expertise at its disposal cannot be put together overnight and no doubt a considerable period of time will elapse before the value of its work is fully appreciated by employers and unions. Nevertheless, there is no doubt in the mind of the present writer that this is the direction in which incomes policy must develop. The only alternatives would be to rely either on a policy of tight control over wage bargaining in the public sector with the government relying on monetary weapons to restrain inflation in the private sector, or on a system of rigid legal controls over individual pay and prices. Neither of these policies would do much, if anything, to improve industrial efficiency, nor would they encourage the parties to adopt a joint problem-solving approach to collective bargaining.

It could, of course, be argued that if an efficiency-biased incomes policy is to be successful, it must result in a shake-out of labour from those industries, companies and public organizations which are at the present time overmanned. Unemployment, however, has already risen to its highest level since the 1930s (approximately 1·6 million in the autumn of 1977) and may never return to the level which was customary during the 1950s and 1960s. In 1976 the Manpower Services Commission estimated that if the level of unemployment in Britain was to be brought down to 700,000 by 1980, no fewer than *one million* new jobs would have to be created during this four-year period. Not even the most optimistic observer, however, would claim that this target is likely to be achieved. The rate of growth which the government is looking for in the manufacturing sector, while extremely high in historical terms, will be achieved – if it is achieved at all – primarily by investing more in labour-saving equipment and by making better use of the existing labour force. In other words, it is unlikely that an expansion in the market sector, even if rapid and sustained, will make much impression on the level of unemployment. Nor will the non-market sector be able to mop up the labour which industry does not want – as it did in the late 1960s and early 1970s – since it is crucial to the government's strategy that public spending should be kept under severe restraint. Productivity bargaining was conceived and practised in an era when labour was thought to be in short supply. Now that the economy has too much labour in relation to its needs, the idea of negotiating improvements in efficiency which may lead to a further contraction of employment is hardly likely to appeal to trade unionists. Consequently it could be argued that the latter will only accept an efficiency-biased incomes policy which offers some safeguards against substantial redundancy, or in other words which has only a limited effect on productivity.

The argument summarized above is one to which there is no easy answer, at least in the short term. If the extra resources which come from North Sea oil are invested in new, high technology industries which have a bright future then clearly *some* new jobs will be created, but not enough to reduce radically the level of unemployment. In the meantime the labour-intensive industries will continue to shed labour as capital investment picks up – a trend which may be slowed down but will not, and indeed should not, be halted by the current framework of employment law. Another wage explosion, however, would simply accelerate the contraction of employment in both the market and non-market sectors. It follows that if the government wishes to use incomes policy in order to improve the level of industrial efficiency, it will have to do two things. Firstly, it must be prepared to invest more resources in a national training strategy, so that the growth industries of the future are not held back by an inadequate supply of specialist labour. Secondly, it must expand its current commitment to job creation, so that those who for various reasons cannot be included in a retraining programme are not left sitting on their hands. The importance of training and retraining has already been recognized in Britain and more resources are now being invested in this field (through the Manpower Services Commission and the Training Opportunities Scheme) than ever before. Nevertheless, the scale of Britain's efforts are still small by comparison with some other European countries, particularly Sweden. In the words of one observer:

Paradoxically, because Sweden has an employment policy, it can operate the economy with quite a high rate of 'unemployment' ... (but) the unemployment equivalent is not made up of people on the scrap heap, wasting and deteriorating away. For every individual who is unemployed in a way comparable with unemployment in Britain, there are two who are occupied in adult training or public relief works programmes which are productive and fruitful pauses between spells of market-generated employment.[45]

The concept of job creation by the government, however, has attracted much criticism from those who believe that employment can only be generated by market forces, i.e. by the operation of supply and demand.[46] But the claim that 'make-work' schemes merely divert resources from the sector of the economy which can generate 'real' employment to the one which cannot assumes that the former would in fact create enough new jobs to absorb most of the surplus labour if it had more resources. For the reasons noted above, this assumption seems increasingly dubious. A policy of simply removing the 'obstacles and distortions' which are thought to inhibit the benign workings of the market will *not* solve our unemployment problem. Once this is accepted, the case for a policy to mitigate the social effects of high unemployment becomes overwhelming. For it must also be accepted that the majority of those in Britain who are currently without a job almost certainly *want* to work, regard being out of work as unpleasant, and may turn to extreme solutions if enough of them remain unemployed for a prolonged period.[47]

In summary, therefore, it should be recognized that in the climate of the late 1970s, the government's strategy in industrial relations cannot be confined to the encouragement of collective bargaining in the hope that employers and trade unions will be able, from positions of relative equality, to solve their own problems without any further advice or intervention from the centre. As long as collective bargaining exists, both sides will expect a reasonable degree of freedom to settle their own problems in their own way. This expectation has been encouraged by the traditional stance of government in Britain towards the conduct of industrial relations and is too deeply rooted in our existing framework of institutions to be ignored. The problem for governments, therefore, is how to persuade employers and trade unions to change their customary practices in accordance with the changing needs of the country as a whole. The experience we have gained since the late 1960s suggests that there are no quick and painless solutions to this problem. Change can only be achieved through involvement, persuasion and agreement. Consequently the government can only indicate to employers and trade unions the direction it would like them to take, give them tangible incentives to take it, and make them fully aware of the consequences of not doing so. For some time now the most urgent problem facing policy makers in Britain and in many other Western Countries has been that of reconciling employees' aspirations for higher standards of living with the need to keep inflation at a level which permits these aspirations to be satisfied and yet does not at the same time damage the competitiveness of industry and weaken the sources of economic growth. No country has as yet been entirely successful in reconciling these conflicting priorities, but Britain has in many ways been less successful than most. These conflicting pressures *can*, however, be reconciled more effectively in the future if the kind of strategy outlined above is adopted. The connection between pay, profitability, employment and efficiency must play the dominant role in the process of wage determination. The government must assist employers and trade unions to recognize the importance of this relationship by establishing a new institutional catalyst for reform and by helping to sustain a constructive dialogue between the parties concerned. Finally, while encouraging the parties to follow its guidelines, the government must also take further action to remove identifiable obstacles to change, in so far as these *can* be removed by government. In short, the government can at least do something to create a climate of opinion on the shop floor which is favourable to change and innovation. In recent years much of its effort has been misdirected, but this is hardly surprising in a country where most politicians and civil servants have had little practical experience of industrial relations and have traditionally made it their business not to obtain such experience. One would hope that the lessons which have been learned so painfully over the past few years will not be forgotten. One would also hope, though with much less confidence, that the ends and means of industrial relations policy at national level might eventually be shaped by a bipartisan consensus. Government intervention in industrial relations has typically reflected short-term priorities. Incomes policies, for example, have usually been introduced in response to an immediate financial crisis, leaving both employers and unions with the impression that they will be discarded or at least relaxed once the crisis is over. No government has yet had sufficient political will to spell out to either side the need for a long-term approach to the regulation of collective bargaining. Until this is done, the credibility and thus the effectiveness of the state as a source of authority within the industrial relations system must necessarily be limited.

Summary

The relevance of a planned approach to change in industrial relations can hardly be exaggerated, whether the focus of action is at national, industry, company or workplace level. How, then, can managements and trade unionists be persuaded to adopt this approach? The Donovan Commission relied on the investigatory work of the CIR which, once it was made known to the industrial relations world at large, would dispel 'ignorance' on all sides and induce managers to initiate reforms. Donovan's model for reform was the formal, written plant agreement covering a relatively wide range of substantive issues and backed by comprehensive procedures. In retrospect, however, one can see that the Donovan approach was both optimistic and superficial. Firstly, while noting the lack of industrial relations policies at company level, the Commission skipped lightly over the problems of formulating and implementing these policies. The development of a company industrial relations policy will in practice have important repercussions for the role and status of line management, for the balance of decision-making authority between workplace and head office, for the attitude of management towards collective bargaining, for the scope of management authority and for the general level of efficiency within the organization. It would therefore be naïve to assume that any management, no matter how competent it may be, will be able to resolve difficulties of this magnitude without a long process of trial and error. Secondly, Donovan greatly underestimated the forces of conservatism within the industrial relations system. The Commission tended to assume that 'ignorance' was at the root of outdated practices and institutions, whereas in reality the situation is much more complex than this. When substantive or procedural change is proposed, there will inevitably be implications for both the balance of bargaining power and the structure of participation within the organization. Should management preserve the right to initiate change unilaterally, while the trade unions retain the right to obstruct or veto that change (perhaps through a *status quo* procedure)? Or should change be planned and introduced as a joint problem-solving exercise, which implies a much greater degree of trade union participation in the management process than has hitherto been customary? Do the unions actually want to become involved in management decision-making to this extent, or do they prefer to retain the right to oppose, which implies a more indirect form of participation? Again, fundamental questions of this kind are not easily answered. Thirdly, Donovan repeatedly emphasized the importance of formalized procedures and bargaining structures in preserving peace and orderly behaviour on the shop floor. But there is no reason to suppose that the formalization of rules will in itself restore order or improve efficiency; indeed it may well generate conflict where none previously existed. Procedures play a dominant role in the conduct of industrial relations at any level, but even where the rules are comprehensive, formal and jointly agreed, there is no certainty that they will always be observed. The effectiveness of procedures depends on there being a strong moral commitment on both sides to the observance of the rules and on the existence of a considerable degree of mutual trust. In workplaces where Fox's 'low-trust' relations are the norm, formalized procedures may simply institutionalize the lack of trust. In short, the process of changing procedural and substantive rules may frequently introduce a greater degree of formality into workplace bargaining and this will in itself have costs as well as benefits.

One of the most outstanding features of industrial relations in Britain is, however, the general absence of direct conflict in the vast majority of workplaces. The concentration of stoppages in a relatively small number of industries and establishments may be explained in terms of the quality of management, the technological characteristics of the work situation, the size of the plant, the quality of the trade union leadership, the effectiveness of the procedural rules, the nature of the payment system, the influence of outside agencies, the historical development of labour relations in the organization and so on. The point is that the reform of bargaining styles and structures as advocated by Donovan can affect only some of these variables and in practice it may not affect them in quite the way that Donovan anticipated. Perhaps the crucial weakness in the Donovan strategy, however, was its thinking on the problem of *motivating* change in industrial relations. One of the most important lessons which has emerged from the experience of recent years is that managements and trade unionists respond not to well-meaning exhortation but to the pressure of external forces and events. If it is indeed the case that most companies and organizations have yet to develop a systematic approach to the management of industrial relations – in other words, a *policy* – then the inference must surely be that they have as yet seen no necessity for such an approach. In other words the pressure from the external environment has been insufficient in many cases to generate the kind of internal changes that are required.

Over the next few years, however, this situation may alter quite dramatically. The framework of employment rights introduced in 1975 should already have given many senior managers an incentive to re-appraise various aspects of their traditional approach to labour relations. Any legislation which increases the overhead cost of employing people and limits management's freedom to dispose of its manpower as it wishes will almost certainly provoke some kind of rethinking in the upper reaches of the organization. This indeed is the best argument for introducing some form of legislation on worker directors and also for compelling companies to disclose more information for collective bargaining purposes. Neither of these innovations will in practice fulfil the expectations of their more uncritical advocates. They will not in themselves bring about a revolution in the management of industrial relations. What they *will* do, however, is concentrate the minds of senior managers on reappraising their approach to industrial relations. They will also tend to raise the expectations of employees and their representatives by introducing new opportunities for joint decision-making and this will bring more pressure to bear on management from within the organization. If incomes policy develops in the direction indicated above, then another and even more compelling form of pressure will be brought to bear on both managers and trade unionists, with far-reaching implications for the substance and style of collective bargaining within the workplace. Taken together, these various pressures for change will almost certainly generate *more* conflict and strikes may become more widespread than hitherto. It is high time, however, that we stopped measuring the effectiveness of our industrial relations system by its ability to avoid strikes. Peace can always be bought if the price is high enough. The kind of changes which managements and trade unions will find themselves under growing pressure to negotiate will not be achieved without a more open and pronounced articulation of conflicting interests. And, as the late Vic Feather was wont to remind us, there is no magic formula, legal or otherwise, for dealing with problems like this.

Postscript

THE course of events during the winter of 1977/8 has in many respects confirmed the analysis presented in the foregoing chapters. The government has succeeded in enforcing the 10 per cent ceiling on pay settlements in the public sector with relatively few prolonged stoppages, although at the time of writing certain key groups have yet to settle. In the private sector (and in coal mining), by contrast, the extensive use of the 'self-financing' productivity deal clauses in the policy have increased average earnings well beyond 10 per cent. The implications of this development for inflation and unemployment have yet to be seen. The number of working days lost through strikes in 1977 as a whole reached nearly 10 million, or more than three times that of the exceptionally peaceful year of 1976. Although most industry groups experienced an increase in strike activity, the biggest upsurge occurred in motor vehicles and engineering. This presumably reflects the increasing frustration of skilled work-groups with the erosion of their differentials over the previous two years. It seems more than likely, therefore, that many of the productivity deals negotiated to date will have been geared to the needs of these groups.

Meanwhile the government has made it clear that when Phase Three expires in July 1978, there will be no question of abandoning incomes policy. Indeed, certain ministers have intimated that they would like to see a movement towards the kind of incomes policy which has been operated in West Germany over the past few years. Presumably the government would indicate the maximum overall increase in earnings compatible with a particular target for economic growth and price inflation and then leave managements and trade unionists to negotiate within that global figure. While there is much to be said for this approach, the present problems of the UK economy require additional measures. If a relatively low ceiling (of, say, 5 per cent) is placed on the growth of earnings in the next round of settlements, there will have to be additional scope for productivity-linked improvements. In recent months public awareness of the relationship between low productivity and low pay has undoubtedly increased. There is a growing realization that, in the absence of a major upswing in world trade, large sections of British manufacturing industry will become even more vulnerable to foreign competition unless managements achieve radical improvements in efficiency. Productivity is, therefore, the key to our present unemployment problem. Unless manufacturing industry becomes more efficient, unemployment will go on rising, and governments will be unable to resort to conventional Keynesian policies in order to reverse this trend. At the time of writing there is no sign of an upturn in manufacturing investment, so that if there is to be a significant increase in productivity during 1978/9 it will have to be achieved mainly through collective bargaining.

If incomes policy is to be a permanent feature of collective bargaining, as certain ministers have now belatedly recognized, then the re-establishment of a central investigatory and monitoring agency cannot be postponed much longer. The problem is, of course, that such an agency will only be successful if trade unions and employers cooperate with it, and the resistance to third-party interference in collective bargaining is still deep-rooted. Like the Habsburg monarchy before 1914, the concept of free collective bargaining has long been moribund, yet it continues to exercise a strong influence over man's minds. This will not easily be dispelled, but the longer the task is postponed the more difficult it will be.

March 1978

NOTES

Notes

Chapter 1

The New Militancy

1. T. Nicholls, *Ownership, Control and Ideology*, Allen & Unwin, 1969, p. 239. See also T. Kempner, K. Macmillan and K. H. Hawkins, *Business and Society*, Penguin Books, 1976, pp. 50–83.

2. Paul Johnson, 'Towards the Parasite State', *New Statesman*, 3 September 1976.

3. An opinion poll conducted by Market and Opinion Research International towards the end of 1975, for example, revealed that 66 per cent of trade unionists and 76 per cent of non-unionists agreed with the proposition that 'trade unions have too much power in Britain today', while 56 per cent of trade unionists and 69 per cent of non-unionists believed that most unions were controlled by a small number of 'militants and political extremists'. (*Economist*, 10 January 1976).

4. Ferdynand Zweig, *The British Worker*, Penguin Books, 1952, pp. 181–2.

5. Allan Flanders, *Management and Unions*, Faber, 1970.

6. Alan Fox, *A Sociology of Work in Industry*, Collier Macmillan, 1971, p. 28.

7. Sidney and Beatrice Webb, *Industrial Democracy*, London, 1898, pp. 597–8.

8. See H. A. Clegg, Alan Fox and A. F. Thompson, *A History of British Trade Unions since 1889*, vol. I, *1889–1910*, Oxford University Press, 1964, p. 9.

9. S. and B. Webb, op. cit., p. 562.

10. Clegg, Fox and Thompson, op. cit., p. 168.

11. See Eric Wigham, *The Power to Manage*, Macmillan, 1973; 'Foreign competitors were working longer hours and often paying lower wages. It was a matter of survival (for the engineering employers) to make the most economical use of new machines, to start enough apprentices to provide the skilled men of the future, to introduce piecework where it would raise output, to make sure that their foremen gave them undivided loyalty. They found it infuriating to be thwarted at every turn by the aggressive district organizations of the Amalgamated Society of Engineers' (p. 30).

233

12. S. and B. Webb, op. cit., p. 391; also Clegg, Fox and Thompson, op. cit, 472–3.

13. Eric Wigham, *Strikes and the Government, 1893–1974*, Macmillan 1976, p. 57.

14. E. H. Phelps Brown, 'New Wine in Old Bottles: Reflections on the Changed Working of Collective Bargaining in Britain', *British Journal of Industrial Relations*, July 1973.

15. Barbara Wootton, *The Social Foundations of Wage Policy*, Allen & Unwin, 1961, p. 160.

16. W. W. Daniel, *The PEP Survey on Inflation* (Broadsheet No. 553), PEP July 1975, p. 18.

17. Wootton, op. cit., p. 161.

18. Daniel, op. cit.

19 Hilde Behrend, 'The Impact of Inflation on Pay Increase Expectations and Ideas of Fair Pay', *Industrial Relations Journal*, Spring 1974.

20. Dudley Jackson, H. A. Turner and Frank Wilkinson, *Do Trade Unions Cause Inflation?*, University of Cambridge (Occasional Paper No. 36), 1972.

21. In Sweden much of the dissatisfaction has been concentrated among white-collar workers, who are generally believed to favour a widening of differentials and lower direct taxation. See Nils Elvander, 'Collective Bargaining and Incomes Policy in the Nordic Countries: A Comparitive Analysis', *British Journal of Industrial Relations*, November 1974. In Germany the growing burden of tax and social security contributions was reported to be a factor in the upsurge of militancy on the shop floor in 1972 and 1973. One source estimated that increased deductions accounted for nearly half of any nominal increase in money wages (*Economist*, 14 April 1973).

22. Robert Price and G. S. Bain, 'Union Growth Revisited: 1948–1974 in Perspective', *British Journal of Industrial Relations*, November 1976. The density of white-collar unionism increased from 29 per cent in 1964 to 39 per cent in 1974 over the economy as a whole. The advance in manufacturing industry alone, however, was even more impressive, from 12.1 per cent in 1964 to 32.0 per cent in 1974.

23. B. C. Roberts, Ray Loverbridge and John Gennard, *Reluctant Militants*, Heinemann, 1972, pp. 323–4.

24. S. and B. Webb, op. cit., pp. 658–9.

25. Robert Bacon and Walter Eltis, *Britain's Economic Problem: Too Few Producers*, Macmillan, 1975, p. 8.

26. See David Wilson, *Dockers*, Fontana/Collins, 1972, and Michael Mellish, *The Docks After Devlin*, Heinemann, 1972.

27. See Eric Wigham, *The Power to Manage*, p. 30. On the eve of the

great lock-out of 1897, the president of the newly-formed Engineering Employers' Federation told union representatives that questions concerning the introduction and manning of machines could no longer be settled locally on the basis of local custom: '... of late years there has been a great number of aggressions made by your Society on the liberty of the employers. The employer had to give way to these aggressions because he stood alone and he could not resist them. That time, I am happy to say, has passed and the employer now meets you on equal terms, and therefore I don't think the local customs which are now existing could be taken as a rule for local customs in the future.'

28. The constraining effect of labour market conditions sharply increased after the General Strike, when it appeared that the trade unions had staked everything on one desperate gamble and had lost. One female trade unionist, speaking from personal experience, has said: 'People left the unions because they left their jobs and became unemployed. Many of the rest didn't bother with the unions, they were just card holders. When there are ten men waiting at the gate for your job, you were not going to be very militant – you only need to say one word out of place and you're out. Unemployment became the main problem.' Quoted in Margaret Morris, *The General Strike*, Penguin Books, 1976, p. 277.

29. Phelps Brown, op. cit.

30. H. A. Turner, G. Clack and G. Roberts, *Labour Relations in the Motor Industry*, Allen & Unwin, 1967, pp. 336–8. The authors estimated that between 1946 and 1964 30 per cent of all the days lost through strikes in the car industry were attributable to disputes over wage structures and work loads, $21\frac{1}{2}$ per cent were due to disputes over trade union status, 18 per cent were caused by redundancy and short-time working, 8 per cent arose from individual dismissals, and 6 per cent were concerned with 'management questions'. Overall, the relative significance of non-wage issues was found to be increasing (pp. 65–8).

31. Huw Beynon, *Working for Ford*, Allen Lane, 1973, p. 138.

32. Turner, Clack and Roberts, op. cit., p. 336.

33. Royal Commission on Trade Unions and Employers' Associations (Donovan Commission), *Report*, Cmnd 3623, HMSO, June 1968, p. 105.

34. Flanders, op. cit., p. 276.

35. William Brown, 'Productive of Change', *New Society*, 14 November 1974. See also Allan Flanders, *The Fawley Productivity Agreements*, Faber, 1964.

36. See Flanders, *Management and Unions*, op. cit., p. 270.

37. W. W. Daniel and Niel McIntosh, *Incomes Policy and Collective*

Bargaining at the Workplace (Broadsheet 541), PEP May 1973, p. 5.

38. Flanders, *Management and Unions*, op. cit., p. 155.

39. B. Towers, T. G. Whittingham and A. W. Gottschalk, eds., *Bargaining for Change*, Allen & Unwin, 1972, p. 12.

40. For a discussion of the limitations of the Redundancy Payments Act see Robert H. Fryer, 'Redundancy, Values and Public Policy', Discussion Paper, Industrial Relations Research Unit, University of Warwick, November 1972.

41. W. W. Daniel, for example, in his investigation of redundancies following the closure of the GEC/AEI factory in Woolwich, found that there was no relationship between the amount of severance payment received and a predisposition to look favourably on redundancy; indeed the reverse was true. (See W. W. Daniel, *Whatever Happened to the Workers in Woolwich?* PEP, 1972, p. 102.) See also Dorothy Wedderburn, *Redundancy and the Railwaymen*, CUP, 1965.

42. H. A. Clegg, 'Mobility of Labour', *National Provincial Bank Review*, May 1965.

43. In *Farthing* v. *Midland Household Stores* (1974).

44. See, for example, W. W. Daniel, *A National Survey of the Unemployed* (Broadsheet No. 546), PEP October 1974. Nearly three quarters of the respondents in Daniel's survey said that it had been 'bad' or 'very bad' for them personally to be out of work; only 28 per cent said that it had 'not been too bad', and they were largely those who had reconciled themselves to being out of work. Nor does the available evidence support the popular view that the financial cushion provided for the unemployed is now so large and comfortable that many are neither inconvenienced by loss of work nor are they motivated to seek another job. Thus Daniel found that those who were most concerned about being unemployed were precisely those who were receiving the *highest* unemployment benefit. See also Frank Herron, *Labour Market in Crisis: Redundancy at Upper Clyde Shipbuilders*, Macmillan, 1975.

45. *Economist*, 1 January 1977.

46. R. W. Revans, 'Participation in What', *Industrial Participation*, Winter 1974/5.

47. Alan Fox, op. cit., pp. 34–9. Fox draws an important distinction between *power* relations which carry 'connotations of pressure or coercion applied against one's consent' and *authority* relations in which sanctions are used to uphold norms which subordinates themselves regard as legitimate.

48. See Kempner, Macmillan and Hawkins, op. cit.

49. A recent survey by Market and Opinion Research International, for example, involving over 1,000 shop floor workers and over 200

managers from a variety of industries, confirms the persistence of conservative attitudes towards conventional managerial objectives alongside more critical attitudes towards the way in which much of industry is managed. Thus 98 per cent agreed that companies needed profits to plough back into investment, 86 per cent said it was important to them to live in a 'free enterprise society' and 89 per cent believed it was 'fair' for a company to pay dividends to its shareholders. But, on the other side of the coin, 86 per cent of the workers felt that the quality of management could be improved, 48 per cent thought that management was not really interested in the opinions of employees, 42 per cent said that they could do more in their present jobs 'without too much effort' (*The Times*, 13 May 1976).

50. Richard Hyman and Ian Brough, *Social Values and Industrial Relations*, Blackwell, 1975, p. 232.

51. Zweig, op. cit., p. 194.

52. Hyman and Brough, op. cit., p. 239.

53. Commission on Industrial Relations, Report No. 18, *Electrolux Ltd.*, Cmnd 4697, HMSO, June 1971, para. 119.

54. Commission on Industrial Relations, Report No. 14, *Standard Telephones and Cables Ltd.*, Cmnd 4598, HMSO, February 1971, para. 104.

55. J. W. Durcan and W. E. J. McCarthy, 'What is Happening to Strikes?', *New Society*, 2 November 1972.

56. Robert Taylor, 'The Cowley Way of Work', *New Society*, 2 May 1974. See also ACAS, *Report No. 1, Dispute Between British Leyland Cowley and AUEW and TGWU concerning Mechanical Rectifiers*.

57. Stephen Cotgrove, 'Alienation and Automation', *British Journal of Sociology*, 1972.

58. Richard Hyman, *Industrial Relations: a Marxist introduction*, Macmillan, 1975, p. 197.

59. ibid.

60. Cotgrove, op. cit. His investigation of attitudes to work among employees in various chemical plants located over a wide geographical area suggests that a significant number of workers (in fact the majority of his sample) do not regard work as 'a salient role': '... Very few found it either the main source of interest, or anxiety, or rated it important, compared with family life ... It is in this sense then that work is instrumental, as a means for the support of the family. It is in his role as father and husband that the worker finds the source of the most important, most worrying and most interesting aspects of his life. And this is for workers whose jobs are probably among the most interesting and least alientaing of any in industrial societies' (p. 446).

Chapter 2

New Pressures and Priorities

1. Allan Flanders, *Management and Unions*, Faber, 1970, pp. 83–4.

2. Richard Hyman, *Industrial Relations: A Marxist Introduction*, Macmillan, 1975, p. 193.

3. Quoted in W. Milne-Bailey, ed., *Trade Union Documents*, Bell & Sons, 1929, p. 55.

4. Marxists, of course, challenge the idea that the state has ever been genuinely neutral towards industrial relations and indeed it cannot be if one accepts the Marxist view that the state is merely an instrument of the dominant class in society. One recent commentator, for example, has argued that the voluntary system in Britain 'was "voluntary" only with an unstated, contradictory proviso: state power could be called back from the sidelines to try to compel labour discipline "in the national interest", if wage earners withheld cooperation' (John Westergaard and Henrietta Resler, *Class in a Capitalist Society*, Penguin Books 1976, p. 383). In fact if one looks back at the period from 1890 to 1906, when 'voluntarism' was firmly embedded in public policy, on the odd occasion when governments did intervene in industrial disputes, it was usually where employers had locked out their workers.

5. The National Union of Manufacturers, the Federation of British Industries and the National Confederation of Employers' Organisations all date from the years 1915–20.

6. In the aftermath of the General Strike the government came under some pressure from certain employers' associations, notably the EEF, to withdraw some of the legal immunities conferred on the unions by the Trades Disputes Act of 1906. Even then, however, none of the employers' organizations wanted the government to take a more active role in collective bargaining. Thus the NCEO argued that 'When the state is the third party with the final say, negotiations between the other two parties who are really immediately responsible becomes unreal and very largely ineffective' (Margaret Morris, *The General Strike*, Penguin Books, 1976, p. 304).

7. Royal Commission on Trade Unions and Employers' Associations (Donovan Commission), *Report*, Cmnd 3623, HMSO, June 1968, p. 21.

8. John Lovell and B. C. Roberts, *A Short History of the TUC*, Macmillan, 1968.

9. Peter Jackson and Keith Sisson, 'Employers' Confederations in Sweden and the UK and the significance of the Industrial Infrastructure', *British Journal of Industrial Relations*, November 1976. The

authors point out that the Swedish employers created a strong central organization in the aftermath of the general strike of 1902 in order to resist the rise of what they regarded as politically extreme trade unionism. Once the employers had taken this step, the trade unions themselves had no option but to do the same.

10. Arthur Marsh, *Manager and Shop Stewards: Shop Floor Revolution?*, Institute of Personnel Management, 1973.

11. In most Western European countries systems of works councils were established in the immediate postwar period through which both joint consultation *and* joint regulation were to be extended. While opinions on the effectiveness of these councils differ, their existence has compelled managements to consult their employees on a wide range of substantive issues and to 'co-determine' certain other issues in direct negotiation.

12. The number of unofficial strikes in engineering rose 'more or less steadily' between 1953 and 1966 to the extent that by the end of the period these strikes were over three times as numerous as they were at the beginning. Yet the *proportion* of firms involved in unofficial strikes remained at less than 10 per cent even in 1966. Even these relatively strike-prone firms usually experienced only 'minor and infrequent dislocations'. See W. E. J. McCarthy and A. I. Marsh, *Disputes Procedure in British Industry* (Royal Commission on Trade Unions and Employers' Associations, Research Paper No. 2, Part 2), HMSO, 1966.

13. R. O. Clarke, D. J. Fatchett and B. C. Roberts, *Workers' Participation in Management in Britain*, Heinemann, 1972, pp. 79–81. The authors found that 70 per cent of their respondents in the public sector reported that they had specific joint decision-making arrangements concerning redundancy and 58 per cent had similar arrangements in respect of discipline and dismissal – compared with only 25 per cent in each case in the private sector.

14. The same authors found that in only 52 per cent of the firms in their sample was it normal for changes in the method of payment to be negotiated; by the same token a large minority did not normally negotiate changes in working arrangements and a clear majority excluded discipline from any kind of joint decision-making arrangement (ibid., pp. 85–93).

15. A survey by the CIR, for example, found little evidence that shop stewards were 'innately hostile' to management and that where there was a lack of cooperation this could sometimes be explained by management's failure to accept the steward's role. See CIR Report No. 17, *Facilities Afforded to Shop Stewards*, May 1971, p. 14. Similarly, the authors of the official survey of workplace relations (1972) reported

that a majority of employees in their sample felt that stewards took a fifty-fifty view between workers and management. Most managers thought that stewards helped in varying degrees to solve industrial relations problems and over half thought they helped with production problems. See Stanley Parker, *Workplace Industrial Relations*, 1972, HMSO, 1974, pp. 52–5.

16. The same survey revealed a clear trend towards an increasing volume of bargaining at workplace and nearly half the stewards wanted to extend their range of bargaining with management (pp. 33–7).

17. Clarke, Fatchett and Roberts, op. cit., p. 87.

18. Royal Commission on Trade Unions and Employers' Associations (Donovan Commission), *Report*, op. cit., p. 33. paras. 127–30.

19. ibid., p. 111, para. 412.

20. Andrew Tessler, 'Britain's Economic Power Failure', *Management Today*, March 1975.

21. Royal Commission on Trade Unions and Employers' Associations (Donovan Commission), *Report*, op. cit., p. 40, para. 162.

22. R. F. Elliott and R. Steele, 'The Importance of National Wage Agreements', *British Journal of Industrial Relations*, March 1976.

23. Parker, op. cit.

24. W. W. Daniel and Niel McIntosh, *Incomes Policy and Collective Bargaining at the Workplace* (Broadsheet No. 541), PEP, May 1973, p. 56.

25. Royal Commission on Trade Unions and Employers' Associations (Donovan Commission), *Report*, op. cit., p. 290, para. 7.

26. Unfortunately their method of formalizing collective agreements was to introduce a presumption that all such agreements would be regarded as legally binding unless the parties specifically expressed a declaration to the contrary. Needless to say, everyone did precisely that.

27. The strategy here rested on the 'sole bargaining agency', under which multi-union bargaining structures would be tidied up by the simple expedient of conferring negotiating rights on *one* of the unions involved. The only difficulty with this otherwise splendid idea was that fragmented bargaining structures are usually based on well-organized workgroups with considerable bargaining strength. Such groups are usually unwilling to agree to any reform of bargaining structures which is likely to weaken their own bargaining position. In any case only a registered union could apply for a Sole Bargaining Agency and most unions did not register.

28. The Act laid down that dismissals should be based on the competence, conduct or redundancy of the employee. Two important limitations, however, were introduced. First, protection was limited to full-

time employees with more than two years' service; second it did not cover employees in very small firms.

29. Only a handful of unions, almost all of them catering for white-collar employees, decided to register under the Act. All were expelled from the T U C in September 1972.

30. Brian Weekes, Michael Mellish, Linda Dickens and John Lloyd, *Industrial Relations and the Limits of Law*, Blackwell, 1975, p. 223.

31. The implementation of the Act coincided with the eruption of a long-festering dispute in the docks over the right of registered dockers to handle container traffic. The dockers were fighting to preserve their jobs from further erosion by container technology; the container companies wanted to avoid using dock labour which they regarded as expensive and inefficient. When shop stewards at Liverpool began to 'black' container lorries which had not been loaded by registered dockers, some of the container companies complained to the National Industrial Relations Court. Under the Act the union involved, the T G W U, was legally responsible for the actions of its 'agents'. There then followed a series of judgements by the N I R C, the Court of Appeal and finally the House of Lords on the complex issue of trade union responsibility, which in itself had little to do with the real point at issue in the docks. For a more detailed discussion see Kevin Hawkins, *British Industrial Relations, 1945–75*, Barrie & Jenkins, 1976, pp. 106–12.

32. *Department of Employment Gazette*, June 1976. The actual annual totals of unfair dismissal applications are 5,197 (1972), 9,350 (1973), 10,109 (1974), 22,632 (1975).

33. Department of Employment, *In Working Order: A Study of Industrial Discipline*, H M S O, 1971, p. 5.

34. *Department of Employment Gazette,* June 1976. In 1972 39 per cent of all unfair dismissal applications were accounted for by construction, transport/distribution and miscellaneous services; by 1975 this proportion had risen to 44·6 per cent.

35. The Act lays down that in redundancy situations involving over 100 workers, the employer must give the unions involved at least ninety days' warning; where fewer than 100 but more than ten workers are involved, the required period of warning is thirty days. Employers must also be prepared to disclose comprehensive information about their redundancy proposals to trade union representatives and to negotiate with them on the basis of this information. If an employer fails to comply with these requirements, he can be taken to an Industrial Tribunal by the union involved and fined.

36. *Economist*, 1 January 1977.

37. Any employee who refuses to join a union which has a closed shop agreement with an employer must be able to prove that he has genuine religious reasons for not doing so. The same applies to a worker who resigns from his union in a closed shop situation and is dismissed. Such dismissals are held to be fair unless the employee can prove otherwise.

38. Michael Moran, *The Union of Post Office Workers*, Macmillan, 1974, pp. 145–7.

39. Aubrey Jones, *The New Inflation*, Penguin Books, 1973, p. 25.

40. S. G. B. Henry, M. C. Sawyer, P. Smith, 'Models of Inflation in the United Kingdom: An Evaluation', *National Institute Economic Review*, August 1976.

41. ibid.

42. D. T. Jones, 'Output Employment and Labour Productivity in Europe since 1955', *National Institute Economic Review*, November 1976.

43. Alan Fels, *The British Prices and Incomes Board*, Cambridge University Press, 1972. The Ministry of Labour (renamed the Department of Employment and Productivity in 1968) was responsible for monitoring the implementation of the policy at plant level but the machinery contained many loopholes. Firms with fewer than 100 employees 'could escape the net with relative impunity if they wished' (Fels, p. 43). Conversely, a few large workgroups with considerable bargaining power (for example, the railwaymen and the dockers) were never subjected to the full rigours of the policy.

44. *Sunday Times*, 1 October 1972.

45. W. W. Daniel, *The PEP Survey on Inflation* (Broadsheet No. 553), PEP, July 1975, p. 11.

46. *Economist*, 29 November 1975.

47. For an account of this dispute, see Kevin Hawkins, 'The Miners and Incomes Policy, 1972–75', *Industrial Relations Journal*, Summer 1975. See also John Hughes and Roy Moore, eds, *A Special Case?*, Penguin Books, 1972.

48. Frank Blackaby, 'Incomes Policy: the Longer View', *New Society*, 9 November 1972.

49. H. A. Turner and Frank Wilkinson, 'The Seventh Pay Policy', *New Society*, 17 July 1975.

50. Robert Bacon and Walter Eltis, *Britain's Economic Problem: Too Few Producers*, Macmillan, 1975. See also *Sunday Times*, 14 November 1976.

51. Bacon and Eltis, op. cit., p. 22.

52. E. H. Phelps Brown, 'New Wine in Old Bottles: Reflections on the Changed Working of Collective Bargaining in Great Britain', *British Journal of Industrial Relations*, July 1973.

53. See, for example, *Reshaping Britain: A programme of economic and social reform* (Broadsheet No. 548), PEP December 1974, pp. 42–9, 79–98.

54. ibid., p. 34.

55. ibid., pp. 37–8.

56. R. F. Elliott and R. Steele, 'The Importance of National Wage Agreements', *British Journal of Industrial Relations*, March 1976.

57. Hugh Clegg, *How to Run an Incomes Policy*, Heinemann, 1971, p. 83.

58. See, for example, William Brown, *Piecework Bargaining*, Heinemann, 1973.

Chapter 3

The Role of Incomes Policy

1. See, for example, C. F. Pratten and A. G. Atkinson, 'The use of Manpower in British Manufacturing Industry', *Department of Employment Gazette*, June 1976.

2. See D. T. Jones 'Output, Employment and Labour Productivity in Europe Since 1955', *National Institute Economic Review*, November 1976. The author observes that after 1973 the UK 'had the lowest level of labour productivity of the EEC countries covered. France and Germany were some 30 per cent higher than the UK and Belgium and the Netherlands 40 per cent and 54 per cent respectively.'

3. See, for example, *Manpower in the Chemical Industry*, NEDO, 1967. The authors of this study concluded that 'on average, each American works has only about 80 per cent of the numbers employed in the average British works, but has nearly twice as much capital invested and produced nearly three times as much'.

4. *Economist*, 20 December 1975.

5. West Midlands Economic Planning Council, 'Industrial productivity – scope for improvement', in *Midlands Tomorrow*, No. 8, 1975.

6. *Economist*, 18 December 1976.

7. NBPI, *Hours of Work, Overtime and Shiftworking* (Report No. 161), Cmnd 4554, HMSO, 1970, p. 52.

8. See Lloyd Ulman, 'Collective Bargaining and Industrial Efficiency', in Richard Caves, ed., *Britain's Economic Prospects*, Brookings Institution, 1968, p. 357. See also NBPI, *Hours of Work, Overtime and Shiftworking*, op. cit.

9. E. G. Whybrew, *Overtime Working in Britain* (Royal Commission on Trade Unions and Employers' Associations Research Paper No. 9), HMSO, 1968, p. 63, para. 180.

10. W. W. Daniel, *Wage Determination in Industry* (Broadsheet No. 563), PEP, July 1976, p. 34. It should also be noted that the position of several groups in the national league table changes quite significantly according to whether or not overtime earnings are included. In April 1974, for example, the transport and communication group ranked ninth if overtime was included; if it was excluded their position dropped to nineteenth. (See W. K. Norris, 'Differentials in Pay', *Lloyds Bank Review*, October 1975.)

11. *Sunday Times*, 3 July 1977.

12. Allan Flanders, *Management and Unions*, Faber, 1970, p. 285.

13. 'The Declining Asset', *Department of Employment Gazette*, April 1977. The authors found that 37 per cent of their sample of former skilled engineers had left their occupation due to redundancy, 28 per cent had left because the prospects for advancement were poor, 13 per cent had left because of low pay, and 9 per cent because of bad working conditions.

14. W. W. Daniel and Niel McIntosh, *Incomes Policy and Collective Bargaining at the Workplace* (Broadsheet No. 541), PEP, May 1973, pp. 55–6.

15. ibid., p. 53.

16. Royal Commission on Trade Unions and Employers' Associations (Donovan Commission), *Report*, Cmnd 3623, HMSO, June 1968, p. 28, para 106.

17. J. T. Winkler, 'The Ghost at the Bargaining Table: Directors and Industrial Relations', *British Journal of Industrial Relations*, July 1974.

18. W. W. Daniel and Niel McIntosh, *The Right to Manage?*, PEP/ MacDonald, 1972, p. 189.

19. CIR, *The Role of Management in Industrial Relations* (Report No. 34), HMSO, 1973, p. 5.

20. CIR, *Industrial Relations Training* (Report No. 38), HMSO, 1972.

21. In 1974 the AUEW reported that one in four of its 1·2 million members were employed in factories which were still not equipped with toilets (*Economist*, 9 November 1974). See Simon Caulkin, 'Industry's Class Divide', *Management Today*, August 1974.

22. Daniel and McIntosh, *The Right to Manage?*, op. cit., p. 193.

23. See Industrial Relations Report and Review No. 109. A survey by the BIM of 328 of its member firms in 1976 revealed that 37 per cent

had negotiated or granted staff conditions for at least some of their manual employees since 1971, while 70 per cent had made changes which reduced status differentials.

24. A report published by the BIM in 1976 (*Managing Manufacturing Operations*) underlines the growing impression that the main weakness in British management nowadays is not so much the neglect of the personnel function as the declining status of *production*. The authors attributed this to the academic bias of the educational system, industry's 'poor image' and the lack of incentives to take risks. They also argued that the acceptance of extra risks in industrial management, compared with the relative security of public service, should be reflected in an appropriate structure of pay relativities.

25. Tom Lupton, ed., *Payment Systems*, Penguin Books, 1972, p. 155.

26. J. R. Crossley, 'Collective Bargaining, Wage Structure and the Labour Markets in the United Kingdom', in *Wage Structure in Theory and Practice*, ed. E. M. H. Jones, North Holland Publishing Co., 1966.

27. Lupton, op. cit., p. 156. See also NBPI, *Payment by Results Systems* (Report No. 65), Cmnd 3627, HMSO, May 1968.

28. ibid.

29. W. W. Daniel and Niel McIntosh, *Incomes Policy and Collective Bargaining in the Workplace*, op. cit., p. 66.

30. William Brown and Keith Sisson, 'The Use of Comparisons in Workplace Wage Determination', *British Journal of Industrial Relations*, March 1975.

31. R. F. Elliott, 'Public Sector Wage Movements: 1950–73', *Scottish Journal of Political Economy*, vol. 24, no. 2, June 1977. See also R. F. Elliott and R. Steele, 'The Importance of National Wage Agreements', *British Journal of Industrial Relations*, March 1976. One of the few sectors in which the gap between basic rates and earnings levels has actually increased since the late 1960s is local government, where incentive schemes for manual workers have been widely adopted. See P. B. Beaumont, 'Incomes Policy, Productivity and Manual Worker Earnings in the Local Government Sector', *Local Government Studies*, January 1977.

32. Brown and Sissons, op. cit.

33. *Sunday Times*, 29 May 1977.

34. Derek Robinson, 'Differentials and Incomes Policy', *Industrial Relations Journal*, vol. 4, no. 1, Spring 1973.

35. W. W. Daniel, in *Reshaping Britain: A Programme for Economic and Social Reform*, PEP, 1974, p. 39.

36. Robinson, op. cit.

37. Alan Schofield and Tom Husband, 'Changing Differentials in

Five Manufacturing Companies, 1973–75', *Industrial Relations Journal*, vol. 8, no. 2, Summer 1977.

38. Robinson, op. cit.

39. Up to the late 1960s there was a remarkable degree of solidarity in the wage policies adopted by white-collar and blue-collar unions in Sweden, which not surprisingly produced an exceptionally egalitarian structure of relativities and differentials. Since then, however, the white-collar organizations have tended to rebel against what they consider to be unfair compression and have pressed for wider differentials. See Nils Elvander, 'Collective Bargaining and Incomes Policy in Nordic Countries', *British Journal of Industrial Relations*, November 1974.

40. Robinson, op. cit.

41. ibid.

42. Between 1970 and 1975 British Leyland gradually replaced its PBR systems with measured day work. The Cowley plant was the first establishment to implement the new pay structure. The most immediate result was a dramatic reduction in the number of small-scale, unofficial strikes, but sectional stoppages by no means disappeared. In January 1975, for example, a dispute involving a group known as engine tuners brought the Cowley plant to a standstill. The AUEW claimed that the tuners should be upgraded to fully skilled production workers. Management resisted the claim on the grounds that if conceded it would upset the entire wage structure. In the post-Ryder era, one of Leyland management's principal objectives was to reduce the number of bargaining units within the company and thereby contain these sectional pressures. The toolmakers' dispute of February/March 1977, however, clearly indicated that some groups still had strong aspirations for *more* separate bargaining units.

43. I. Boraston, H. A. Clegg and M. Rimmer, *Workplace and Union*, Heinemann, 1975.

44. A. W. J. Thompson and L. C. Hunter, 'The Level of Bargaining in a Multi-Plant Company', *Industrial Relations Journal*, vol. 5, no. 2, Summer 1975.

45. Boraston, Clegg and Rimmer, op. cit.

46. W. W. Daniel, *Wage Determination in Industry*, op. cit., pp. 50–51.

47. In the year July 1975/July 1976 average earnings rose by 14 per cent compared with the estimated increase of 10 per cent; a similar degree of slippage occurred in the following pay round. *Economist*, 26 March 1977.

48. A. J. H. Dean, 'Earnings in the Public and Private Sectors, 1950–1975', *National Institute Economic Review*, November 1975.

49. *Economist*, 3 September 1977.

50. *New Society*, 9 November 1972.

51. PEP, *Reshaping Britain*, op. cit., p. 40.

52. Daniel, *Wage Determination in Industry*, op. cit., pp. 43–5, p. 121.

53. ibid., p. 122.

54. Although the Accounting Standards Committee has recommended that companies should include statements of Added Value in their annual reports.

55. See R. J. Ball, 'The Use of Value Added in Measuring Managerial Efficiency', *Business Ratios*, August 1968.

56. Daniel, *Wage Determination in Industry*, op. cit., p. 117.

57. W. E. J. McCarthy and N. D. Ellis, *Management by Agreement*, Hutchinson, 1973, p. 108.

58. W. W. Daniel and Niel McIntosh, *Incomes Policy and Collective Bargaining at the Workplace*, op. cit., p. 57.

59. ibid., pp. 57–8.

60. Department of Employment, *The Reform of Collective Bargaining at Plant and Company Level* (Manpower Papers No. 5), HMSO, 1971, p. 87.

61. Flanders, op. cit., p. 68.

Chapter 4

The New Legitimacy

1. R. O. Clarke, D. J. Fatchett and B. C. Roberts, *Workers' Participation in Management in Britain*, Heinemann, 1972, p. 5.

2. ibid, pp. 7–8.

3. CBI, *The Road to Recovery*, October 1976, p. 64.

4. David Guest and Derek Fatchett, *Worker Participation – Individual Control and Performance*; Institute of Personnel Management, 1974, p. 24.

5. ibid. The authors conducted a survey of managerial opinion and found that 32 per cent of their sample believed that money was the only thing that the majority of workers were interested in; 42 per cent said that money was important 'up to a point' but that what most workers *really* wanted was 'a chance to do a challenging and responsible job' (p. 91).

6. ibid, pp. 71–2.

7. One of the pioneering studies in Britain was that by Trist and Bamforth (1951) in the coal-mines, which underlined the danger of introducing new methods of working which ignored the existing structure of inter-personal relations in the workplace. See E. L. Trist and K. W. Bamforth, 'Some Social and Psychological Consequences of the

Longwall Method of Coal-getting', *Human Relations*, vol. 4, no. 1, 1951·

8. See, for example, C. Argyris, *Integrating the Individual and the Organization*, Wiley, 1964.

9. Guest and Fatchett, op. cit., p. 81.

10. J. H. Goldthorpe, D. Lockwood, F. Bechhofer, J. Pratt, *The Affluent Worker: Industrial Attitudes and Behaviour*, Cambridge University Press, 1968.

11. J. H. Westergaard. 'The Rediscovery of the Cash Nexus', in R. Miliband and J. Saville, eds., *The Socialist Register, 1970*, Merlin Press, 1970, p. 120.

12. Huw Beynon, *Working for Ford*, Allen Lane, 1973, p. 121. The following observation on instrumentalism and priorities in work is significant: 'People, living their lives, develop a pretty accurate idea of their own life chances, of the odds they face and the hopes that they can realistically entertain ... If you're young, with family responsibilities and want to move out of the house you know to be a slum you attempt to get as much money as you can by selling to the highest bidder ... This doesn't mean that you are not aware of alternativē things, better ways of living, but merely that these are unlikely to be open to you. If you work at Ford's on the line, you let your mind go blank and look forward to pay day and the weekend' (p. 113).

13. Dorothy Wedderburn and Rosemary Crompton. *Workers' Attitudes and Technology* (Cambridge Papers in Sociology No. 2), Cambridge University Press, 1972, pp. 147–8.

14. Stephen Cotgrove, 'Alienation and Automation', *British Journal of Sociology*, vol. 23, December 1972.

15. W. W. Daniel and Niel McIntosh, *The Right to Manage?*, PEP/ MacDonald, 1972, pp. 37–8.

16. Alan Fox, *A Sociology of Work in Industry*, Collier Macmillan, 1971, pp. 22–3.

17. Daniel and McIntosh, op. cit. The authors investigated the introduction of a productivity agreement in a petrochemical works and observed a significant change in the balance between extrinsic and intrinsic satisfactions: 'The agreement had been negotiated and implemented in the face of strong opposition and only after hard wage–work bargaining backed by a national incomes policy. Yet nine months after the agreement, the majority of the men favoured the changes because of job enrichment, heightened interest and satisfaction in their work rather than because of increases in wages ... in the negotiating context they were not more – perhaps even not at all – interested in job satisfaction. They wanted to make the best deal in the terms that the negotiating context defines ... But once agreement had been reached and once the

changes had been implemented, the formal benefits that it had furnished were taken for granted and what then became important were the changes that had been generated in the context and meaning of their day-to-day activities and relationships at work' (pp. 35–6).

18. B. C. Roberts, Ray Loveridge, John Gennard, *Reluctant Militants*, Heinemann, 1972, p. 142.

19. ibid, pp. 142–4.

20. ibid. pp. 147–8.

21. Wedderburn and Crompton, op. cit., p. 23.

22. ibid. p. 144.

23. Harvie Ramsay, 'Participation; The Shop Floor View', *British Journal of Industrial Relations*, July 1976. It is significant, however, that these reported aspirations for more influence over a range of substantive issues were closely related to collective bargaining. The majority of workers in the sample expected management to take the initiative on these issues, but not to proceed to action without their agreement.

24. Peter Brannen, Eric Batstone, Derek Fatchett, Philip White, *The Worker Directors*, Hutchinson, 1976, pp. 36–46.

25. Daniel and McIntosh, op. cit., p. 48.

26. ibid. p. 46.

27. David Weir, 'Radical Managerialism: middle managers' perceptions of collective bargaining', *British Journal of Industrial Relations*, November 1976.

28. See Guest and Fatchett, op. cit., pp. 151–72.

29. The experience of Volvo, the Swedish motor-car manufacturers, with the much-publicized experiment at their Kalmar plant is relevant in this context. In 1974 Volvo abolished the continuous assembly-line production technology at this plant in favour of 'island assembly' by semi-autonomous workgroups. The main purpose of the new system was to induce the workforce to take more interest in their jobs, thereby reducing the high levels of absenteeism and labour turnover and simultaneously improving the quality of the product. Two years later, however, it was reported that the experiment had only been a qualified success. Absenteeism and labour turnover had both fallen, but the level of output had not improved; nor had the quality of the output proved to be as good as was anticipated. Consequently the extra investment costs incurred by the abandonment of the traditional assembly line had not been offset by greater efficiency (*Financial Times*, 23 November 1976).

30. Royal Commission on Trade Unions and Employers' Associations (Donovan Commission), *Report*, Cmnd 3623, HMSO, June 1968, para. 212.

31. Fox, op. cit., pp. 169–70.

32. Clarke, Fatchett and Roberts, op. cit., pp. 95–102.

33. ibid., pp. 98–9.

34. ibid., pp. 119–20.

35. In the survey by Clarke *et al.* over 70 per cent of firms still retained some form of joint consultation. The larger the company, the more likely management was to have a formal system of consultation; small companies, by contrast, tended to rely on informal arrangements (ibid., pp. 72–3).

36. Eric Batstone and P. L. Davies, *Industrial Democracy: European Experience* (two reports prepared for the Industrial Democracy [i.e. Bullock] Committee), HMSO, 1976, pp. 32–3. See also Commission on Industrial Relations, *Worker Participation and Collective Bargaining in Europe* (Study No. 4), HMSO, 1974, pp. 133–8. The tendency for old consultative institutions to be absorbed into an emerging framework of workplace bargaining is most marked in Italy and Denmark; elsewhere existing works councils are increasingly dominated by shop stewards and trade union members.

37. Allan Flanders, *Management and Unions*, Faber, 1970, p. 137.

38. The 1972 Survey of Workplace Relations found that in most industrial groups a decisive majority of employees and shop stewards did *not* feel that they could obtain better and quicker results by striking than by using the established disputes procedure. There was also strong disapproval of the use of the strike weapon for purely opportunistic reasons. In general a majority of employees, and an overwhelming majority of shop stewards, felt that strikes in breach of procedure were only justified if either (1) management had broken an agreement, or (2) management had resorted to unreasonable delay in dealing with grievances or (3) there was no other way of preventing the unfair dismissal of a workmate (Stanley Parker, *Workplace Industrial Relations, 1972*, HMSO, 1974, pp. 69–70).

39. Flanders, op. cit., p. 138.

40. Batstone and Davies, op. cit., p. 35.

41. Brannen *et al.*, op. cit., p. 57.

42. ibid., p. 138.

43. ibid., p. 170.

44. Batstone and Davies, op. cit., p. 25.

45. ibid., pp. 18–22.

46. ibid., p. 234.

47. ibid., p. 21.

48. ibid., p. 40.

49. *Economist*, 29 January 1977.

50. Batstone and Davies, op. cit., p. 42.

51. J. T. Winkler, 'The Ghost at the Bargaining Table: directors and industrial relations', *British Journal of Industrial Relations*, July 1974.

52. ibid.

53. Batstone and Bavies, op. cit., p. 40.

54. A. J. Eccles, 'Industrial Democracy and Organizational Change', *Personnel Review*, Winter 1977.

55. Ramsay, op. cit.

56. A survey by MORI in January 1977 suggested that while there was strong support among the general public for the *idea* of workers on company boards, there was an equally strong feeling that worker directors should constitute less than half the total board membership and that they should be elected by all the employees in the enterprise rather than nominated through trade union machinery (*Sunday Times*, 30 January 1977). An ORC poll conducted about the same time indicated that in thirty large companies only seven out of every hundred workers rated board representation as one of their four most important priorities. Better financial incentives, more information from top management, better chances for promotion, higher pay and a 'bigger say' in how their work is planned and organized were all rated as much more important than board representation. It could of course be argued that support for participation at board level would increase considerably if workers were convinced they would have a better chance of realizing their expressed aspirations if they had their own representatives on the board. However, it would appear from the ORC poll quoted above that the respondents had little understanding of the procedural aspects of board representation, particularly if this was presented in terms of a two-tier structure (*The Times*, 26 January 1977).

Chapter 5

The Role of Law

1. S. D. Anderman, *Employment Protection: A New Legal Framework*, Butterworth, 1976, p. 3.

2. The labour correspondent of the *Sunday Times*, for example, has argued that, 'There is now evidence, much of it admittedly fragmented and anecdotal, that many of the country's 800,000 small firms are becoming weighed down with legislation they cannot either understand or implement. There are claims that these laws, especially the Employment Protection Act, which makes sacking-on-the-spot virtually a thing of the past, are stopping businesses taking on new men and women' (28 August 1977). This statement – by a leading industrial journalist – in

itself illustrates how the current legal framework has acquired its own mythology. There is nothing in either the 1975 Act or the ACAS Code of Practice which prevents *summary* dismissals (i.e. one without notice). The Code does say, however, that while summary dismissal may be an appropriate penalty in cases of gross misconduct, management should hold some kind of investigation in order to ensure that the employee concerned was in fact guilty of gross misconduct. The presumption is, therefore, that *instant* dismissal (i.e. one without any kind of investigation) will rarely be justified. It would be difficult to argue, however, that this basic requirement constitutes an intolerable burden on any management.

3. *Earl* v. *Slater & Wheeler (Airlyne)* (1973).

4. *Grundy (Teddington)* v. *Willis* (1976).

5. In *Devis* v. *Atkins* (1975, 1976), for example, the EAT upheld the employer's appeal against the finding of unfair dismissal by an industrial tribunal: 'What the industrial tribunal ought to do is not to ask itself "Are we satisfied that the offence was committed?", but to ask itself the question "Are we satisfied that the employers had at the time of the dismissal, reasonable grounds for believing that the offence put against the applicant was in fact committed?"'

6. The same point was reinforced by the EAT in *Cook* v. *Thomas Linnell & Sons* (1977): 'It is important that the operation of the legislation in relation to unfair dismissal should not impede employers unreasonably in the efficient management of their business, which must be in the interest of all.'

7. In *Durrant* v. *Baker Oil Tools Ltd* (1973), for example, an industrial tribunal held that the applicant was entitled to refuse to accept a change in the organization which required him to hand over part of his responsibilities to another manager: 'He would have suffered substantial loss of job satisfaction and status had he accepted the reorganization ... less work for the same salary did not appeal to (him) ... For the respondents to alter his contract against his will amounted to a repudiation ... commercial reorganization is within the province of the employer but his discretion is limited by the just interests of his employees.'

8. See, for example, *Robinson* v. *Flitwick Frames Ltd* (1975). An unreasonable refusal to cooperate with management, as in Robinson's case, where the applicant refused to work 'voluntary' overtime without giving a reason for doing so despite the fact that his colleagues had agreed that the overtime was necessary, may fall within the catch-all category of 'some other substantial reason' for dismissal. Where an employee's contract does not allow for a particular change, but refusal to cooperate could jeopardize the company, his dismissal will probably

be fair. Thus the EAT rules in *Ellis* v. *Brighton Cooperative Society* (1976), that 'where there has been a properly consulted-upon reorganization which, if it is not done is going to bring the whole business to a standstill, a failure to go along with the changes may well – it is not bound to but it may well – constitute some other substantial reason (for dismissal)'.

9. *Moon and others* v. *Homeworthy (Furniture) Northern* (1976).

10. *Grundy (Teddington)* v. *Willis* (1976).

11. See, for example, *Quinton Hazell* v. *Earl* (1976) and *George M. Whiley* v. *Anderson* (1976).

12. *O'Connell* v. *Hilltop Steel Structures* (1976).

13. *Industrial Relations Review and Report*, no. 89, 25 May 1977.

14. Anderman, op. cit., p. 4.

15. ibid.

16. Allan Flanders, *Management and Unions*, Faber, 1970, p. 178.

17. A questionnaire issued by ACAS to the staff of the Legal and General Assurance Co. Ltd, was successfully challenged in the High Court by the L & G. Staff Association, who contended that the form in which the questions were asked was biased against the Association and in favour of the trade union involved, ASTMS.

18. See Bernard James, 'Third Party Intervention in Recognition Disputes: the Role of the Commission on Industrial Relations', *Industrial Relations Journal*, vol. 8, no. 2, Spring 1977. In the dispute between Grunwick Processing Laboratories Ltd and APEX, for example, it transpired that ACAS was only able to sound the attitudes of the ninety-one workers who had been dismissed from their employment with the company for taking strike action. The company refused to provide ACAS with access to the majority of employees who remained at work and instead commissioned Gallup and MORI to poll the workforce on their preferences. The results of the polls showed an overwhelming rejection of APEX's claims that the union should be recognized and the dismissed strikers reinstated. The Scarman report, however, put less weight on the results of these polls than it did on the ACAS ballot, eliciting the following caustic comment from Grunwick: 'The inquiry was so convinced that the role of trade unions in industry is wholly beneficial, so concerned to have the APEX strikers back inside Grunwick, that instinctively it shied away from examining the most important piece of evidence in front of it'. (*The Times*, 30 August 1977.)

19. Department of Employment, *Industrial Relations Procedures* (Manpower Papers No. 14), HMSO, 1975, p. 5.

20. The CIR conducted some thirty-seven inquiries into recognition

disputes, and in twenty-three cases recommended that an independent trade union should be given sole negotiating rights on behalf of defined groups of employees. The CIR's recommendations, however, were carried out in only fourteen of these cases; in the others it would appear that the 'extreme anti-union stance' of the employer prevented further progress towards collective bargaining (James, op. cit.).

21. See, for example, CIR *Coventry Economic Building Society*, (Report No. 45), HMSO, 1973.

22. In the spring of 1977, for example, one of the last big non-union companies left in Britain – IBM – easily defeated a challenge from four trade unions. The unions had claimed sufficient support within the company for collective bargaining to be established. A ballot by ACAS, however, resulted in a vote of only 566 in favour of collective bargaining out of a total workforce of 13,000: 'The ballot, which attracted a 95 per cent poll, was therefore a huge vote of confidence in the IBM ethic – described by the unions as paternalistic – that talent and hard work should be measured and rewarded individually' (*Sunday Times*, 12 June 1977).

23. In the reports it has issued to date, it would appear that ACAS is looking for a level of *support* for collective bargaining (as opposed to actual trade union membership) among the employees concerned of about 50 per cent in order to justify a recommendation in favour of collective bargaining. In several cases, however, the expressed level of support was considerably less than this, and ACAS therefore declined to make any recommendations.

24. CIR, *Recognition of White Collar Unions in Engineering and Chemicals* (Study No. 3) HMSO, 1973, p. 8, para. 29.

25. *Industrial Relations Review and Report*, No. 133, August 1976.

26. W. E. J. McCarthy and N. D. Ellis, *Management by Agreement*, Hutchinson, 1973, p. 91.

27. Stanley Parker, *Workplace Industrial Relations*, 1972, HMSO, 1974, p. 71.

28. Robin Smith, *Current UK Practice on Disclosure*, BIM, 1975. One significant point emerging from this survey is that only about 25 per cent of British companies regularly disclose information on general performance or future plans on a regular basis.

29. Arthur Marsh and Roger Rosewell, 'A Question of Disclosure,' *Industrial Relations Journal* vol. 7, no. 2, Summer 1976.

30. ibid.

31. ibid.

32. *Lomax* v. *Ladbroke Racing Ltd* (1975), *Derving* v. *Kilvington Ltd* (1973). However, it has also been held that an employer who threatens

to close down his business rather than concede a claim for union recognition is contravening the rights of his employees under S.53 of the EPA – *Brassington and others* v. *Couldon Wholesale Ltd* (1977).

33. *Tynan* v. *Balmer* (1966). 'The only indisputably lawful pickets after this judgement are those who attend in small numbers near the chosen place and who keep out of everyone's way. Meanwhile, the workers whom they have come to persuade to join them can sweep past in vehicles which the pickets have no right to stop' – K. W. Wedderburn, *The Worker and the Law*, Penguin Books, 1971, p. 325.

34. ibid., p. 321.

35. *The Times*, 30 August 1977.

Chapter 6

Policy and Practice

1. Allan Flanders, 'The Future of Voluntarism', *Personnel Management,* December 1966.

2. Royal Commission on Trade Unions and Employers' Associations (Donovan Commission), *Report*, Cmnd 3623, HMSO, June 1968, p. 41 para. 169.

3. Michael Terry, 'The Inevitable Growth of Informality', *British Journal of Industrial Relations*, March 1977.

4. CIR, *The Role of Management in Industrial Relations* (Report No. 34), HMSO, 1973, para. 31.

5. J. T. Winkler, 'The Ghost at the Bargaining Table: Directors and Industrial Relations', *British Journal of Industrial Relations*, July 1974.

6. CIR, *Industrial Relations in Multi-Plant Undertakings* (Report No. 85), HMSO, 1974, para. 82.

7. C. G. Gill and H. M. Concannon, 'Developing an Explanatory Framework for Industrial Relations Policy within the Firm', *Industrial Relations Journal*, Winter 1976/7.

8. Department of Employment, *The Reform of Collective Bargaining at Plant and Company Level* (Manpower Papers No. 5), HMSO, 1971. The authors noted that in the cases they studied 'There was a marked reluctance on the part of both managements and trade unions to take their disagreements "outside the factory". Involvement of third parties in their "domestic" affairs was viewed as undesirable, and on occasions they went to considerable lengths to prevent such an intrusion.'

9. C. G. Gill, 'Industrial Relations in a Multi-Plant Organisation: Some Considerations', *Industrial Relations Journal*, Winter 1974.

10. ibid. The authors found some evidence that this was happening in the firms they studied.

11. Department of Employment, *The Reform of Collective Bargaining at Plant and Company Level*, op. cit., pp. 5–6.

12. Alan Fox, *Beyond Contract: Work, Power and Trust Relations*. Faber, 1974, p. 284.

13. ibid., pp. 314–15.

14. ibid., p. 332.

15. ibid., p. 321.

16. Dewi-Davies Jones, *Wages and Employment in the EEC*, Kogan Page, 1973, p. 145.

17. Department of Employment, *Industrial Relations Procedures* (Manpower Paper No. 14), HMSO, 1975, p. 4.

18. Alan Fox, *A Sociology of Work in Industry*, Collier Macmillan, 1971, p. 149.

19. ibid., p. 150.

20. M. G. Wilders and S. R. Parker, 'Changes in Workplace Industrial Relations, 1966/1972', *British Journal of Industrial Relations*, March 1975.

21. Fox, A *Sociology of Work in Industry*, op. cit., p. 150.

22. ibid., p. 151.

23. Huw Benyon, *Working for Ford*, Allen Lane, 1973, p. 140.

24. Terry, op. cit.

25. ibid.

26. ibid.

27. Department of Employment, *Industrial Relations Procedures*, op. cit., p. 76.

28. ibid., p. 38.

29. ibid., p. 67. In a survey of more than 200 collective agreements in firms with more than 300 employees, spread over twenty-seven industries, the author found that only 17 per cent had *status quo* clauses.

30. *Industrial Relations Report and Review*, no. 134, August 1976.

31. Department of Employment, *Industrial Relations Procedures*, op. cit., p. 77.

32. J. H. Andriesson, 'Developments in the Dutch Industrial Relations System', *Industrial Relations Journal*, vol. 7, no. 2, Summer 1976.

33. Solomon Barkin, *Worker Militancy and its Consequences, 1965–1975*, Praeger Publishers Inc., 1975, p. 385.

34. In 1976 the average level of absenteeism in Swedish industry was 10 per cent, having steadily risen since 1960 – *Economist*, 28 August 1976.

35. *The Times*, 19 August 1975.

36. *Economist*, 16 July 1977.

37. A recent survey by *The Times* (22 June 1977) concluded that 'the German worker has become one of the least mobile in Western Europe'.

38. Barkin, op. cit., p. 256.

39. ibid., p. 270.

40. ibid.

41. Allan Flanders, *Management and Unions*, Faber, 1970, pp. 239–40.

42. See, for example, Michael Moran, *The Union of Post Office Workers*, Macmillan, 1974.

43. *Sunday Times*, 12 June 1977.

44. Aubrey Jones, *The New Inflation*, Penguin Books, 1973, pp. 170–71.

45. Santosh Mukherjee, *Making Labour Markets Work* (Broadsheet No. 532), PEP, January 1972, pp. 135–6.

46. Sir Keith Joseph, for example, has argued that 'The aim of production is ... consumption. It has been increasingly violated in our own day by the chimera of "job creation", which probably destroys as many jobs as it creates ... More and more resources which should be devoted to producing goods and services which people want, are diverted to producing work. So the total output stagnates while incomes rise' (*The Times*, 31 August 1977). The assumption is, of course, that job creation cannot by definition perform a necessary or desirable service since, if the function or service in question had really been in demand, market forces would already have supplied it. To argue thus, however, is to take an unduly simplistic view of the way in which the market for work operates. Many 'job creation' projects, for example, have been concerned with the reinstatement of derelict land – a service which is both socially and economically desirable but which, traditionally, has been performed only to a very limited degree by the private sector.

47. A survey of the unemployed by Daniel in 1973/4 found that three quarters of them attached considerable importance to finding a job as soon as possible and had been unable to do so for over a month. Less than a third of the sample either had no intention of finding a job or attached little importance to doing so. Daniel concluded that lack of *motivation* to work reflected lack of *opportunity* to work. Moreover, nearly three quarters of the respondents said that it had been 'bad' or 'very bad' for them personally to be out of work. Those who felt that it had not been 'too bad' were largely those who had reconciled themselves to the idea of being unemployed – W. W. Daniel, *A National Survey of the Unemployed* (Broadsheet No. 546), PEP, October 1974, pp. 144–51. Confirmation of Daniel's findings may be found in the *Department of Employment Gazette*, June 1977, which conducted its own survey in June 1976, when the level of unemployment was nearly three times as great as when Daniel's research was undertaken. The

D of E survey found that 55 per cent of the men and 70 per cent of the women in the sample were 'keen or relatively enthusiastic' to find work and were judged to have good, fair or reasonable prospects for doing so; 21 per cent of the men and 16 per cent of the women were equally anxious to find work but had poor prospects for doing so; 24 per cent of the men and 13 per cent of the women were judged to have poor prospects for finding work and were 'somewhat unenthusiastic' in their attitude to work.

INDEX

Index

Added Value, 109–13, 219

Advisory Conciliation and Arbitration Service (ACAS), 64 ff, 151, 157, 166–7, 171–2, 180, 183

alienation, 42–3, 122–3, 126

Associated Society of Locomotive Engineers and Firemen (ASLEF), 100

Association of Professional, Executive, Clerical and Computer Staff (APEX), 66, 183

Association of Scientific, Technical and Managerial Staffs (ASTMS), 66

British Institute of Management (BIM), 151–2, 173

British Leyland, 41, 78, 84, 101–2

British Rail, 100

British Steel Corporation, 137–9

Bullock Report (1977), 117, 137, 143–51

car industry, *see* motor-car industry

closed shop, 64, 65–6, 170–71

coal mining, 16, 38, 39, 95

Code of Practice (1971), 32

Code of Practice (ACAS), 172, 176

collective bargaining
'free', 107, 115–16, 186, 217–18
growth of, at work-place level, 26, 52, 57, 187–8, 193–4
growth of, in Western Europe, 210–11
and industrial order, 43, 156
industry level, 13, 34, 51, 57, 77
and management, 135–6
and worker participation, 134
see also procedures; productivity bargaining; wage bargaining

Commission on Industrial Relations (CIR, 1969–74), 39, 59, 91, 165–6, 169, 189, 191, 224

Confederation of British Industries (CBI), 48, 49, 76, 119, 172, 218

conflict, 14, 55, 187
see also strikes

craft tradition, 15, 16, 87–8

craftsmen, 28, 29, 125

Daniel, W. W., 19, 20, 59, 70, 76, 91, 94, 108, 111, 123, 126

Department of Employment, 53, 64

differentials, 77, 97–8, 108
see also relativities

directors, company, 90–91, 134, 146–9, 188–9
see also worker directors

disclosure of information
in UK, 32, 111, 118, 171–7, 183
in Western Europe, 172
dismissal, 62, 64, 65, 160–63
Donovan Commission (Royal Commission on Trade Unions and Employers' Associations, 1968), 28, 29, 41, 54, 57, 60, 63, 77, 102, 130, 188 ff, 200 ff, 224

economic growth, 13, 28, 37, 54–5
Economist, 33, 71, 105, 145
effort bargain, 24, 28, 30
see also wage-work bargain
Electrical, Electronic, Telecommunications and and Plumbing Trades Union (EETPU), 98, 149
Electrolux Ltd, 39, 40
employers' association, 48
employment
full, 27–8, 34, 50–51, 90
growth in public sector, 74
growth in white-collar occupations, 22, 128
see also unemployment
Employment Appeals Tribunal, 160–64, 182
Employment Protection Act (1975), 32, 64, 66, 155–7, 159, 171
Equal Pay Act (1970), 96
expectations, employees
in UK, 15–35, 63, 90, 125–7, 131–2, 197–8
in Western Europe, 207–15
see also orientations to work

fairness, 37, 38, 98–9
see also wage bargaining
Fawley productivity agreements, 29
see also productivity bargaining
Feather, Lord, 227
Flanders, Allan, 28 ff, 45, 87, 115, 187, 216
Fox, Alan, 14, 36, 123, 131, 196 ff, 201, 225

General Strike, 48
government, role of, 17, 19, 215–24
see also voluntarism
Grunwick dispute (1976–7), 178, 180–83

incomes policy
objectives of, 81–2, 98, 186, 218
of 1965–70, 30, 59, 69–70, 94, 218
of 1972–4, 70–71, 107
since 1974, 73, 83–4, 104–8
and structure of collective bargaining, 83, 94, 102
in Western Europe, 211–12
see also inflation; social contract; wage bargaining
Industrial Relations Act (1971), 32, 61–2, 66–7, 72, 155, 164, 172, 177, 180
industrial tribunals, 32
industrial relations policy, 91, 114, 147, 169, 182–3, 187–95, 225–6
inflation, 58, 68–9, 75
see also incomes policy; wage bargaining

information, disclosure of, *see*
disclosure

job enrichment, 121
job evaluation, 108–9
job property rights, 26–9, 31, 33,
35, 39, 90
joint consultation
in UK, 132, 173
in Western Europe, 133, 208–9
Jones, Aubrey, 68, 219

labour costs in manufacturing
industry, 56
Lesney Products v. *Nolan* (1977),
161
'Living Wage', idea of, 16–17

management
attitudes of, 11, 14, 40, 195
quality of, 114
rights of, 36, 63
style of, 113, 195
and trade union recognition,
167–9
see also directors
manpower policy, 33, 221–2
Manpower Services Commission,
220
motor-car industry, 26, 27, 51, 85,
97–8, 100

National Board for Prices and
Incomes (NBPI, 1965–71),
58, 63, 77, 86, 107–8, 115,
218–19
National Industrial Relations
Court (NIRC, 1971–4), 160,
161

National Union of Bank
Employees (NUBE), 66
National Union of Mineworkers
(NUM), 95, 98, 179
National Union of Railwaymen
(NUR), 100

orientations to work, 43, 122–4
see also expectations
overtime, 29, 77–8, 86–7

participation, 37, 52, 118–21, 129
see also collecting bargaining;
worker directors
Pay Board (1973–4), 108
payment by results, 93–6, 101,
110–11, 120
see also wage bargaining
Phelps Brown, E. H., 17, 26
picketing, 178–81
procedures
and discipline, 64, 204–5
formalization of, 40–41, 57, 60,
65, 175, 198–200, 201–4,
225
functions of, 199–204, 207, 225
informality of, 52, 131, 188–9,
203–4
see also collective bargaining;
status quo clauses
productivity, 28, 58, 69, 84–6,
92–3, 113, 186
productivity bargaining, 30, 35,
40, 59, 83, 89–90, 104, 115,
172, 220–21

relativities, 77, 97–8, 104–5, 108
see also differentials

redundancy, 65, 162–3
Redundancy Payments Act
(1965), 31
Ryder Report (1975), 84

Shonfield, Andrew, 60
shop stewards, 45, 52, 61, 65, 67,
102, 201–3
see also collective bargaining,
growth of, at workplace level
social contract
of 1972, 72
of 1974/5, 72–3, 158
in Western Europe, 212–14
see also incomes policy
social wage, 21, 73
staff associations, 66
Standard Telephones and Cables
Ltd, 40
status quo clauses, 205–7
strikes
distribution of, 53
duration of, 179
and full employment, 34
in motor-car industry, 26–7
and pay issues, 18, 19
'post-Donovan', 41
and redundancy, 32
unofficial, 29, 45
in Western Europe, 211, 215
Sweden, 21, 55, 99, 206

taxation, 21, 70, 73–4, 105–7, 185,
213
technology, 42, 54–5, 96, 123, 129
trade unions
'excessive' power of, 12, 60, 187
functions of, 76, 216–17
growth of, 12, 22, 197–8

recognition of, 61, 63, 65 ff,
130, 164–70, 180–81, 195
structure of, 49, 99
white-collar, 22–3, 39, 50, 66,
100, 128
Trade Union and Labour
Relations Act (1974), 64, 160,
178
Trades Union Congress (TUC),
33, 49–50, 62–3, 76, 134, 205
Transport and General Workers'
Union (TGWU), 97, 100
trust relations, 196–8, 225

unemployment
in inter-war years, 16–17
in 1969–72, 19, 30–31, 89–90
since 1974, 64, 73, 113, 157,
220
USA, 51, 55, 107
Union of Post Workers (UPW),
67

voluntarism, 51, 54, 214
see also government

wage bargaining
fair comparison in, 17, 21, 24,
26, 38
and payment systems, 41, 78
and relativities, 19, 20, 104–5
and wage 'explosions', 30, 103,
105, 221
see also collective bargaining;
incomes policy; inflation;
payment by results
wage–work bargain, 23–5
see also effort bargain

Webb, Sidney and Beatrice, 15, 16, 24
Whitley Commission (1917), 34, 133
Wilson, Nicholas, 149–50
Woodcock, George, 175

worker directors
  in UK, 134, 136–43
  in Western Europe, 137–8, 140, 143
  see also directors; participation

MORE ABOUT PENGUINS
AND PELICANS

Penguinews, which appears every month, contains details of all the new books issued by Penguins as they are published. From time to time it is supplemented by our stocklist, which includes around 5,000 titles.

A specimen copy of *Penguinews* will be sent to you free on request. Please write to Dept EP, Penguin Books Ltd, Harmondsworth, Middlesex, for your copy.

In the U.S.A.: For a complete list of books available from Penguins in the United States write to Dept CS, Penguin Books, 625 Madison Avenue, New York, New York 10022.

In Canada: For a complete list of books available from Penguins in Canada write to Penguin Books Canada Ltd, 2801 John Street, Markham, Ontario L3R 1B4.

Pelican Library of Business and Management

AN INSIGHT INTO MANAGEMENT ACCOUNTING

John Sizer

Management accountancy is the key to modern business strategy and technique. No department specialist – and certainly no general executive – can cope without an insight into its principles and practices. This book is designed to give just such an insight: to enable every businessman to understand the finances and internal costing of his company – and to keep its accountants on their toes.

John Sizer, who has practical experience of several industries, is now Professor of Financial Management and Head of the Department of Management Studies at Loughborough University of Technology. In this book he discusses such subjects as stewardship, cost accounting, the measurement and control of profitability, long-term planning, capital investment appraisal, budgetary control and marginal costing. Other chapters cover the accountant's contribution to the pricing decision, and company taxation. But whilst he provides an admirably succinct description of modern accounting techniques, John Sizer's main achievement has been to relate them all to essentially functional and practical situations within the firm. This is a no-nonsense manual which firmly removes from accounting all the mystique which overawes managers and often merely masks muddle.